CREDIT RISK MANAGEMENT

A Guide to Sound Business Decisions

H. A. Schaeffer Jr., C.C.E., C.E.W.

John Wiley & Sons, Inc.

New York • Chichester • Weinheim • Brisbane • Singapore • Toronto

658.88
S29c

This book is printed on acid-free paper. ∞

ISBN 0-471-35020-6

Printed in the United States of America.

10 9 8 7 6 5 4 3 2 1

CONTENTS

iii

PREFACE

Here is the book every credit professional has been waiting for, a book that tells all in some "real-life" case studies and reveals not only what other credit professionals thought and how they arrived at their decisions but also the actual facts behind the final outcome of the case.

The cases are 12 of the best from this 28-year veteran of the credit trenches. They were originally assembled for a dynamic course for one of the leading educational organizations in the country, the American Management Association (AMA). This course, a three-day seminar, first provided both novice and seasoned pro a four-part refresher on analyzing a case from all possible points of view. It showed how to arrive at not just a credit decision but a sound business credit decision using far more than just basic credit and financial information to arrive at the final resolution. It also showed participants how to accept the fact that in real life there can be a decision other than a credit decision or a sound business credit decision.

Occasionally top management makes business decisions that cannot be justified by credit. This type of override can cause hard feelings and the wrong attitude in some credit staff. This book shows readers how to be "team players" yet still do what is the most basic yet important directive in the life of credit professionals—maximize sales yet minimize risks. If a credit professional's decision is overridden as a team player, he or she must make every effort to minimize the fallout from a business decision. The first four chapters guide readers through this process and prepare for these twelve cases.

While readers may be tempted to skip directly to the case studies, *don't*. Readers who overlook these tools will not have what they need to properly attack these challenging cases.

The cases provide readers not only with the opportunity to solve credit issues in a number of different industries but also the chance to see how others have treated the same problems. Since this book is based on a course I taught for the AMA, I am also able to share the recommendations of other credit professionals who looked at these very same problems. In each case study, after presenting the facts and the financial information available, I share the recommendations of three of my students. Each attendee brought a unique perspective based on his or her own experiences.

As most reading this know only too well, top management often is swayed by a persuasive sales department and ignores credit's impeccable recommendations. After reviewing the recommendations made by the three sample students, I then assume that top management has overridden the recommendation from credit and the students make a second recommendation. The students also indicate how they will try and minimize the fallout from poor management decisions.

The many students who attended this AMA course shared not only their enjoyment of the cases but their experiences while working in the credit profession. Their experiences have been profound and surprising, sad and hilarious, and inspiring and demeaning. But they could not be prouder of the profession that they had chosen. I truly enjoyed working with them and know readers will enjoy their insights.

This book throws the gauntlet at your feet—it asks you to do the work necessary to make a sound business credit decision from the facts presented. And, just as in real life, some of the facts are missing. Readers may need to make assumptions or suppositions to fill in the missing information. The ability to do this accurately separates the rookie from the credit professional, so read carefully. However, even the most experienced get taken once in a while.

The other motto that should be remembered by every credit professional is that "every sale can be made." Notice I did not say that credit would be extended, just that every sale could be made. This fact is prominently reviewed and considered in each case. Sometimes credit professionals must be extremely creative to find the means necessary to make that sound business credit decision.

The types of cases included cover a plethora of today's topics, including the threat of bankruptcy, marginal customers, fraud, domestic and international credit, and even a case on how to be a credit consultant.

After readers have worked up a sweat in digging though cracks and crevasses to find that one elusive piece of information that will make the "light" come on, I will explain what really happened. Readers will have a chance, just as my AMA students did, to see how truth can be stranger than fiction and how sometimes the smallest, most insignificant piece of information can be the answer to the whole case.

I received the Certified Credit Executives designation from the National Association of Credit Management over 13 years ago; sometimes I feel that I may have been in credit too long. But every time I talk to one of my former students who has just received a professional designation, a promotion, or landed a great new position, it all becomes worthwhile. I used the material in this book to help those very same credit professionals become what they are today, successful and proud of their choice of a career. I hope that you will find the same help and enjoyment that they and I shared when we worked as a team to solve the mysteries of the 12 case studies.

ABOUT THE AUTHOR

H. A. Schaeffer Jr., C.C.E., C.E.W., is president of D&H Credit Services, Inc., a credit and financial customer service consulting firm to all sizes of manufacturers, wholesalers, government agencies, and credit organizations located in Port Washington, New York. He has served as a credit consultant for a number of midsize companies as well as Fortune 500 companies, including Bausch & Lomb and Mobil, Inc. Schaeffer is a certified expert witness in bankruptcy preference actions. He represents creditors who have been served with a preference action by a trustee and has negotiated on behalf of several companies that faced difficult large collection issues. He has taught credit courses for the American Management Association (AMA), the National Association of Credit Management (NACM), and Dun & Bradstreet. He also has taught customized courses for Fortune 500 companies and noncredit organizations.

PART ONE

STEPS FOR A SOUND BUSINESS CREDIT DECISION

INTRODUCTION

The first section of this book reviews some of the tools used by every credit professional to arrive at a sound business credit decision. This book uses the "A, B, C, D" method to prepare readers to make this type of decision not only for the case studies provided herein but also for those situations that cross readers' desks on a daily basis. Some of these concepts may appear basic to a seasoned pro, but the back-to-basics approach plus some more advanced concepts in these initial four chapters can prove useful to all. Even the seasoned pros need to return to the basics occasionally in order to avoid overlooking a danger sign that to a novice might appear blatant.

On many occasions when I taught two courses for the American Management Association (AMA), I was surprised by a question from a person who had only two or three months of credit experience. After 28 years in this field, I am proud to say that I do not know everything and never will. But what I do know is where to find the answers. Over the years I have established many ties and relationships with all types of individuals and organizations that can help me.

This book will provide not only my own insights but also the visions of those exceptional individuals who took my course. They came from all over the country and from all different types of firms. This diversity helped to make the learning experience not only enjoyable but also very beneficial to all. I always opened my classes by saying that I would learn more from the session than any one student there as I would gain insight from all of those who attended the session. I usually finished this speech by saying that it is in the best interest of all who attend seminars paid for by their firms to take advantage of all the opportunities that their companies will provide. The firms are gaining a more knowledgeable employee and the student secures not only more knowledge and experience but also new contacts to use for the future.

The value of taking courses (and reading books) that improve skills and abilities is that you can never lose them and no one can take them from you. You are an asset to many firms. A table is also an asset. When a table is worn out, the company discards it. When you are of no use to the firm . . . well, you know what happens. Take advantage of all that your firm provides and obtain as many credentials, degrees, knowledge, skills, and most important contacts that you can. Although you may not need any of these tools today or tomorrow, one of these days . . .

1

A IS FOR ANALYSIS FOR CREATIVE CREDIT MANAGEMENT

INTRODUCTION

This chapter sets the groundwork for solid financial credit analysis. Specifically:

- What techniques are used for obtaining financial data while controlling the cost of acquiring it? How can the worth of the data obtained be evaluated?
- What is common-size analysis?
- What is trend analysis?
- How can you make sure that "apples" are compared to "apples" when equating ratios to industry averages?
- What is the benefit in determining the value of ratios in financial analysis?

This chapter covers techniques for obtaining financial data on customers while controlling the always-important aspect of cost. The chapter also determines the value of the data and how important it is in making a sound business credit decision. Tools such as vertical and horizontal (trend) common-size analysis are discussed, and the text will leave readers with an appreciation of what these figures do and do not tell you about a customer. A clear understanding of what it means to compare "Apples to Apples" when comparing data will help readers appreciate the value of industry numbers. Finally, readers will gain an appreciation and understanding of the value of ratio analysis through a review on ratios that cover solvency, profitability, and efficiency and how these ratios work in tandem with each other to provide a clearer "picture" of the customer.

TECHNIQUES FOR GETTING FINANCIAL DATA WHILE CONTROLLING COSTS

To prepare readers for managing the case studies and those that are faced daily, we begin by looking at techniques for gaining financial data while controlling costs in obtaining it. The following sources can be used to make that all-important sound business credit decision. Their prices and value vary.

Customer.   While being the ultimate free source of information, customers rarely provide all the data needed to help credit executives make that decision. If the customer is a publicly traded firm on any of the stock exchanges, easy access to data is available from its annual report or any of the reports that are submitted to the Securities and Exchange Commission (SEC). These include the 10K (detailed audited annual report) or a 10Q (limited detail unaudited quarterly report) and so on. If the customer is a privately held company, then the whim of the owners determines whether financial data can be obtained. The customer's need for your product will greatly enhance or detract from its willingness to provide this information.

Depending on the size of the firm, some customers will complete the credit application; larger firms will provide a fact sheet of basic information, usually their bank, possibly a trade reference or two, and their Duns number (Dun & Bradstreet reference number for their credit report). Credit executives can never obtain financial information on a division of a company; only sometimes will financial data on a subsidiary be provided. Typically the smaller the company, the more it needs the services of the credit executive's firm, and the more information the client will provide. Also proportionally, the larger a firm is, the more likely that its financial information will be audited.

Internet.   One of the greatest sources of information (and occasionally disinformation) available today is the Internet. It provides access to information from numerous firms, government agencies, colleges, news publications, libraries, and elsewhere. Search engines help users find the different web sites that will provide large quantities of data that can support research toward making a sound business credit decision. Some firms have web sites that include product information, financial data, history of the firm, and who owns or runs the firm.

All this can prove quite useful, but at times the amount of data and the time it takes to separate out the chaff from the wheat is overwhelming. A vast amount of these data is raw, unverified, or unaudited, which means that it must be taken with a grain of salt. Always be careful of what you read and the source that it comes from before accepting it as fact.

Brokerage firms. Brokerage firms are the place to go for information on publicly traded firms. They have prospectuses on all firms traded on the New York, American, and NASDAQ stock exchanges. Prospectuses provide not only financial data but also background information on the firm's makeup.

State government. Some state governments require that companies doing business in their state submit certain financial or business data in order to continue to conduct business there. None of the information is audited, and it tends to be very limited in nature. Some examples include balance sheet information, profit-and-loss statements, and intelligence only on the principles that run the firm. Since the information is unaudited, it should serve as nothing more than a good starting point to initiate your overall credit check.

Dun & Bradstreet/Experian. These two companies supply credit and other informational reports on firms across the United States (their strength) and across the world (less accurate and up to date). Both provide trade reference information as well as audited financial data on publicly traded firms; public records on companies that have judgments, suits, tax liens, bankruptcy filings, and date and state of incorporation (if applicable); and UCC-1 filings. Dun & Bradstreet also provides information on the principals of the firm, notes on any significant changes to a firm, analysis of the financial data, unaudited financial data, terms of sale, who and where they sell, and information on the location of the facility and its ownership. How good is this extra information supplied by D & B? It is unaudited and generally obtained directly from the customer itself. Does this mean that it is inaccurate or valueless? Like the unaudited information supplied to the state, it can serve as a good starting point to initiate your overall credit check.

International financial information is more difficult to obtain in countries other than the United States due to local customs, government regulations, and data availability. Thus, these reports tend to be less accurate or current. Most countries do not have access to the level of detail and the rigorous nature of a U.S. audit of financial information.

Securities and Exchange Commission (SEC). This wing of the federal government oversees firms that are publicly traded on the various stock exchanges. Firms that sell stock on these exchanges must supply certain audited and unaudited information on a regular and timely basis. These records and reports can be obtained directly from the SEC or through their web site Edgar.gov, and are free of charge. They can be downloaded to a computer for analysis.

EVALUATING THE WORTH OF THE DATA ACQUIRED

Once credit executives have the information, the next step is to evaluate its worth. If the data are audited, then an independent accountant's opinion will be stated, which confirms the validity of the information presented in the financial package. There are four levels of opinions for audited statements and other levels for unaudited statements.

1. **Unqualified:** This audit confirms that the financial data that was investigated totally conformed to generally accepted accounting principles (GAAP), which is the highest level of audit that can be performed on financial data. Rigorous testing of data is performed as outlined by the guidelines stated in GAAP. The firm that has completed the audit certifies that the data as presented meet all standards without exception according to those set by GAAP.
2. **Qualified:** This rating indicates that an independent accounting firm certifies that the audit performed met all GAAP standards with a notable exception. This exception can be for a variety of reasons and is noted because the way that the firm accounts for one aspect of its operation may not meet GAAP standards. This may or may not be significant in the eyes of the credit professional, but the facts relating to this failure to comply with GAAP should be investigated.
3. **Adverse:** The auditing firm confirms that the information audited does not conform to GAAP, which means that the value of the information

does not meet these requirements. An adverse opinion can mean, for example, that the firm is financially insolvent and may be out of business soon.

4. **No Opinion:** When an account provides no opinion, it simply means that the level of the audit was insufficient to provide an opinion. GAAP has set standards regarding, the degree of investigation required to qualify for an accountant's opinion. Within this level there exist sublevels of "nonopinion." They are:

   • **Reviewed:** Some checks of the data have been made but they were of insufficient depth of audit to provide an opinion.

   • **Compiled:** No auditing was done. The company provided the accounting firm with enough information to create a balance sheet and income statement.

   • **No accountant's report:** No outside independent accounting firm reviewed the information.

Assuming no audited, unqualified opinion financial report was available, what data might be obtainable?

Complete annual report. Some privately held companies do have audited annual reports. This information is just as good as that supplied by any publicly traded company. Some private firms have statements that are reviewed or compiled by an outside accounting firm, and they will state that it does not comply with GAAP.

Annual balance sheet and income statement. Some firms will provide a year-end balance sheet and income statement. While this information is helpful, it is unaudited and lacks the notes necessary to clarify some numbers on the two reports. Without previous years to compare against, credit professionals cannot determine trends in the way that the firm is performing from just one year's numbers.

Quarterly balance sheet and income statement. A greater problem exists for the credit professional in using these reports, for they lack certain year-end adjustments without which the net income appears inflated. To get the best trend contrasts, comparisons should be made only from the same quarter previous year to same quarter present year. Quarter-to-quarter comparisons will show trends within the year but will not be a true comparison of like times.

One-month balance sheet and income statement. A one-month balance sheet provides a snapshot of the business on that day. The lack of something to compare it against and the fact that it is not audited decreases its value tremendously. A one-month income statement is merely an interim statement. Because it lacks final adjustments, it does not enable credit professionals to judge accurately how profitable the business is. Likewise, trend analysis cannot be performed on it.

Balance sheet only. This provides a snapshot picture but offers nothing to compare against and is unaudited.

Income statement only. This has the same problems as in the one-month income statement reviewed earlier.

Partial numbers only. Partial numbers have literally no value as they are taken out of context and tell precious little.

How good is the source of the financial information? Depending on who the source is will greatly vary the value the information will have. The following are the various levels of audit offered by various organizations:

- Customer: audited for public companies; audited to totally unaudited for private companies
- Internet: audited (public company from Edgar.gov, a brokerage firm, or the public company itself) to totally unaudited (company web site to news article)
- SEC/Brokerage Firm: audited annual, unaudited quarter numbers, public companies
- State Government: unaudited, varies could be balance sheet, income statement, and/or principals of company
- Dun & Bradstreet/Experian: audited (both) to totally unaudited (D & B only) to none at all

WHAT IS COMMON-SIZE ANALYSIS?

Common-size analysis was created to compare firms of different sizes against each other to determine how successful they are. It reduces a company's numbers down to the level of a percentage, which can be readily compared to a firm of a totally different size. It uses three different bases (denominators) as the divisor for computing these percentages.

1. In the case of assets, total assets is used as the denominator (i.e., cash/total assets as a percentage).
2. For liabilities or any part of the shareholder's equity (retained earnings, etc.), the denominator is the total of liabilities and shareholder's equity (i.e., accounts payable/total liabilities + shareholders' equity as a percentage).
3. For the income statement, net sales is used as the denominator (i.e., operating profit [loss]/net sales as a percentage).

Common-size analysis allows a company to compare its percentages for each item against the previous year's results. This will help when using trend analysis. Common-size analysis becomes much more focused when two or more firms that have the same Standard Industrial Classification Code (SICC) number are compared. This number is used to identify what type of business a particular company conducts. The level of comparison can be sharpened even more if the level of annual sales falls within a specific range and there are a particularly large number of members in the same code and same size range to compare against.

WHAT IS TREND ANALYSIS?

Trend analysis compares parts of the balance sheet, income statement, statement of cash flows, and ratios from the present year to those of previous years. It also can compare these same numbers against industry standards from those same years to see how they have improved or deteriorated not only against themselves but also against the industry as a whole.

This type of analysis is best when there is at least three to five years' worth of data to compare. This comparison can be of value when, by contrasting the present year against either the previous year or against industry norms, unusual items are discovered in the financial data. Such a discovery can be the difference between approving credit immediately (assuming all other work has been done and is satisfactory) and either asking more questions or quickly declining credit.

RATIO ANALYSIS AND THE MOST IMPORTANT RATIOS

Ratio analysis compares certain parts of the balance sheet with the total balance sheet, the balance sheet with the income statement, or a certain part of the income statement with the total income statement in a mathematical formula that can be used to compare against previous years or industry standards. Formulas can be calculated in number of days, number of times that something is turned over, comparison to a $1.00, or as a percentage. These ratios usually fall into three types of categories:

1. *Solvency* is the level at which a firm can meet its obligations.
2. *Efficiency* is how effective a firm is at turning over its debts and assets.
3. *Profitability* reflects level of income a firm generates from its daily operations.

Certain ratios are more important to some organizations than others. Ratios used by those firms that extend long-term credit or brokerage firms are totally different than the ratios used by a trade creditor. Some examples of ratios important to trade creditor are:

Quick ratio. This ratio is computed by taking cash, marketable securities, and accounts receivables and dividing them by current liabilities. This provides a dollar amount of current assets compared to $1.00 of current liabilities. The ratio defines the degree to which a company's current liabilities are covered by the most liquid current assets. It was thought in past days that a quick ratio of $1.00 to $1.00 was great. However, this can be misleading, depending on the outcome of the days sales outstanding ratio and what is normal for that particular industry.

Days sales outstanding. DSO is computed by taking the accounts receivable and dividing it by the net sales number times 365 days. This provides an average number of days it takes for a customer to collect receivables. When comparing this number to industry standards, it can be seen if the receivables appear to be collected slowly or if longer terms are being offered. If the customer's industry rarely has variable terms, then it is likely a sizable portion of its receivables may be either delinquent or nonperforming.

Using this ratio in conjunction with the quick ratio will help credit professionals make a better determination of a customer's liquidity. Trend analysis on both of these ratios will reflect the overall liquidity status over the last few years. These two ratios are extremely important to the short-term trade creditor. If a firm does not have solid receivables turnover, it will not have the necessary liquidity to meet its trade debt.

Accounts payable turnover. This ratio is calculated by taking accounts payable and dividing it by the cost of sales times 365 days. This ratio presents the average days that a customer takes to pay its trade suppliers. Why is this important to a trade creditor? The higher this number, the longer the trade creditor will have to wait for payment. While a company that has managed its cash flow well can be defined as one that gets its payment before it has to pay its creditors, that situation can make for some very unhappy trade vendors and credit professionals.

Inventory turnover. This ratio is calculated by taking inventory and dividing it by the cost of sales times 365 days. Why is this important to the trade creditor? This is easy; this is the creditor's inventory. This is the average days that the customer takes to turn its inventory once. The longer the inventory sits, the less the chance that it will ever move. Low inventory turnover also decreases the trade creditor's ability to sell new additional product to a customer. While a slightly higher than industry average is not bad, a number that is vastly higher than industry average is dangerous, as it could mean that the inventory is being sold at "fire sale" prices. In such a circumstance, the customer will not have the funds necessary to meet its obligations, as the funds received will most likely be used to cover costs.

Debt to tangible net worth. This ratio is computed by dividing the total liabilities by tangible net worth (net worth minus intangible assets). It indicates a firm's ability to leverage itself while still meeting its obligations. It shows how much the owners and creditors have invested in the firm. The higher the number, the higher the potential danger to all creditors, for if the owners have little invested in the firm, there is far less incentive to do much to salvage the firm.

In the case of a leveraged buyout, the owner(s) typically have only one percent invested in the firm. In the past, bankruptcy courts were littered by these types of firms.

Gross profit margin. This ratio is computed by taking gross profit and dividing it by the net sales of a firm. This is an example of common-size analysis. The value of this ratio can be shown only when it is compared to the industry standard. Is a company profitable? The answer depends on how it did in the previous years as well as how it is doing against its competition. This ratio also tells how much a firm can afford to lose on a sale before the profits of that sale are completely eaten away.

Return on investment. This ratio is computed by taking profit before taxes, dividends, and interest, and dividing them by the tangible net worth. It reflects the efficiency of management's performance by stripping away all other nonoperations and cost-of-sale items from net sales and shows just how much management has made through its efforts. If management ends up costing the firm profits through poor leadership, that situation will be reflected in these numbers when compared with industry standards.

HOW RATIOS CAN BE USED TO PREDICT FUTURE PERFORMANCE

By mapping the changes that have occurred over the stretch of data available, a prediction can be made. (Note: Predictions are only as good as the data used. The greater the number of years of data available, the better the prediction.) The data must be devoid of any large, unusual, or nonrecurring items. Any known (or unknown) major changes that have occurred recently or will occur to a company or its industry or a change due to a major legal ruling (i.e., a major acquisition, a bankruptcy filing, a spin-off of a major product line, etc.) will make future forecasting less accurate or totally inaccurate.

Apples with Apples Comparison

Obviously, the worth of any evaluation depends on the validity of the ratio comparison. How do you make sure that "apples" are compared to "apples" when equating ratios to industry averages? The use of the same formulas as are used to compute the ratios of the industry standards is the first step. The matching of ratios of companies in the same SIC code and in a similar narrow dollar sales range also will keep this comparison valid.

An attempt to discern "commonality" in how industry members value inventory and compute depreciation versus the customer's methods (this will be reflected in the annual report's notes section) will aid in making these comparisons more factual. The last and one of the most important tasks involves checking the annual report's notes for unusual or one-time occurrences that affect the company's results. Doing so prevents miscalculations in determining true annual net income, especially when comparing income from the previous year to the present year. It also provides an accurate picture as to a company's "real" income from operations.

Benefits of Ratio Analysis

Ratios provide a means of comparing a firm's performance to that of an industry. Without this, there is literally no way to tell how the customer is achieving its goal to be the best in the industry. Ratios provide a means of comparing a firm's performance to that of its industry. This can help a firm to prove that it is on the right track as an operation that is successfully run.

Ratios view a company in light of solvency, efficiency, and profitability. These three areas are the most critical to a firm's survival. Ratios can provide a method to tie all the parts of a balance sheet and income statement together. Since parts of both kinds of data are used at times to calculate these ratios, and since they can be tied together by some additional ratios, they provide the "binding" that locks these two reports together.

One such example of a ratio that binds these two reports together is the DuPont method. It takes the total asset turnover (sales/assets) and ties it to the net profit margin ([net income/net sales] income statement) to give the return on investment (net income/assets). It then takes and multiplies the return on investment times the financial leverage ([assets/equity] [balance sheet]) to arrive at the return on equity (net income/equity). The DuPont method shows how efficiencies can be developed in both sides of a financial statement when they are reflected by the trend movement over a five-year period in the return on equity.

Ratios can show trends in all the parts of a balance sheet and income statement and can tie the results together and focus on the weakest link in the chain. The advantage of using ratios is that exceptional items or areas where the numbers are unusual will tend to stand out when compared against the industry numbers.

Ratios also can help to identify some tricks companies use to make their numbers look good, such as:

- Recording revenue too soon: This makes a firm appear more profitable than it really is.

- Recording bogus revenue: This can make a company appear profitable when it may or may not be profitable and can be a form of fraud.
- Boosting profits with one-time gains: This can make a customer appear more profitable than it is.
- Shifting current expenses to a later period: By doing this, a firm makes itself appear to be more profitable than it really is.
- Failing to record or disclose all liabilities: This is an attempt by a firm to appear financially sound when it may or may not be solvent and can be a form of fraud.
- Shifting current income to a later period: Playing games with profit using the "saving of income for a rainy day" method of accounting deceives shareholders into believing that income is consistently improving.
- Shifting expenses into the current period: This likewise uses the "saving of income for a rainy day" accounting technique and deceives shareholders into believing that income is consistently improving.

CONCLUSION

Using the four main forms of financial analysis—common, ratio, trend, and comparison to industry standards—provides the ability to determine the financial strength or weakness of a firm. It furnishes insights into how well a firm is being managed and can give a "look" into the future using past trends as a guide. These analyses are by no means the only sources of information that credit professionals have at their disposal for arriving at a sound business credit decision. Many other factors within and outside of the firm can and will influence the final decision. These factors are reviewed in Chapters 2 and 3.

2

B IS FOR BUILDING ESSENTIAL BUSINESS CREDIT INFORMATION

INTRODUCTION

This chapter guides the credit professional in the right direction to get the very best information available. Specifically it focuses on:

- How can the availability of sources of business and credit information be determined?
- How sound are these sources of information?
- How cost effective compared to value are these sources to an overall business credit decision?
- How can checks be executed and the information provided by the customer substantiated?
- What are some internal facts that could alter a business credit perspective?

This chapter provides information on where to acquire new sources of information on customers. Each source is reviewed and its soundness considered. The cost/effectiveness of these sources is taken into account to determine the most effective information sources for making a sound business credit decision. The chapter explores how to perform the checks effectively, efficiently, and expeditiously while confirming the information given by the customer. Readers will gain a new appreciation for the value of customers' references and see the big picture by considering other internal factors that can affect a sound business credit decision.

Here we focus on the sources of business and credit information that are available to the credit professional. As mentioned, obtaining information on firms outside of the United States is more difficult; first reviewed will be some of the domestic sources followed by the international ones and then a discussion of what type of information is available to both. Unlike financial statements that have been audited and verified by an independent auditing firm in the United States, the information supplied by firms outside the country has not been confirmed by an independent third party. Does that make the information worthless? No, but less faith should be put into some types of information.

DOMESTIC SOURCES OF BUSINESS CREDIT INFORMATION

Some suppliers obtain part of their information directly from government agencies; they receive other parts via monthly computer tapes and still other information directly from the customer. A general rule of thumb is never to base an entire credit decision on either one piece of information or on only one source of information. A thorough investigation should use multiple sources, and the credit decision should be based on all of that information. Now first let us look at domestic sources of information.

Dun & Bradstreet. This firm provides multiple types of reports, from very detailed to very limited, from very general to very specific, and from preformatted to a very customized one. Some of the information that can be obtained from Dun & Bradstreet includes SIC code, a rating based on financial information and paying habits, references, financial information, legal information, status of incorporation, and general information on the principals and the firm. Not all of this information is available on every report. Some reports lack financial information, some have minimal trade information, and not all tax liens, judgements, lawsuits, UCC-1 filings, or bankruptcies show up. Credit professionals can request custom reports that include only the sought-after information, if it can be obtained. If the firm is privately held, D & B cannot obtain financial information from a firm that is not willing to give it out. D & B reports can be a good starting point for launching a credit investigation.

Experian. Experian is a D & B competitor that provides reports with reference information, legal information, and only audited financial information. This information, like that from D & B, is obtained from the computer tapes of the customer's trade creditors and from government agencies. The financial information provided is audited. Experian gives information on the principals only if this information is reflected in the firm's audited annual report.

NACM affiliates. Some National Association of Credit Management (NACM) affiliates run industry trade groups. The groups are made up of credit managers in the same industry. The affiliates compile trade data on firms that are customers of their trade group members. These members may supply computer tapes that can be used for providing credit reports to other members and nonmembers. In the case of nonmembers, those providing the data are not identified in the report.

Trade exchange groups. Similar to the NACM affiliates (and some affiliate-run trade groups), these firms create trade reference reports that members of that particular trade group use as a guide for how customers pay. In the industries that have a trade association, members use this report to check the paying habits of potential customers before approving their credit line.

Trade references. Trade references usually are requested on all credit applications and most times are checked by credit professionals. The drawback to these references is usually potential new customers include only their best-paid creditors. While this does indicate how high a credit limit the customer has, it does not ensure that another firm will be paid near as well as the best-paid creditors. If your credit application requires references that will be paid in the same manner as you anticipate being paid, the value of these references will grow exponentially.

Banks. This reference likewise does not add much in the way of how well you may anticipate being paid in the future. Most banks' working capital lines of credit are fully secured by all the assets of the customer. Customers who default on the bank most likely will not be in business very long. It is helpful to find out what credit line the bank has granted and what the current balance outstanding is. If there is a great deal of room left on the line, a new marginal customer may be able to obtain a standby letter of credit to secure your credit limit.

Attempting to confirm that all assets are being used as collateral also might be valuable information. Free assets could provide you with something to use as collateral. Likewise, if the balance outstanding on the working capital line of credit is low against the limit, then a purchase money security interest in your inventory might not be a great problem, as the bank will have more than sufficient collateral to cover the loan.

Internet. This vast and wide-open, relatively new source of financial, business, and credit information can be overwhelming at times. The Internet provides users access to government agencies that have financial data, newspapers that have information on potential and current customers, access to the firm's own web site as well as many other credit and business web sites. Some information will be at your fingertips while other information will require a vast amount of "digging." Internet access should be required of all credit professionals.

Newspapers, business publications, industry association newsletters. These sources help to not only provide sound information for the credit professional but also are a very beneficial training and new ideas' area. These publications pass along new techniques and tools that can help the credit professional stay on the cutting edge of all areas that affect their job.

Customer and the salesperson. These people are not the first choice for the most accurate information, but you have to start somewhere. While the first contact with customers is usually the best time to obtain the most information, what customers are willing to provide depends in large part on who has the greatest need of the other. Generally I take the salesperson's buildup of a new customer and divide it by four; the result may be reasonably close to reality. The outcome of this "calculation" likewise can vary depending on your relationship with the sales force, whether your company is marketing oriented or cash oriented, and on the individuals themselves. Many salespeople are extremely professional. Many are concerned not only with getting the sale but with seeing that the invoice is paid for on a timely basis. Some salespeople are quite adept at getting the proper information and documents that the credit professional needs to approve the sale.

INTERNATIONAL SOURCES OF CREDIT INFORMATION

Credit Reports Latin America (CRLA) and the World. This firm provides custom, fresh investigations of firms around the globe. It provides help with specific needs and can offer country risk assessments that will help credit professionals judge the risk in selling goods to a firm in a particular country. Credit Reports can address not only country risk but political and monetary risk as well. These custom reports address the credit professional's needs when considering the terms to offer customers residing outside of the United States.

Dun & Bradstreet. D & B provides packaged reports similar to those for U.S. firms and provides information on the type of company, SIC code, principals, bank and trade information (if available), and the company itself. Custom reports are also available and are cost sensitive based on the part of the world the report pertains to and how fast the information is needed. D & B also provides country risk assessments as well.

Experian. It is branching out into the international market.

FCIB (division of NACM). This wing of NACM provides country risk assessments and terms recommended in various areas of the world. Customer information typically is not available, but information on problems within certain industries is available. It is also an excellent source of education for credit professionals who deal in international credit.

Graydon America. This company provides customized and fresh reports as well as country risk assessment.

Veritas. This company is similar to CRLA in providing customized and fresh reports for credit professionals. It specializes in the Latin American reports and can also do country risk assessment.

Internet. Once again, a vast ocean of information is available on the Internet. Creditworthy.com provides weekly information on events happening around the globe, while news sources such as the *Wall Street Journal* and many other daily domestic and international newspaper companies make the job of the credit executive a little easier. Minute-by-minute updates from news reporting agencies such as CNN and other news networks provide almost instantaneous access to information around the globe.

With the amount of information available, the greatest challenge for credit professionals is avoiding information overload.

International Chamber of Commerce (ICC). This is a highly regarded source of country data and laws governing selling and shipping internationally. A great deal of data is available through this organization on the "dos" and "don'ts" of selling outside the United States.

U.S. Department of Commerce. Similar in nature to the International Chamber of Commerce, this agency has a large amount of information on how to stay out of trouble when selling into a foreign country.

Local and national international trade associations. These associations work like other trade credit associations but tend to deal more with assessing country risk rather than with specific customers with the exception of the country's government itself. These groups meet monthly, quarterly, or semiannually to discuss problems that members are experiencing in particular countries and ways they have used to deal with these risks. Such associations are excellent places to learn how to escape the pitfalls of selling internationally.

Trade references. Many firms outside the United States do not provide trade references and request that any information be obtained from their banks. Trade references are not as common.

International banks. Most international banks will provide references, but just to another bank. Credit professionals can have their bank contact the international banks for this information. There usually is a fee for this service.

***Wall Street Journal*, IOMA's "Managing International Credit and Collections," S.J. Rundt & Associates Inc. publications:** These organizations sell daily newspapers or monthly newsletters that provide information on international events and country risk information. All information available will help in assessing the other forms of credit risk related to international sales that firms typically do not experience when selling within the United States.

HOW SOUND ARE THE DOMESTIC SOURCES OF INFORMATION?

Credit reporting agencies. Some information in credit reports is verified (audited statements, government records [UCC]), and some is hearsay (information direct from the customer, unaudited financial statements). Some information is up to date, some is not. Some information can be extremely useful (i.e., audited statements), while other information can be totally valueless ("customer business is on a well-traveled street") or very limited (few references or facts). Ratings may be based on out-of-date information, unverified (unaudited annual reports), or skewed toward larger balanced references compared to the overall rating of all credit references listed.

Trade references, trade groups, and banks. These can be excellent sources of up-to-date information of companies' paying habits. Some information, however, is limited usually to references only. If a customer supplies trade references, generally all information will be positive. Banks are generally fully secured and are usually the best paid.

Internet, newspapers, the customer, and salespeople. These can be excellent sources of information, generally on larger companies. Customers usually are excellent sources of information when they want something or when the supplier has control over them. The salespeople can be the "eyes, ears, and nose" of the credit group and can supply on-the-spot information on a customer.

HOW SOUND ARE THE INTERNATIONAL SOURCES OF INFORMATION?

Credit reporting agencies. As in domestic reports, some information is verified, some is hearsay; some information is up to date while other parts may not be. Information varies from extremely useful to totally valueless, or it may be very limited. Some agencies reports are based on a database, while others do fresh investigations. Ratings may be based on out-of-date information, unverified information, or may be skewed toward larger balanced references compared to the overall rating of all references listed.

Internet, International Chamber of Commerce, and U.S. Department of Commerce. These sources can be excellent suppliers of information, generally on larger companies. The International Chamber of Commerce usually has more information on country risk than company information. Information from the U.S. Department of Commerce may be out of date.

Local and national international trade associations, trade references, and international banks. These organizations are an excellent source of information on companies of all sizes plus an excellent source of up-to-date country risk information.

***Wall Street Journal,* IOMA's "Managing International Credit and Collections," S.J. Rundt & Associates Inc. publications.** These organizations can be excellent sources of information, generally on larger companies, and can provide an up-to-date evaluation of country risk.

COST EFFECTIVENESS OF THE DOMESTIC INFORMATION

Credit reporting agencies. These firms can require a one-year contract, which has a minimum contract amount and allow only a partial carry-over of any unused part. If credit extensions are for low-dollar, high-volume sales then using a "rating" system for automatic approval can save time and money. Ratings are obtained through books or CDs supplied by the credit information supplier. These reports can be a good starting point for investigations of larger dollar transactions.

Trade references, trade groups, and banks. Trade and bank references are time costly but generally supply only "prompt payment" results. Trade groups supply limited but timely information on slow-paying customers and can be expensive to participate in; however, savings may more than offset the cost of membership.

Internet, newspapers, the customer, and salespeople. The Internet and newspapers generally are good sources of information, ranging from background information to audited annual reports, mostly on large corporations. Costs are monthly or tied to an annual subscription. The customer can supply all types of information but unless the financial information is audited, credit professionals will be taking it on blind faith. Time spent may vary greatly depending on the dollars connected to the sale from a phone call to a personal visit. An alert salesperson can supply specific information on the building, upkeep, and inventory, and any costs involved will be part of their initial sales calls.

COST EFFECTIVENESS OF INTERNATIONAL INFORMATION

Credit reporting agencies. A new investigation may provide excellent information on a company. Some agencies supply country risk information and provide a recommended credit limit based on their findings. These types of reports tend to be more expensive than off-the-database reports. Generally they require payment in advance for a one-year contract, which has a minimum number of reports and allow only a partial carry-over of the contract. The credit reporting agency may be able to obtain financial data; those data may be the only source other than a visit by the salesperson or the credit person to determine a company's size and financial strength. Information may not be audited, and accounting rules can differ greatly from those of the United States.

Internet, International Chamber of Commerce, and U.S. Department of Commerce. Generally, these are inexpensive sources of information on large companies and on country information. For large transactions, the additional information supplied by these organizations may change the type of terms that credit professionals may offer to a customer.

Local and national international trade associations, trade references, and international banks. An association's annual fee may be high, but generally membership is worth the cost as the exchange of information on country risk and the access to others that have "survived" international transactions can prove invaluable in preventing losses. A trade reference from a U.S. company on a foreign customer will be of great value. Some firms outside of the United States are reluctant to supply credit references on their customers. Cost of getting a trade reference is not more than a fax and the time to follow up if no reply. Banks can be excellent sources of country as well as customer risk. Sometimes they can obtain information on the foreign customer from the customer's bank, which can prove very valuable. Some banks do not offer this service and others charge a fee for it.

Wall Street Journal, IOMA's "Managing International Credit and Collections," S.J. Rundt & Associates Inc. publications. These types of publications are excellent sources of up-to-date information on the political and economic condition as well as a country's currency exchange rates. They may even contain information on large international firms and any problems they may be experiencing with selling in that country. Costs are usually tied to an annual subscription rate.

SUBSTANTIATING INFORMATION PROVIDED BY DOMESTIC CUSTOMERS

Credit reporting agencies. Generally, credit reports can be obtained by downloading data by modem via a mainframe to PC access or through the Internet. A total report or parts of a report can be obtained, depending on what information is needed to approve or deny credit.

Trade references, trade groups, and banks. Trade and bank reference forms (see Exhibits 2.1 & 2.2) usually can be faxed to the respective firms but should always include a customer signed authorization form (see Exhibit 2.3), allowing that firm to release credit information on them.

Internet, the customer's auditor, the customer, and salespeople. A quick Internet check may provide some general background information on the customer. A confirming call to the customer's auditors may provide some additional insight to the customer's current financial condition. A call to the customer may help to fill in any gaps in information received from trade references, credit reporting agencies, or on financial information. The salesperson may provide the names of other companies that the firm does business with after seeing the facility and reviewing the inventory on hand.

Exhibit 2.1. Bank Credit Inquiry

Your Company Name
Street Address
City, State & Zip
FAX#: ( ) -

BANK CREDIT INQUIRY

Bank Name
Street Address
City, State & Zip
( ) -

Ref: <u>Customer Name</u>
<u>Street Address</u>
<u>City, State & Zip</u>

The above-referenced company has given your concern's name as a credit reference. Please provide us with your experience with them so that we may determine their credit worthiness. Please fax this information back to us as soon as possible. Thank you in advance for the information that you provide and be assured that it will be kept confidential.

Sincerely,

I. M. Tracer
Credit Department

If business is not incorporated, please provide owner's name & address:

<u>SAVINGS ACCOUNT</u>   LOW ___   MEDIUM ___   HIGH ___ $___ FIGURE

OPEN ___   CLOSED ___

<u>CHECKING ACCOUNT</u>   LOW ___   MEDIUM ___   HIGH ___ $___ FIGURE
SATISFACTORY ___   UNSATISFACTORY ___

<u>CREDIT EXPERIENCE</u>

Loans are granted: Frequently ___   Occasionally ___   Seldom ___

Type: Working Capital ___   Mortgage ___   Installment ___

Maximum Credit Extended $ _____   Secured ___   Unsecured ___

Present Outstandings: Secured $ _____   Unsecured $ _____

Relationship: SATISFACTORY ___   UNSATISFACTORY ___

Have "NSF" checks been issued: Yes ___   No ___

Prepared By: _____   Title: _____

Exhibit 2.2. Credit Inquiry

Your Company Name
Street Address
City, State & Zip
PHONE (   )   -
FAX   (   )   -

CREDIT INQUIRY

*Trade Reference Company   Ref: <u>Trade Reference Name</u>
*Street Address   <u>Street Address</u>
*City, State & Zip   <u>City, State & Zip</u>

The above-referenced company has given your concern's name as a credit reference. Please provide us with your experience with them so that we may determine their credit worthiness. Please fax this information back to us as soon as possible. Thank you in advance for the information that you provide and be assured that it will be kept confidential.

Sincerely,

_____
 Credit Department

Sold from _____   MANNER OF PAYMENT
                                                                 __ Discounts
Terms of Sales _____   __ Prompt & Satisfactory
                                                                 __ Prompt to ___ Days Slow
Largest Amount Now Owing $_____   __ Pays on Account
                                                                 __ Asks for More Time
Amount Past Due $_____   __ Slow but Collectible
                                                                 __ Accepts COD's Promptly
Recent Trend Toward ___Promptness   __ Settles by Trade Acceptance
               __ Slowness   __ Notes Paid at Maturity
Makes Unjust Claims (State) _____   __ Account Secured
_____
Credit Refused (State Cause)
_____
_____
Remarks: _____   ____ Average Days Paid
_____
_____
Information Given By: _____ Date _____

WE REQUEST THE RETURN OF THIS FORM TO FACILITATE OUR SYSTEM OF FILING REPORT.

Exhibit 2.3.　Credit Release Form

CREDIT RELEASE FORM

Complete EACH of the forms below. They should correspond to the four credit references in your credit application. Please TYPE or PRINT clearly.

BANK REFERENCE: AUTHORIZATION TO RELEASE CREDIT INFORMATION
Name of Bank _____

Dear Mr. or Ms. _____We are at present making
application to purchase products or services from
_____. We would appreciate your completing the attached reference form
and returning it to them with this authorization.
　　　　Company _____
　　　　Signature _____ Date:_____

SUPPLIER: AUTHORIZATION TO RELEASE CREDIT INFORMATION

Name of Supplier _____

Dear Mr. or Ms. _____
We are at present making application to purchase products or services from
_____. We would appreciate your completing the attached reference form
and returning it to them with this authorization.
　　　　Company _____
　　　　Signature _____ Date:_____

SUPPLIER: AUTHORIZATION TO RELEASE CREDIT INFORMATION

Name of Supplier _____

Dear Mr. or Ms. _____
We are at present making application to purchase products or services from
_____. We would appreciate your completing the attached reference form
and returning it to them with this authorization.
　　　　Company _____
　　　　Signature _____ Date:_____

SUPPLIER: AUTHORIZATION TO RELEASE CREDIT INFORMATION

Name of Supplier _____

Dear Mr. or Ms. _____
We are at present making application to purchase products or services from
_____. We would appreciate your completing the attached reference form
and returning it to them with this authorization.
　　　　Company _____
　　　　Signature _____ Date:_____

SUBSTANTIATING THE INFORMATION PROVIDED
BY YOUR INTERNATIONAL CUSTOMER

Credit reporting agencies. Generally, credit reports can be requested by downloading data by modem via a PC to mainframe access. Some reports from databases can be immediately downloaded, whereas fresh investigations may take from three to 30 business days depending on the country and your need.

Internet, International Chamber of Commerce, and U.S. Department of Commerce. A quick Internet check may provide some general background information on the customer. Information obtained from the International Chamber of Commerce and the U.S. Department of Commerce may be able to be faxed. If a fee is involved, a check could be shipped overnight with an authorization for the return of the information by prepaid overnight express, which will help to speed up needed reports.

Local and national international trade associations, trade references, and international banks. A quick phone call to other members of local and national trade associations may help to obtain updated information on a customer. A check of the trade exchange reports also may provide some insights into the customer's paying habits. By faxing trade references with a credit release authorization form, a quick verification of terms of sale (open account, sight draft, letters of credit, etc.) can be obtained from a customer's U.S. suppliers. References requested from companies outside of the United States may take longer due to time zone differences as well as cultural differences. Allow a reasonable amount of time for receipt of the information and then follow it up. International banks may provide information only to your bank. Attempt to obtain information first by fax directly to the customer's bank. If there is no reply or if instructions are received to go through your bank, do so and be prepared for delays.

***Wall Street Journal*, IOMA's "Managing International Credit and Collections," S.J. Rundt & Associates Inc. publications.** A quick scan of these publications might help to obtain status on recent problems in a customer's country as well as the current exchange rates.

"INTERNAL" FACTS THAT COULD ALTER A BUSINESS CREDIT PERSPECTIVE

Company philosophy. A marketing-oriented (sales first, credit last) or cash-oriented philosophy drastically affect the way the credit professional runs the department. In a marketing atmosphere, credit tends to be looser and collection efforts more restrained. In a cash environment, credit can be restrictive and collections tight. Most firms tend to be somewhere in the middle with a slight lean toward the marketing side.

Position in the industry. If a firm is an industry leader, its influence on the market can be the driving force behind what information, security, and collection pace the credit professional can set. Even being one of a few can help to keep controls in place over customers. If, however, a firm is one of many, its ability to control the behavior of customers may be limited.

Type of product. Typically, highly technical products are sold to firms that are financially sound or can afford large down payments before these types of items are sold. Unique (customized) products also tend to fall into this type of category. Somewhat technical or commodity products can be sold to all types. Credit professionals may have to do more thorough investigations of the firms that are interested in such products. Professional products can also be sold to a great deal of marginal or problem accounts, so credit extension should be carefully scrutinized. Easily identifiable products (assuming there is no general blanket lien) can be used as collateral to help support your credit decision.

Customer location. Selling to local customers provides greater control through easy access to them. By selling nationally, some of that control is exchanged for a larger area to expand sales growth. International sales allow the least amount of controls possible, thus entailing the greatest risk, which should result in the greatest profits and the largest possible area to sell products.

Type of customer. Selling to manufacturers and distributors is similar, as these firms pass on the costs of products to the end user. Retailers do likewise but tend to add on other charges not common to manufacturers or distributors. Service firms may also be similar to manufacturers and distributors and will pass costs on to end users. Nonprofit companies survive on donations and fees charged to members and at times are limited by very tight cash flow. Agricultural firms have to deal with environmental conditions, commodity-pricing conditions, and weather conditions, which can seriously stifle their cash flow.

Terms of sale common to the industry. Net terms (i.e., net 10, net 15, net 30, etc.) are from the date of invoice and offer no financial benefit for paying early. On the other hand, discount terms (i.e., 1% 10, net 30, 2% 10, net 30, etc.) provide an incentive to pay early. Discount terms can create problems when customers take the discount without paying within the discount period.

Extended terms (i.e., net 60, net 90, etc.) offer customers additional time to pay a debt. The additional time may be required due to the distance the product may need to travel or may be standard for an industry. It also may be needed because of slow turnover of certain types of products. Extended terms cost sellers money, as they must carry these receivables longer than what may be a normal 30 days. The cost of these terms should be built into the price of the goods. Extended terms may allow a firm to buy product where normal terms would not. They also may be a source of greater exposure and potential for a larger loss, as greater credit limits will be needed by customers receiving extended terms. Firms may need to offer extended terms to meet the competition of a rival firm as governed under the Robinson-Patman Act.

Costs of shipping products (your location versus that of the customer). High shipping costs due to weight and bulk of products (i.e., concrete) and customer location can play a large role in determining to whom a firm will sell a product. High shipping costs due to volatility of products (i.e., a hot new toy at Christmas time) may occur if products must be at the customer's location to meet seasonal or emergency needs. Perishable goods (i.e., bread) incur high shipping costs due to their short life spans. Fragile goods (i.e., glass products) can result in high shipping costs due to the special packaging materials needed to protect these items from damage.

Average to low shipping costs due to the ease of shipping goods (i.e., canned goods) can help to keep goods flowing more readily. Ease of shipping from plant due to location of customer base can help to keep costs low (i.e., customer base is local).

Government regulation of an industry. Alcohol, drugs, firearms, and hazardous materials are regulated by federal and/or state government agencies, and strict regulations add to the cost of producing and selling of these goods. Some agencies involved in these types of products include the Drug Enforcement Agency (DEA), the Food and Drug Administration (FDA), the Alcohol, Tobacco, and Firearms (ATF) Agency, and the Environmental Protection Agency (EPA).

Production lead time. Long production time can provide credit professionals with the time needed to complete some investigations, provided that large expenditures are not made quickly for raw materials needed to create a finished good. Short production time can limit the ability of credit professionals to stop a shipment to a problem customer. Off-the-shelf products leave no time for action and can force credit professionals to be alert to financial problems on marginal or bankruptcy-prone customers. A time delay involved in receipt of raw materials and/or goods for sale can create additional problems for credit professionals if the items are time sensitive due to seasonal or emergency needs or are perishable.

Financial condition and size of the company. Working for a large company provides certain strengths and access to more information and tools needed to make better credit decisions and react faster to collection risks. Medium-size firms can have access to most options that are available to larger firms but may be less able to use more expensive options, such as larger credit reporting contracts. However, these medium-size firms may have better control over operations due to a reduction of red tape. Small companies, on the other hand, may have very limited access to credit tools. Financially sound and cash-rich companies can more easily afford to provide their credit professionals with all the necessary tools to meet all their needs. Cash-poor companies, such as leveraged buyout (LBO) firms, will be very restrictive on expenditures. They will also demand tight controls over the collection efforts made by their credit professionals.

Costs of sale. Profit margin (profit made after overhead costs are deducted) on some goods are a major factor in whether credit can be approved. If margins are high, greater risks can be taken and vice versa. Labor and overhead costs (plant and machinery upkeep, tooling expenses, etc.) along with raw materials costs directly affect this profit margin. The lower these costs are in relation to the selling volume and profit of the goods, the greater the gross profit of the goods being sold. Higher profit margins provide credit professionals with some flexibility to make a credit sale.

CONCLUSION

We have looked at the tools and the internal and external factors that can directly influence the decision of credit professionals. The degree that any one of these aspects influences a professional's decision depends on the industry he or she is in, the size and financial condition of the firm, the firm's philosophy, and the type of customers sold to, among other factors. With all of these things influencing credit professionals on a daily basis, how can a sound business credit decision ever be made? Chapter 3 provides the answer to this question.

3

C IS FOR CONSIDERING ALL FACTORS THAT IMPACT THE BUSINESS CREDIT DECISION

INTRODUCTION

Once the information has been assembled and the calculations completed, credit professionals need to do something with the information. This chapter takes a look at the following issues:

- Weighing financial, credit, and business factors in formulating a sound business credit decision
- Possible costs to the company based on credit decision rendered
- Possible value to the company based on credit decision rendered
- Developing best-case/worst-case scenarios
- Consolidating and ordering facts to vindicate the decision/recommendation
- Ascertaining any gaps in the data

This chapter provides the ability to assign weights to the value of different types of information uncovered through investigation and evaluation of data. Readers will gain an appreciation of the strength of certain factors common to their industries that affect sound business credit decisions. Is a sound business credit decision too expensive for the firm (costs), or is it preventing a much greater cost (bad debt)? Readers will learn to provide multiple best-case/worst-case scenarios to explain their decisions, gain a sixth sense for locating gaps in data, and figuring out how to plug them.

WEIGHING FINANCIAL, CREDIT, AND BUSINESS FACTORS

Now it is time to weigh the importance of each factor that goes in arriving at a sound business credit decision. The text will ask questions to help readers to focus on the different factors that affect the rendering of such decisions. Readers' answers will help them to weigh each point and understand how to arrive at a final decision. The answers will also provide a logical trail to follow and the means to defend the decision (if necessary) to not only top management but also the customer.

A credit decision cannot be made in a vacuum. A number of questions must be asked and answered before a conclusion can be drawn. Sometimes the issues will have nothing to do with the customer. Here are some questions that must be answered in order to make a sound financial credit decision.

Will the company be able to accommodate the order? This time we will first consider our own firm's financial status, which will affect its ability to obtain and pay for the raw materials and/or finished goods. If a firm is not financially strong enough, if it does not have the factory capacity to handle the order, or if it does not have the labor available to process the order, then it must consider other alternatives.

Other factors along this same line include ease of shipping, including any special handling needed due to regulation of certain types of products and due to the customer's or the supplier's location. Other shipping concerns include the need to complete accurately certain paperwork required (i.e., certificate of origin, bid bonds, performance bonds, additional invoice copies, etc.) and the size and weight or type of material being shipped.

Will the order generate sufficient profit to make it worthwhile?
After looking at all the costs involved in the creation and handling of the order, will the order help the firm to cover overhead or create other incre-

mental and more profitable additional sales? If a company does not make money on the sale, then it may not be worth accepting.

What will be the turnaround time for creation and/or receiving of goods followed by the shipping of the finished product? The longer it takes for a firm to realize its profit on this sale, the less money it will make. If there are long delays in the manufacture or receipt and shipping of the finished goods, the anticipated profit margin goes down in direct proportion to these delays.

When will payment be received? This factor considers not only the paying habits of the customer but also whether extended terms were offered in order to get the sale. Any delays, whether authorized or unauthorized, cost part of the anticipated profit margin. The longer it takes to collect the funds even after extended terms are considered, approved, and elapsed, the lower the profit on the final sale.

Are extended credit terms being requested, or are they common for the industry? If offering extended terms of sale is the norm for the industry, then this should be computed into the cost of doing business. If, however, the customer is requesting terms, then the all-important question to ask is: Why? This aspect must be addressed immediately or the collectability of the sale may be in jeopardy. Terms should never be "sold" to get an order but should be used to equalize competition. The answer to the all-important Why? question will directly affect how this aspect of extended terms is reflected in the firm's overall approval equation.

CREDIT CONSIDERATIONS

How much credit does the customer need? Before answering this question, determine exactly what the firm considers to be a large, medium, and small order. What may be huge to one firm may be almost nothing to another. Once credit professionals have established these levels, the amount of effort in the investigation and consideration of a sale should be in direct proportion to the dollars involved in the sale. The following questions will help determine the level of investigation.

Is the sale to a new, current, or former customer? For current customers, on top of all other factors to be considered, the added weight of recent experience with that company can lessen or increase the degree of difficulty in approving credit for this sale. If the sale is to a new or former customer with whom the firm has had no experience in over a year, the level of investigation basically starts at ground zero.

Is the customer located in the United States? Is it in a politically or financially unstable country? Depending on the location of the customer, the degree of risk rises proportionately. Once outside of the country, three additional risks occur: economic, political, and monetary. Economic risk deals with status of the country's financial condition (i.e., high unemployment, hyperinflation, large trade deficits, etc.). Political risk involves problems with the stability of the government currently in power. Finally, monetary risk involves the value of the local currency against the U.S. dollar. If the local currency drops or goes into free-fall, then it will cost the customer far too much to buy U.S. goods. Inside of the United States, the only risk comes from credit risk; sometimes that is risk enough.

When are the goods to be shipped? Long time lags allow for a closer monitoring of problems whereas shorter ones can keep problems coming at a pace that sometimes cannot be handled properly.

Is the sale for a small or large amount (based on the company's definition of a large or small sale)? The larger the sale, the greater the amount of investigation that will be needed with few exceptions. The chances of having a large loss if all the "I's" are dotted and the "T's" are crossed are lower than for a smaller sale that probably is watched less carefully.

How long will it take to obtain a credit report? Domestically, credit reports are virtually instantaneous. Outside of the United States, the country in which the customer is located and also whether a "fresh" report or one off a database is needed greatly affect the length of time required to get a credit report. Pricewise, fresh reports cost more, and the faster they are needed the more expensive they become. Typically, even in the worst possible areas, the longest time for a report will be from 21 to 30 days.

What is the turnaround time for obtaining references, background information, and country risk status (if needed)? Obtaining references in the United States can take hours to a maximum of one or two days. Background information can be obtained from a credit report that can be downloaded instantly. If international references can be obtained at all, they may take a week to two weeks or longer. Numerous sources within the United States can supply country risk information, as can the firm's own bank in a matter of minutes to hours.

Is the sale a one-time deal or will continuous sales be made? In the case of a one-time deal, depending on the dollars involved, it is best to make a thorough investigation, as a firm will have no leverage to rely on in the future if it cannot hold orders. As for continuous business, holding orders as a last resort can work in some cases; therefore, the investigation does not need to be so thorough.

If the sale is to a current or former customer, is it within their credit limit? Credit limits should be looked at annually as a normal course of business. Granting the maximum amount of credit possible when a customer requests a credit line is the best way to handle credit extension; it eliminates the need to review the limit during that year. If the customer needs an amount of credit higher than what was granted, then security of some kind will be needed to increase the amount beyond the limit set.

What is the profit margin on the sale? This is critical to know, as it can be the reason that an order is approved at all or will be considered for a lesser amount. With high margins, credit extension can be more liberal; with low margins, credit extension should be more conservative.

Have terms other than standard terms been requested? This also can be a factor that may be addressing competition. If this is the case and a firm is required to meet competition, the terms other than standard may be in order. If, however, nonstandard terms are requested to help a marginal customer survive long enough to make the sale but not necessarily make payment to the firm, then other terms should not be offered.

If open account terms are not recommended, can the credit extension be secured? This depends greatly on the status of any working capital line of credit that a customer may have with its bank, the status of the agreement with the bank, the balance owed, the amount of collateral used, and the customer's ability and desire to supply it. If open account terms are not recommended and the customer cannot offer any security, can a cash sale be made? Cash sales always can be made if the customer has the cash. Can additional discounts be offered in exchange for a cash-in-advance payment? This aspect is always recommended if the margin on the product is not too low and a firm is willing to offer the same terms to all customers in the same class.

Can the order be broken up, making it easier to manage cash payments? This depends greatly on the size of the order and whether the purchase order requires a complete shipment. Only by working closely with the customer can this fact be determined.

After rejecting all the usual ways to make a sale, is there an unusual way to clinch the deal? The credit professional should always try to be creative.

BUSINESS CONSIDERATIONS

Credit is only part of the equation. As amazing as this may be to credit professionals, some companies also take certain business issues into consideration when they decide whether to extend credit. Here are some of the business questions that may be asked.

Is this sale important to the well-being of the company? Literally every sale that is not a loss is important to the well-being of a company. The question, however, implies that the sale is significant enough to make it valuable to the firm. This goes hand in hand with the larger the sale, proportionately, the greater the risk and rewards involved.

Will the sale go to a competitor? In most cases, this is not "what the doctor ordered." If the order represents a sure loss, then losing the sale may not be such a bad thing.

What control does the company have over its customers? A company may have some control over its customers, depending on the nature of the industry that the firm is in, the type of products that it sells, and whether it has a one-of-a-kind product or one that its customers would have limited access to. Otherwise, the firm probably has no control; it is just one of many that is fighting to get the order.

What control does the company have over the marketplace? The same factors that applied in the previous question will hold true for this question.

What control does the company have over its suppliers? Typically, only firms that purchase a large quantity of product on a regular basis or that buy product that is not readily sellable to others, have any control over suppliers.

Does this sale represent new incremental business or is it a one-time sale? Both types of business are desirable, but obviously continuous business is always the most desirable.

Will this sale lead to other new unrelated business? This factor always must be considered in every sale that is made. Being able to draw additional sales from a base sale is the goal of every good salesperson and every growing firm.

Will this sale create new recognition for the company from other potential customers? Brand recognition is extremely desirable for every firm. Keeping the firm's products and name in the forefront of business is critical to survival.

Will this sale open new doors to other marketplaces for the company's products? Breaking into new territories especially in markets where the number of competitors is small and the only way to gain market share is "over the dead body" of the competition may be reason enough to pursue certain customers.

Will this order result in new product development? Expansion into new products increases the salability of a company. Firms always need new products to meet the continuous needs of customers. New products also can reflect favorably on the firm, as it will appear to be an innovator within the market that it sells to.

Will this order require possible expansion of the company? This is always a difficult question to address, especially if it requires that a firm grow quickly. Without proper support and funding by a bank or investors, orders that cause major expansion can drive a business into the ground.

Will this order require partnership agreements with other companies? Another hard decision to the firm is one that tends to shy away from anything that would tie it to another firm. Considering the number of successful joint ventures, the potential partnership issue is a decision that may need serious consideration.

Will this order require subcontracting part of the work to others? Work should be subcontracted out only if the firm that will do the subcontracting has a solid reputation and can be trusted. If a subcontractor's work is shoddy, your firm's reputation will suffer.

Could hidden expenses or liabilities arise as a result of accepting this order? Some products carry their own type of problems. An example is asbestos. Although it performs well in many areas, its side effects can make it too risky to sell or even use. Due to the number of lawsuits being brought, it may be wiser to obtain a more expensive safer substitute than to use it.

What are the warranty requirements for this order? Is anything besides the firm's standard warranty required? If so, some costly expenses may come back later to haunt future profitability. Always anticipate what this additional warranty will cost and set up a reserve to cover it.

What is the company's liability in accepting this order? If the liability goes beyond the normal warranty, then, as suggested above, a reserve should be set up or liability insurance should be obtained to cover this risk.

Are there time limits on this order, and can they be met without unusual expenses or hardship on the company? Time limits on large orders can be the death knell for many firms that, in their desire to obtain the order, overlook time constraints. Pressures from deadlines that the firms are unable to meet destroy them. Each order must be looked at realistically and not taken on blindly because on the surface they appear profitable.

POSSIBLE COSTS OF THE CREDIT DECISION

Few people stop to consider the possible financial effects of making a credit decision. However, credit decisions can have negative consequences. Here is a look at what can go wrong.

Total loss of the sale. This is obviously the ultimate loss in not approving an order, but it may not end there. A firm that is declined may be tempted to "bad-mouth" your firm, which can cause your firm to lose other sales. Every effort to make the sale should be made to prevent this negative situation from ever occurring. Every credit professional knows that it is in not only in their firm's best interest to make every sale but it is also in their best interests as well.

Partial loss of the sale. This also can result in some long-term problems similar to total losses of sales. Nevertheless, not all sales can be made, especially if the total sale requires the inclusion of goods that are not made by your firm or add significant expense to the overall sale. Still, every effort should be made to make every sale.

Extra carrying costs of receivables for the total order amount, due to extended terms requested by the customer. If there is a need to offer extended terms, this factor should be built into the costs of making the sale. Extended terms should not be used to sell an order unless total loss of a profitable piece of business or future incremental profitable business would occur without them.

Extra carrying costs of receivables for a partial order, due to extended terms requested by the customer. As above, these extra costs should be built into the costs of making the sale. Since the size of the entire order approved was reduced, so also is the expense involved in approving the order.

Possible loss of future sales from that customer. Every credit decision must consider this factor. If those sales would have been profitable, then the denial of credit can indeed be costly. As stated before, every effort must be made to approve all sales.

Possible bad debt if the sale is made regardless of the terms extended. Every credit decision is based on the risk factor. While foolish and rash decisions always can cost a company (and a credit professional!), some losses can and should occur or a firm may be passing up some profitable business.

POSSIBLE VALUE REALIZED BASED ON THE CREDIT DECISION

There are gains to be had as well as losses, and many companies have profited handsomely due to the actions of their credit professionals. Here is a look at some of the things that can go right.

Profit made on sale after expenses. This is the bottom line in every sale, and credit professionals should make all efforts to help improve profitability. Keeping credit investigations cost effective while minimizing the risks involved will help to improve the firm's bottom line.

Possible gains from future sales made to that customer. Using every means to encourage sales by maximizing the customer's credit limit will help to increase the gains from future sales while keeping expenses of reinvestigating a customer to a minimum.

Cost savings from utilization of plant facilities (manufacturing). Making every sale possible (not necessarily extending credit on them all) will help to keep the firm's plant both busy and fully utilized.

Reduction in the costs of carrying inventory. This falls under the same results as plant utilization. It is always better to keep inventory on the shelves of the customers and its customers than on your own.

Possible increase in cash flow (if terms can be reduced). Firms can accomplish this increase by offering discounts, but they should be considered only if they are cost effective. If a firm wants extended terms but the credit professional is convinced that this is either not possible or not in their and the firm's best interests, then this approach cannot increase the cash flow and the profitability of that particular order.

DEVELOPING BEST-CASE/WORST-CASE SCENARIOS

This area entails dealing with the success or failure of a sale based on the decision that is rendered. A sale can be approved as is, approved with a variation to the terms requested by the customer, approved for a lesser amount while granting the customer's terms request, or approved for a lesser amount with terms other than what was requested by the customer. Let us look at what the credit professional will be faced with in dealing with each decision.

Sale Is Approved as Ordered and Company Is Committed to Filling the Order

The credit professional must make every effort to ensure that the order is made to the exact specifications that were stated in the purchase order to prevent deduction problems before they can occur. Such efforts on the part of the credit professional, obviously, can happen only in the case of a large custom-made order that represents a sizable profit to the firm. Generally, the credit professional can act on these kinds of problems only after the deductions have been taken. If, however, there seems to be a trend of deductions from many different customers for similar products, then the credit professional must take steps to correct whatever causes these deductions.

Company is liable for all terms and conditions as reflected in the customer's purchase order. Unless there is an overriding agreement, such as when a distributor agreement supercedes the customer's purchase order, once a shipment is made against the purchase order, the firm is bound by its terms and conditions. Special customized or large dollar orders from first-time or irregular customers should be reviewed for any possible exceptional terms that may appear on the order. Such terms must be addressed before a shipment is made, by either a signed letter of change that confirms any changes by both parties or by a revised purchase order that can be submitted in place of the original one.

Credit must police the payment of this order in accordance with the terms of the customer's purchase order and according to company policy and procedures. Normal collection procedures should be followed when handling an order unless special terms were accepted. Also, if there is a concern that default might occur, credit must watch the account closely.

Credit may need to solve disputes between the customer and the company in order to effect payment of the debt. A public relations call should be made either before the due date of a discount time, if discount terms are offered, or at the halfway point in the time of the net terms being due. This call can help to resolve disputes before the invoice becomes due or past due. It also helps to eliminate nearly 95% of all excuses that a customer can use to not pay you.

Sale Is Approved with Variation to Terms Requested by the Customer; Terms Are Changed to Comply with the Company's Standard Terms

Customer may refuse to accept standard terms, thus canceling the order. At this point the credit professional has two alternatives, renegotiate or pass. The solidity of the investigation and the decision as well as the obvious pressure that will result from the loss of this order will determine which of the two options Credit will take.

Customer may counteroffer with other terms that may or may not be acceptable. The credit professional must be prepared to negotiate and settle the deal before things get out of hand and the sales and marketing group gives the store away. If the deal can be made with different terms that are acceptable to the credit professional and top management, and that do not violate the Robinson-Patman Act, then the deal may be saved. If, however, the deal does violate the Robinson-Patman Act and top management still wishes to go forward with the different terms, then the credit professional should duly note these facts in his or her records and obtain a signature from the top manager on the business decision.

Customer may accept new terms but demand price concessions. This is the same as above, with price concessions being substituted for terms. The same procedure needs to be followed.

Customer may accept new terms as is. All procedures that were stated in the section "Sale Is Approved as Ordered" should be followed here.

Sale Is Offered for a Lesser Amount with Acceptance of Terms Requested, Customer Is Offered Less Product Than Ordered

Customer may accept as is. All procedures that were stated in the Section "Sale Is Approved as Ordered" should be followed here.

Customer may refuse to lower amount of goods, thus canceling the order. Once again, at this point the credit professional has two alternatives, renegotiate or pass. The solidity of the investigation and the decision, as well as the obvious pressure that will result from the loss of this order will determine which of the two options Credit will take.

Customer may counteroffer with other terms for the entire shipment that may or may not be acceptable. Once again, here is where the credit professional must be prepared to negotiate and settle the deal before things get out of hand and the sales and marketing group gives the store away. If the deal can be made with different terms that are acceptable to the credit professional and top management, and that do not violate the Robinson-Patman Act, then the deal may be saved. If, however, the deal does violate the Robinson-Patman Act and top management still wishes to go forward with the different terms, then the credit professional should duly note these facts in records and obtain a signature from the top manager on the business decision.

Customer may be willing to offer security for larger shipment amount. Assuming that the security is acceptable and sufficient, then follow what was stated in the section "Sale Is Approved as Ordered." If it is not, then the credit professional has two alternatives, renegotiate or pass. The solidity of the investigation and the decision as well as the obvious pressure that will result from the loss of this order will determine which of the two options Credit will take.

Customer may be willing to offer a down payment on the larger shipment amount. The answer is the same as above.

Sale Is Offered for a Lesser Amount with a Variation to the Customer's Requested Terms or Customer Is Offered Less Product Than Ordered and Standard Company Terms

Customer may accept as is. Follow what was stated in the section "Sale Is Approved as Ordered."

Customer may refuse the offer, thus canceling the order. Once again, at this point the credit professional has two alternatives, renegotiate or pass. The solidity of the investigation and the decision as well as the obvious pressure that will result from the loss of this order will determine which of the two options Credit will take.

Customer may counteroffer with other terms for the entire shipment that may or may not be acceptable. Assuming that the terms are acceptable, follow what was stated in the section "Sale Is Approved as Ordered." If not acceptable, at this point the credit professional has two alternatives, renegotiate or pass. The solidity of the investigation and the decision as well as the obvious pressure that result from the loss of this order will determine which of the two options Credit will take.

Customer may be willing to offer security for larger shipment amount and accept offered terms. Assuming that the security is acceptable and sufficient, then follow what was stated in the section "Sale Is Approved as Ordered." If it is not, then the credit professional has two alternatives, renegotiate or pass. The solidity of the investigation and the decision as well as the obvious pressure that will result from the loss of this order will determine which of the two options Credit will take.

Customer may be willing to offer a down payment on the larger shipment amount and accept offered terms. Assuming that the down payment is acceptable and sufficient, then follow what was stated in the section "Sale Is Approved as Ordered." If it is not, then the credit professional has two alternatives, renegotiate or pass. The solidity of the investigation and the decision as well as the obvious pressure that will result from the loss of this order will determine which of the two options Credit will take.

Customer may be willing to offer security for larger shipment amount while requesting the original credit terms. Assuming that the security is acceptable and sufficient, then follow what was stated in the section "Sale Is Approved as Ordered." If it is not, then the credit professional has two alternatives, renegotiate or pass. The solidity of the investigation and the decision as well as the obvious pressure that will result from the loss of this order will determine which of the two options Credit will take.

Customer may be willing to offer a down payment on the larger shipment amount while requesting the original terms. Assuming that the down payment is acceptable and sufficient, then follow what was stated in the section "Sale Is Approved as Ordered." If it is not, then the credit professional has two alternatives, renegotiate or pass. The solidity of the investigation and the decision as well as and the obvious pressure that will result from the loss of this order will determine which of the two options Credit will take.

CONSOLIDATING THE FACTS TO VINDICATE A DECISION/RECOMMENDATION

Every credit professional should consolidate and order facts to vindicate a decision/recommendation in order to deal with the situation of being overridden by top management. This documentation process tends to be more of an issue the more important that an order is or depending on the time when it is being shipped out (end of the month, quarter, year compared to beginning of the month, quarter, or year). Credit professionals who know they will be overridden must document the facts of how they arrived at their decision and note that a business decision, not a credit one, was responsible for the approval of the order. Let us look at the factors now and address their effects on the decision.

Size of the order. The larger the order, the more effort that should be made to bring the sale to a successful conclusion. This does not mean that credit must be extended!

Completeness and quality of data supplied on application (new customer) and from sales personnel. If the salesperson has been properly trained by the credit professional in the ways of obtaining the maximum credit information possible and the customer has cooperated fully, then this is certainly a plus on the side of approval.

Amount, degree of verification, and quality of information obtained in the investigation. The more proof available due to the investigation, the sounder the decision.

Details on the order (or credit limit requested by a new customer) such as margin, terms, and conditions requested by the customer. All the facts must be known in order to make a sound business credit decision. Things such as margin, terms, and conditions can make or break a deal, especially if the terms are nonstandard, the margin is low, and the conditions are unreasonable.

Potential for additional orders. This factor must enter into all decisions made on new customers. The fact that future orders may be more profitable than the first order will add weight to approving credit for the order. If margin of future orders is exceptionally higher than the initial order, this may be a way to help to offset future risk with this customer.

Time constraints for developing information to make a decision. The bane of all credit professionals is lack of the necessary time to make a sound business credit decision. One way to help with this problem is to develop solid ties to the sales and marketing staff by attending weekly sales meetings to keep informed of any new or pending business. Credit professionals should build the same type of bridge with the customer service area, which likewise has access to information on pending orders.

Is the order for a domestic customer, and is there a sales rep near the customer? Having the customer in the United States improves the odds that collection will be successful. Having the watchful eyes, ears, and nose of a local sales rep will also help to make those odds even better.

For an international customer, what country is the customer located in, what bank does it use, and does your bank have a corresponding relationship with the customer's bank? For an international sale, the three additional risks enter the picture to make collection more difficult. Political risk is one of these three additional risks and, depending on the status of the country, will directly impact the degree of difficulty of collecting this sale. If there is a correspondent relationship between the customer's bank and yours and your bank is willing to confirm the customer's letters of credit, this will improve the options for making the sale on a credit basis. If your bank can obtain credit information from the customer's bank due to its relationship with the customer's bank, you will gain additional information on that particular customer.

INFORMATION IS REQUIRED TO MAKE A SOUND BUSINESS CREDIT DECISION

Most companies require more information from customers attempting to place large orders and are willing to accept less from those placing small orders.

Large Dollar Order (or High Credit Limit Needed)

Complete credit application (new customer). The more details provided, the better the chances for working out a decision that will be acceptable to both parties. Sales staff needs to be trained to obtain the maximum amount of information from every new customer with few exceptions.

Updated audited annual financial statements. These will provide verified information that can be analyzed and checked against industry standards. They will help in determining how the customer has progressed in the past few years (trend analysis) and how well it is doing against the competition (industry analysis).

Detailed verified credit report. This information serves as a starting point for information. Credit professionals should compare their investigation with the information the credit reporting agency was able to compile.

Updated credit references. Comparing these against the credit reports and seeing the high credit provided and whether it is secured or unsecured will help the credit professional determine how the customer's largest creditor feels about it.

All details on the order. These include terms and conditions, profit margin, shipping date requested, domestic or international, off-the-shelf or custom-made products, production time for goods ordered, and any special shipping instructions.

All of these areas can be deal makers or deal breakers for a major sale. Credit professionals must have access to all this information and must scrutinize all purchase orders and contracts for anything out of the ordinary that will cause the firm problems in meeting requirements that will prevent it from being paid.

Medium Dollar Order (or Medium Credit Limit Needed)

Complete credit application (new customer). Fewer details may be acceptable here, but every effort should be made to have the application be as complete as possible, in order to maximize the potential new customer's credit line.

Annual financial statements (audited if possible). Obtaining audited reports is always helpful but as long as balance sheet, income statement, statement of cash flow, and accompanying notes are available, then the value of this information is still good.

Credit report. This area should be the same as for a large order, but less financial information and fewer trade references are required.

Updated credit references. These should always be obtained unless the size of the order is insignificant.

Details on the order (if unusual). These include terms and conditions, profit margin, shipping date requested, domestic or international, off-the-shelf or custom-made products, production time for goods ordered, and any special shipping instructions.

If a significant number of new customers and orders are processed daily, then the degree of watching that is done may be reduced considerably. If, however, there are special terms, if the sale is international, or if the purchase order lists some unusual requirements, then significantly more attention should be paid to this order.

Small Dollar Order (or Low Credit Limit Needed)

Complete credit application (new customer). A complete credit application should always be insisted on but the level of investigation may be far more limited. By training sales staff to obtain the maximum amount of information on every credit application, the life of the credit professional will be much easier.

Credit report (or rating if dollars are very low). For firms with a high volume of small dollar orders, ratings may be used to save time in approving or declining orders. If volume is low, then the trade reference part of the report may be enough to use for considering the order.

Updated credit references. These should always be obtained unless the size of the order is insignificant.

Details on any special or unusual terms or conditions on the order. These aspects always need to be watched to prevent violations of the Robinson-Patman Act and to prevent fraud.

ASCERTAINING ANY GAPS IN YOUR DATA

Obviously, the size and degree of importance to the firm of the order will directly affect the effort made to plug the holes in any decision rendered. Credit professionals can use the following questions as a general guide to ensure that they are making every effort based on the client's size and degree of importance to keep from making a sound business credit decision with anything less than what is absolutely needed. Extenuating circumstances may require going the extra mile, regardless of the size of the sale; such circumstances include suspicion of fraud.

Large Dollar Order (or High Credit Limit Needed)

- Has all requested information been received and checked, including credit application, credit report, and trade and bank references?
- Has a financial analysis been done and a summation of its results, strengths, and weaknesses been created?
- What are the details on the order? Have all areas of special handling been addressed? These might include:
  - Has the order been accepted and acknowledged?
  - Is this a one-time order or continuous business?
  - Have special terms been requested by the customer (addressing legal issues, i.e., the Robinson-Patman Act)?
- If the goods are custom made, can they be produced in time to meet the conditions of the purchase order?
- If the goods are custom made, is there any other possible buyer for them?
- If the order is international, is a payment and/or a performance bond needed, and does the margin allow for delays in shipping or consider a customer's request for extended terms?

Medium Dollar Order (or Medium Credit Limit Needed)

- Has all requested information been received and checked, including credit application, credit report, and trade and bank references?
- If financials were obtained, has a financial analysis been done and a summation of its results, strengths, and weaknesses been created?
- What are the details on the order? Have all areas of special handling been addressed? (These are the same as for a large dollar item.)

Small Dollar Order (or Low Credit Limit Needed)

- Has all requested information been received and checked, including credit application, credit report or rating, and trade and bank references?

- What are the details on the order? Have all areas of special handling been addressed? (These are similar to the issues discussed for large and medium orders.)

SUMMARY

Despite the distractions and pressures placed on credit professionals every minute of every day, the decision to extend credit can mean a firm's life or death. In major deals, the wrong decision may cause employees to lose their jobs, plants to shut down, and companies to go under. Such catastrophes can happen over a significant piece of business or develop on a small, slow scale over a longer period of time. Credit professionals must make every effort to maximize sales and minimize risks and must be determined that every sale can be made.

They also must never be afraid to incur some losses. If loses do not occur, some profitable business may be passing out of the firm's reach and into the wide-open arms of competitors. They likewise must not be afraid to let some business flow out to their competition, for in some cases competitors will be the ones to incur losses rather than the credit professionals' firm. The motto for credit professionals: Be vigilant, be observant, be diligent, and never give up or in.

4

D IS FOR DECISION (OR RECOMMENDATION)

INTRODUCTION

Finally, we reach the point where the credit professional has gathered all the relevant information and is ready to make the decision. This chapter will review:

- Making a sound business credit decision that is high in value and cost effective
- Developing alternatives as a fallback safeguard

The skills you acquired in the earlier chapters should give you confidence in your ability to render a sound business credit decision. This chapter will help you render a decision that is both cost effective and innovative. You will learn how to sell a win-win innovative decision. The fine art of "making a tactical retreat" by providing alternative sound business credit decisions will become another tool in your arsenal to minimize losses and maximize sales.

This chapter reviews how to eliminate loopholes in your decision, thus preventing the need to defend your decision. It also explores how to gracefully accept a decision not acceptable to your analysis yet still minimize the potential for a loss. The art of educating upper management on the dangers of making unsound credit decisions rather than exhibiting an I-told-you-so air will be fully considered. Readers will be skilled in picking up the pieces after the decision unravels by the chapter's end.

It is time to pay the piper and not only make the decision but live with the consequences. Credit professionals also may have to learn how to eat crow and be a team player. Top management sometimes overrules credit and makes a business decision. If the credit professional's decision is overridden, he or she, as a team player, must minimize the fallout from the decision that was made.

MAKING A SOUND BUSINESS CREDIT DECISION THAT IS HIGH IN VALUE AND COST EFFECTIVE

What value is gained by making a sound business credit decision? The most significant aspect of any sound business credit decision is reduction of risk of a loss. A large potential sale and subsequent loss could have a devastating effect on the bottom line and could result in the firm's failure.

Credit professionals can prevent this potential for a loss by anticipating problems that would destroy the profit margin. Managing the details that result in future problems, such as deductions, collection problems due to document errors (international), and compliance with terms and conditions of the purchase order, can substantially reduce number of losses that occur. Confirming changes to purchase orders that would violate either company policy or federal law (the Robinson-Patman Act) is one additional way to remain in compliance and to prevent future collection problems.

How can a sound business credit decision be cost effective? Sound business credit decisions are based on more than just credit factors. Some notable outside aspects that are considered include profit margin, inventory costs, capacity usage (labor and overhead, manufacturing, etc.), and future potential business. An additional consideration could be opportunities into new markets or growth of penetration into the current ones. Sound credit decisions also look at credit factors, such as costs of credit reports, time needed to conduct credit investigations in relation to size of order, the collection staff needed, and the computer systems costs used in controlling this additional delinquency. Using the time value of money to determine the true profitability of a sale, credit professionals who make sound business credit decisions determine whether the order is as good as it appears on the surface.

What are some of the short-falls of making just a credit decision? The shortfalls that can have the greatest impact on the bottom line include loss of a sale, reduction of a sale, loss of some profitability of a sale, and, most important, the loss of some or all of the "goodwill" of a customer.

DEVELOPING ALTERNATIVES AS A "FALLBACK" SAFEGUARD

Amazing as this may seem, occasionally top management overrides the very sound decisions made by fine credit professionals. When this happens, the credit professionals are asked to devise a new solution so the sale can be made. Credit professionals in this situation can ask these questions.

What are some possible strategies to use as an alternative to the first sound business credit decision? The strongest forms of collateral available to the credit professional are standby letters of credit, filing a UCC-1 on company inventory, and a purchase money security interest filing on inventory and proceeds. All can be used as security to make a sale. Some additional less secure alternatives include a personal guarantee or corporate guarantee, if a parent or sister company can sign this agreement. Some nonsecurity-related techniques include breaking up the order into smaller shipments depending on the profit margin, obtaining a down payment or shorter terms, or offering a large cash discount for cash with order or at time of shipment, depending on whether the goods are off the shelf or custom made. In the case of an international sale, a confirmed irrevocable letter of credit, sight draft, a financing plan under the Export Import (EXIM) Bank, or credit insurance (also available for domestic sales) will work as an alternative to rejecting an order.

How can the credit professional appraise the cost factors of these alternatives to both the company and the customer? In the case of the company, the following could happen:

- Loss or reduction of a sale
- Loss of some profitability of a sale

- Loss of some or all of the goodwill of a customer
- Cost of insurance fees

The customer would experience some or all of the following:

- Increases in its bank fees
- Tying up of available capital (L/C)
- Reduction of the customer's cash available for other purchases
- Delays in the completion of an order to its own customer that could result in the reduction of the profit for the sale

MAKING AN AIRTIGHT RECOMMENDATION

Before making any recommendations, credit professionals should consider the following questions to eliminate any loopholes.

- Does the decision reflect the best interests of the company?
- Can the sale be made safely without loss of profit?
- Have all alternatives been looked at and weighed against the good of the company?
- Would any additional information not available at this time change the decision being made now?
- Would direct discussion with the customer's top officers, either by phone or in person, provide other possibilities for altering the decision (assuming that the amount of the sale warrants a personal visit)?
- Would a second opinion with colleagues in the field (NACM) help to alter the final decision?

BRACING FOR REJECTION AND BEING OVERRIDDEN BY MANAGEMENT

To prepare to defend a decision to top management, the first step is to summarize the reasons for the decision. Credit professionals should keep their thoughts and words brief, focused, and to the point. They should have all documents available to back up their reasoning in a short presentation format and be prepared to offer an alternate recommendation that can be defended. They must be prepared to defend any legal or moral reasons related to the decision and be prepared to advise on the fallout potentials of other decision possibilities.

DEALING WITH BEING OVERRIDDEN BY MANAGEMENT

Once credit professionals are overridden by top management, they should assume a team attitude and advise management on precautions that might be taken to minimize damage caused by other decision possibilities. They should guarantee the support of the credit department in making the sale as profitable as possible, and take every step possible to prevent being overridden in the future. Credit professionals should strengthen ties to the sales and marketing area to stay in the loop before potential problems develop. They should keep credit records updated generally on all customers but specifically on large customers. Also, credit managers should work to improve the turnaround time in completing a credit investigation. They also should provide top management with regular reports on the status of any decision on which they were overridden, detailing any deterioration and all steps that are being taken to monitor and prevent a possible loss.

GATHERING THE PIECES AFTER MAKING A BAD DECISION OR BEING OVERRIDDEN

When a management override turns out to be a bad decision, credit professionals always must maintain the right attitude. They should determine what went wrong with management's decision and report to top management on the steps taken to make the sale a success and recommendations for preventing the recurrence of this type of loss.

No matter whose decisions go south, the credit professional should first confirm that all possible cost-effective efforts have been made to collect the account. The next step is to advise top management, sales, and marketing on the details of the loss immediately and notify order entry/customer service on the status of the account, to stop all future sales. If the account is in dispute, attempt to negotiate a settlement, which might include a return of merchandise. If a lawsuit will be required to collect the account, proceed immediately. Accept and recognize the loss immediately by writing it off.

MAKING SURE IT DOES NOT HAPPEN AGAIN

Communications must be kept flowing among sales, marketing, top management, and credit on the status of the account. Credit professionals should strengthen sources of information within the industry (trade associations, etc.). In general, they should sharpen their own and staff's credit skills, knowledge, and contacts by attending credit seminars, credit association meetings, trade credit meetings, and so on. Credit policy and procedures should be revised to reflect any changes to the customer base, market, economics of the times, competition, technology, and the like. Daily procedures should be reviewed specifically to make sure they adequately cover the requirements of making sound business credit decisions while remaining cost effective.

SUMMARY

You did your best to make a good decision and got your teeth kicked out. That happens to the best of us. Being the credit professional that you are, you will take all the proper steps to minimize any future losses. If a loss occurs, no recriminations will be made. You will take advantage of the situation to make important changes, including attending all sales and marketing meetings and improving communications to prevent a future recurrence of these events. As a team player, you will gain the respect of top management and your opinion will not only be sought out but will be implemented most of the time.

Now it is time to tackle the case studies.

PART TWO

CASE STUDIES

INTRODUCTION

This section will give readers the opportunity to see how other credit managers make decisions. Twelve real-life cases were selected from a course I developed for the American Management Association. In this three-day seminar, students were given the opportunity to make decisions in a simulated credit environment. For each case, I present the conclusions of three students. As in real life, they do not all reach the same conclusion.

Before we delve into the mysteries of the cases, let us look at the class setting. The typical class size was about 20 to 30 students. For the case studies, they were subdivided into separate groups that consisted of one person acting as the vice president of finance, one as marketing and sales manager, and two to three individuals as the credit committee. Everyone in the group reviewed the cases, and the members of the credit committee worked as a team to make a presentation for the vice president of finance. The marketing and sales manager did his or her own review in order to defend the need to make the sale. The vice president of finance also reviewed the case to make his or her own decision but could be swayed as to the pros and cons of the case. Ultimately, the finance VP presented the group's decision and reasoning to the entire class. He or she informed the class of other arguments presented by other factions in the group.

My usual criteria for picking who got which job was that if anyone had an accounting background, the individual ultimately was my first choice for vice president of finance. In a rarer case, if someone (or more) had some sales or marketing background, then that person was the instant choice for marketing and sales manager. I tried to balance the level of expertise on the credit committee so that at least one more seasoned credit individual was in each group. If no background in either accounting or marketing and sales existed in the class, I started with the most seasoned credit pros to take the two noncredit positions. By doing this I discovered that there really were some "closet" marketing and sales managers working in credit.

Each person, though, depending upon the class size would have a chance in each position. I would also rotate the credit committee members to different groups as this kept people from getting too used to dealing with each other and would also maximize the exposure to different backgrounds for each person in class. Over a two-day period we covered eight cases and depending on the backgrounds of the attendees, I would choose from the inventory of cases those that would be the best fit for the class. I extended the option to the class to either "role play" these cases in a normal day-to-day atmosphere or simply present them as they saw fit.

One such group chose not to role-play but almost ended up in what at times really happens in a normal day under the pressure to make a decision in credit. In this particular class, I had the good fortune to have an individual who had twenty years of experience as a marketing and sales manager but had switched to credit one year earlier. The vice president of finance was a controller who had credit reporting to him and I had three seasoned credit managers in the "Credit Committee." Having had such perfect people for the group, I felt that they would excel in not only their creativeness in making a decision but would be outstanding in their presentation of it. Nothing could be farther from the truth.

After deliberating among themselves the "credit committee" presented their very sound thoughts on the case to the vice president of finance. Their leader was most elegant in her logic and flexibility on the "proper" way to structure the sale. The marketing and sales manager had his turn. Within five minutes, he had twisted and torn the credit committee's entire recommendation to shreds and had backed the vice president of finance into a corner. It would have been extremely difficult for the vice president of finance to extradite himself from this mess.

Before I describe the events that followed, I must describe the characters and the surroundings of the classroom. The gentleman that played the role of marketing and sales manager was tall, bearded, well groomed, and unflappable. The seasoned credit manager was about five feet tall and equally elegant. The chairs that everyone sat in were on wheels and would recline back to a 45 to 90 degree angle. Now that I have painted the picture let us continue with the story. At this point, the leader of the credit committee jumped up, leaned over the marketing and sales manager forcing him to recline almost vertically and waived her finger in his face menacingly and shouted that she knew what he was doing and that she didn't like it. Her eyes (and his I might add) were huge and her voice was filled with pure rage at the way he had adeptly, through slight of hand, made the credit committee look like a bunch of rank amateurs.

Seeing that this was no role-playing but one of my students about to kill another one, I proceeded to take her out into the hallway and attempted to calm her down. She immediately relayed to me that she had been in the exact situation the week before in front of her boss and that she had lost control over the thought that it was occurring all over again. I quickly explained to her that this was role playing only. After regaining her wits she apologized profusely to me, to the class, and then in particular to the marketing and sales manager.

Needless to say at the break, he asked me if he could be in a different group the rest of the class and I quickly accommodated his request. The moral to this story is that no matter where you are or what the situation is, you should always be prepared to duck when dealing with an irate credit manager.

Besides the narrative facts of each case, I also supply (if available or needed) a credit report, a bank and three trade references, and a two-page financial analysis report. (See Exhibit II.1.) The first page of the financial analysis report takes information from a balance sheet and income statement and lists the information vertically in its normal order.

The second column compares the percent of change from the previous year to the current year.

The third column takes the percentage of each category, such as cash as a percent of total assets. This percentage is then compared against the fourth column, which is industry standard for this type of company using SIC (Standard Industrial Classification) codes as the guide for the product or services that the firm offers for sale.

The percent in the fourth column is the industry average for that SIC code. The computation of these percentages is called common-size analysis. Liabilities or equity items are compared against total of liabilities and net worth.

The income statement categories are compared against the net sales or revenues total. There are three sets of these comparisons using four years' worth of data (if available).

At the bottom of page 1 is a recommended credit limit that was computed using a software package copyrighted by this author, which is available directly from D&H Credit Services (dandhcredit@earthlink.net). It bases its recommendation on the comparison to industry standards and other factors.

Page 2 of the analysis presents a list of computed ratios broken down by solvency, efficiency, and profitability categories. The top half (with a few exceptions) have industry standards to compare against, and the standards are broken down from a range of the best (UQ, upper quartile), to the average (Med, median), to the worst (LQ, lower quartile).

The column to the right of the ratios computed is the percent change of these ratios from the previous year to that of the present year. Like the first page, there are three sections of comparisons using four years' worth of financial data (if available). How these ratios are computed and what information they reveal will not be covered in this book but can be researched in a number of accounting and financial analysis books.

After explaining the relevant facts for each case study, I provide an overview of the case and then some of the thought patterns used by students to arrive at their decisions. These thought patterns were based not only on group teamwork but also reflected the industries that these students worked in. Finally we review what truly happened in each "real-life" case. Of course, the company names have been changed to protect the innocent.

As you go through each case you will come to realize that not all facts are present in each case. This is to make the cases as true to life as possible because it is quite normal for a credit manager to have very few facts to work from and some assumptions will need to be made. In many situations, more research will be needed before an answer can be given; nevertheless, an answer was required in each of these cases, based on the facts as presented. Each answer given by my students is looked at for its validity and ease of usage.

Each case plays on a facet that can "upset the apple cart" and cause what looked like a "no-brainer" decision to turn out to be terribly wrong. In each case, you must understand that the sale being considered is critical and that it is for a large extension of credit. In some industries, a large sale may be tens of millions of dollars; in others, a $5,000 sale is large. You also must remember that the number-one duty of a credit manager is to make every sale a reality. This does not always mean that credit should be extended on every sale. Being creative is the most important aspect in arriving at a decision.

Exhibit II.1

Leakproof Seals Co., Inc.
123 Stopflow Gap
Watertown, NY 12345

SIC 3053   ACCOUNT # 123456

$3,868,310.00
$480,673.00

Page 1

	12/31/98 $	% Change	% Assets	Ind % Assets	12/31/97 $	% Change	% Assets	Ind % Assets	12/31/96 $	% Change	% Assets	Ind % Assets
Cash	$247,675.00	6.77	19.03	4.70	$231,971.00	23.12	18.04	5.10	$188,406.00	100.00	16.24	8.80
Accounts Receivable	$427,247.00	32.69	32.83	34.30	$321,980.00	0.98	25.04	31.80	$318,866.00	100.00	27.49	30.80
Inventory	$501,425.00	-17.92	38.53	37.60	$610,917.00	17.30	47.52	29.00	$520,823.00	100.00	44.89	28.00
Due from Shareholder	$0.00	0.00	0.00	---	$0.00	0.00	0.00	---	$0.00	0.00	0.00	---
Due From Affiliate	$0.00	0.00	0.00	---	$0.00	0.00	0.00	---	$0.00	0.00	0.00	---
Other Current	$4,834.00	67.44	0.37	1.00	$2,887.00	-93.66	0.22	1.20	$45,571.00	100.00	3.93	0.80
Total Current	$1,181,181.00	1.15	90.77	70.10	$1,167,755.00	8.76	90.83	67.10	$107,366.00	100.00	92.55	68.40
Fixed Assets	$72,033.00	-19.56	5.54	21.10	$89,546.00	35.70	6.97	24.20	$65,987.00	100.00	5.69	24.50
Notes Receivable	$0.00	0.00	0.00	---	$0.00	0.00	0.00	---	$0.00	0.00	0.00	---
Deposits	$0.00	0.00	0.00	---	$0.00	0.00	0.00	---	$0.00	0.00	0.00	---
Cash Value of Life Insur.	$48,069.00	69.65	3.69	7.90	$28,335.00	38.28	2.20	6.50	$20,491.00	100.00	1.77	4.70
Intangible Assets	$0.00	0.00	0.00	0.90	$0.00	0.00	0.00	2.20	$0.00	0.00	0.00	2.40
Total Assets	$1,301,283.00	1.22	100.00	100.00	$1,285,636.00	10.82	100.00	100.00	$1,160,144.00	100.00	100.00	100.00
Account Payable	$446,325.00	-0.18	34.30	18.20	$447,109.00	85.03	34.78	17.90	$241,640.00	100.00	20.83	15.20
Bank Loans + N.P.	$119,000.00	14.08	9.14	10.80	$104,311.00	-19.87	8.11	11.00	$130,177.00	100.00	11.22	9.10
Cur. Mat.-L.T.D.	$24,176.00	-4.66	1.86	5.20	$25,357.00	86.39	1.97	6.20	$13,604.00	100.00	1.17	6.70
Income Tax Payables	$1,414.00	-63.17	0.11	0.10	$3,839.00	-10.35	0.30	0.90	$4,282.00	100.00	3.39	0.50
Accrued Expenses	$9,033.00	1.06	0.69	6.40	$8,938.00	-27.33	0.70	4.70	$12,299.00	100.00	1.06	8.30
Total Current	$599,948.00	1.76	46.10	40.70	$589,544.00	46.65	0.00	40.70	$402,002.00	100.00	34.65	39.80
Long Term Debt	$220,662.00	3.53	16.96	12.30	$213,145.00	5.66	16.58	12.20	$201,725.00	100.00	17.39	11.10
Deferred Taxes	$0.00	0.00	0.00	0.10	$0.00	0.00	0.00	0.60	$0.00	0.00	0.00	0.40
All Other L.T. Debt	$0.00	0.00	0.00	0.00	$0.00	0.00	0.00	0.90	$0.00	0.00	0.00	2.70
Net Worth	$480,673.00	-0.47	36.94	46.90	$482,937.00	-13.21	37.56	45.60	$556,417.00	100.00	47.96	46.00
Total Liab. & Equity	$1,301,283.00	1.22	100.00	100.00	$1,285,636.00	10.82	100.00	100.00	$1,160,144.00	100.00	100.00	100.00
Net Sales	$3,868,310.00	3.20	100.00	100.00	$3,748,239.00	13.10	100.00	100.00	$3,313,955.00	100.00	100.00	100.00
Cost of Goods Sold	$2,987,467.00	6.91	77.23	70.00	$2,794,406.00	13.70	74.55	68.10	$2,457,705.00	100.00	74.16	66.70
Gross Profit	$880,843.00	-7.65	22.77	30.00	$953,833.00	11.40	25.45	31.90	$856,250.00	100.00	25.84	33.30
Depreciation	$22,970.00	-0.09	0.59	---	$22,991.00	6.94	0.61	---	$21,498.00	100.00	0.65	---
Lease Payments	$0.00	0.00	0.00	---	$0.00	0.00	0.00	---	$0.00	0.00	0.00	---
Other Operating Exps.	$825,094.00	-6.13	21.33	---	$878,961.00	12.12	23.45	---	$783,928.00	100.00	23.66	---
Tot. Operating Exps.	$848,064.00	-5.97	21.92	29.00	$901,952.00	11.98	24.06	28.10	$805,426.00	100.00	24.30	25.10
Operating Profit	$32,779.00	-36.82	0.85	1.00	$51,881.00	2.08	1.38	3.70	$50,323.00	100.00	1.53	8.20
Interest Inc./(Exp.)	$0.00	0.00	0.00	0.00	($13,567.00)	-41.83	-0.36	0.70	($23,323.00)	100.00	-0.70	1.50
G/(L) on sale of Fxd Assets	$0.00	0.00	0.00	---	$0.00	0.00	0.00	---	$0.00	0.00	0.00	---
Profit Before Taxes	$32,779.00	-14.45	0.85	0.90	$38,314.00	39.32	1.02	3.00	$27,501.00	100.00	0.83	6.70
Taxes	$10,043.00	-14.85	0.26	---	$11,794.00	10.59	0.31	---	$10,665.00	100.00	0.32	---
Net Profit	$22,736.00	-14.27	0.59	---	$26,520.00	57.52	0.71	---	$16,836.00	100.00	0.51	---
Other Data:												
Working Capital	$581,233.00	0.52	44.67	29.40	$578,201.00	-13.92	90.83	26.40	$671,664.00	100.00	57.89	28.60
Tangible Equity	$480,673.00	-0.47	36.94	46.60	$482,937.00	-13.21	37.56	43.40	$556,417.00	100.00	47.96	43.60
Recommended Credit Limit:	$54,796.72	-2.18	---	---	$56,020.69	-3.19	---	---	$57,867.37	---	---	---

Leakproof Seals Co., Inc.
123 Stopflow Gap
Watertown, NY 12345

RATIOS		12/31/98 Value	98 % Change	98 UQ	98 Med	98 LQ	12/31/97 Value	97 % Change	97 UQ	97 Med	97 LQ	12/31/96 Value	96 % Change	96 UQ	96 Med	96 LQ
SOLVENCY																
Current Ratio	($)	1.97	-0.60	2.40	1.70	1.20	1.98	-25.84	2.40	1.80	1.30	2.67	100.00	2.30	1.80	1.30
Quick Ratio	($)	1.12	-34.82	1.50	0.80	0.50	0.94	-25.54	1.30	0.90	0.80	1.26	100.00	1.50	1.00	0.60
Net Profit B4 Tax + Depr./Cur LTD	(X)	2.31	-4.62	2.60	1.00	0.00	2.42	-32.88	3.80	2.10	0.50	3.60	100.00	7.30	3.30	1.30
Sales to Fixed Assets	(X)	53.70	274.04	35.30	16.90	10.20	14.36	-71.41	17.50	11.10	7.80	50.22	100.00	38.80	14.30	4.80
Sales to Total Assets	(X)	2.97	1.96	3.50	2.80	2.60	2.92	2.06	3.00	2.60	1.90	2.86	100.00	2.90	2.40	1.50
Total Liab. to NW	(X)	1.71	2.71	0.70	1.20	2.20	1.66	53.19	0.80	1.20	2.20	1.09	100.00	0.60	1.80	3.30
Fixed Assets to NW	(X)	0.15	-19.18	0.20	0.50	1.10	0.19	56.35	0.30	0.50	0.90	0.12	100.00	0.20	0.50	1.10
Tot. Liab. to Tot. Assets	(%)	63.06	1.00	N/A	N/A	N/A	62.44	19.98	N/A	N/A	N/A	52.04	100.00	N/A	N/A	N/A
Oper. Prof. to Int. Exp.	(X)	0.00	-100.00	N/A	N/A	N/A	3.82	75.49	N/A	N/A	N/A	2.18	100.00	N/A	N/A	N/A
Oper Prof+Lease Py to Int Exp+LP	(X)	0.00	-100.00	N/A	N/A	N/A	3.82	75.49	N/A	N/A	N/A	2.18	100.00	N/A	N/A	N/A
EFFICIENCY																
Sales to Receivables	(X)	9.05	-22.22	10.30	8.40	7.50	11.64	12.01	9.80	8.20	6.20	10.39	100.00	9.20	7.40	6.40
Days Sales Outstanding	(D)	40	29.03	35	43	49	31	-11.43	37	45	59	35	100.00	40	49	57
Cost of Sales to Inv.	(X)	5.96	30.25	9.30	6.20	5.10	4.57	-3.07	9.30	6.00	3.90	4.72	100.00	9.60	5.50	4.00
Days' Sales in Inventory	(D)	61	-23.75	39	59	72	80	3.90	38	66	91	77	100.00	38	66	91
Sales to Net Working Cap.	(X)	6.66	2.67	6.30	10.70	30.10	6.48	31.39	5.70	9.70	16.60	4.93	100.00	5.40	8.80	18.00
Cost of Sales/Payables	(X)	6.69	7.10	22.00	10.20	7.20	6.25	-38.55	19.30	9.90	7.00	10.17	100.00	15.10	12.00	9.20
A/P Turnover	(D)	55	-5.17	17	36	51	58	61.11	24	30	40	36	100.00	25	30	40
PROFITABILITY																
Depreciation to Sales	(%)	0.59	-3.19	0.70	1.60	3.10	0.61	-5.45	1.10	2.30	3.10	0.65	100.00	1.30	2.00	3.70
Prof bef Tax to Tot.Assets	(%)	2.52	-15.48	12.40	7.50	0.00	2.98	25.72	15.70	7.00	0.30	2.37	100.00	19.30	13.70	7.00
Profit before Taxes to TNW	(%)	6.82	-14.04	23.90	16.10	0.00	7.93	60.52	29.80	15.70	2.50	4.94	100.00	65.10	35.40	21.00

RATIOS		12/31/98 Value	98 % Change	98 UQ	98 Med	98 LQ	12/31/97 Value	97 % Change	97 UQ	97 Med	97 LQ	12/31/96 Value	96 % Change	96 UQ	96 Med	96 LQ
SOLVENCY																
Inv. to Net Work. Capital	(X)	0.86	-18.35	N/A	N/A	N/A	1.06	36.27	N/A	N/A	N/A	0.78	100.00	N/A	N/A	N/A
Current Liab. to NW	(X)	1.25	2.24	N/A	N/A	N/A	1.22	68.97	N/A	N/A	N/A	0.72	100.00	N/A	N/A	N/A
LT Debt to Tot. Debt & Capital	(%)	16.96	2.29	N/A	N/A	N/A	16.58	-4.66	N/A	N/A	N/A	17.39	100.00	N/A	N/A	N/A
Fixed Assets to LT Debt	(X)	0.33	-21.43	N/A	N/A	N/A	0.42	27.27	N/A	N/A	N/A	0.33	100.00	N/A	N/A	N/A
EFFICIENCY																
Net Sales to NW	(X)	8.05	3.74	N/A	N/A	N/A	7.76	30.20	N/A	N/A	N/A	5.96	100.00	N/A	N/A	N/A
Net Sales to Inventory	(X)	7.71	25.57	N/A	N/A	N/A	6.14	-3.46	N/A	N/A	N/A	6.36	100.00	N/A	N/A	N/A
Cost of Sales/Working Capital	(X)	5.14	6.42	N/A	N/A	N/A	4.83	31.97	N/A	N/A	N/A	3.66	100.00	N/A	N/A	N/A
Short Term Loan Turnover	(X)	15.00	7.14	N/A	N/A	N/A	14.00	-26.32	N/A	N/A	N/A	19.00	100.00	N/A	N/A	N/A
LT Liabilities Payback *	($)	$21.53	-10.86	N/A	N/A	N/A	$24.15	-2.33	N/A	N/A	N/A	$24.73	100.00	N/A	N/A	N/A
PROFITABILITY																
Gross Profit on Net Sales	(%)	22.77	-10.53	--	30.00	--	25.45	-151.00	--	31.90	--	25.84	100.00	--	33.30	--
Net Oper Inc on Net Sales	(%)	0.85	-38.41	--	1.00	--	1.38	-9.80	--	3.70	--	1.53	100.00	--	8.20	--
Net Profit on Net Sales	(%)	0.59	-16.90	N/A	N/A	N/A	0.71	39.22	N/A	N/A	N/A	0.51	100.00	N/A	N/A	N/A
Net Prof on Total Assets	(%)	1.75	-15.05	N/A	N/A	N/A	2.06	42.07	N/A	N/A	N/A	1.45	100.00	N/A	N/A	N/A
Tot Assets to Equity	(X)	2.71	1.69	N/A	N/A	N/A	2.66	27.68	N/A	N/A	N/A	2.09	100.00	N/A	N/A	N/A
Net Prft on Stkhldrs Eqty	(%)	4.73	-13.84	N/A	N/A	N/A	5.49	81.19	N/A	N/A	N/A	3.03	100.00	N/A	N/A	N/A

(X) = TIMES   ($) = DOLLARS   (D) = DAYS   (%) = PERCENT

* IN THOUSANDS

5

CASE STUDY 1:
SURE PROGRESS, INC.

Creative Alternatives to the Direct Extension of Credit

INTRODUCTION

This case provides new insights into the methods to render a sound business credit decision that may not involve the direct extension of credit to a customer. Here we explore methods commonly used in some industries that can be applied to others. The techniques used for dealing with customers, the sales/marketing staff, and upper management are discussed, viewed through the eyes of three students who completed this course. The goal of graciously accepting the final decision of upper management while minimizing the possibility of a loss is explored throughout this case.

By reviewing this real day in the life of a credit department, readers will learn to make effective use of data, facts, and alternative methods in reaching a decision. An appreciation for how other people in marketing or finance think will hone negotiating skills. Readers can use new insight into the creation of a sound business credit decision to prevent gaps or weaknesses in their decision-making processes.

65

Case study 1 looks at selling to a marginal customer on an order that has a high margin. Now comes the tough part: How do you make the sale without losing everything, including the end user? Every credit professional faces this task when selling to companies that have cash-flow problems and lack the financial strength to deal with a lot of new business. Making the sale while minimizing the credit risk is the ultimate goal of today's credit professional. With this in mind, review the following case, consider the facts, answer the questions, and compare your answers with those of some of my students. Then see what really happened in this case and determine if the real events are close to your decision or if truth is stranger than fiction.

THE FACTS

I.M. "Skip" Tracer, credit manager of New Deal Products (a manufacturer), received a call from his regional sales manager, Joe Fastbuck, in Houston. His distributor, Sure Progress, Inc., was trying to clinch a $5 million yearlong contract with Jackson Company (a Fortune 200 Company with a 5A1 rating) for our product. That was the good news. The bad news was that this distributor had a $100,000 credit limit and a net worth of about $125,000 from its 1994 financial statement. It had been in business for 25 years and was growing but recently had been experiencing some growing pains. Cash flow had not been as good as it should have been, which resulted in some 30 to 60 day past-due balances. Our terms of sale are 1% 10 net 30 days, and at 45 days the account is placed on credit hold.

The customer's bank has first lien on virtually everything. The only reason the company had a strong chance to obtain this order was that it was a minority business. Sure Progress was requesting that we increase its line of credit to $1 million and give it net 90-days terms. Our margin on this order is 55%, which is above our normal 35% margin; Sure Progress's margin is 40%, which is 10% higher than average. An updated credit check was made and year-end financials were obtained on Sure Progress.

INSTRUCTIONS

1. Analyze all data available on the case. Summarize findings using the following:

A. Trend analysis, common-size analysis, ratio analysis, and comparison to industry standards

B. Summarize the information available in the credit report, references, and information available above

2. Will you approve the sale according to the terms and conditions requested by the customer?

3. If approved, state your reasons for agreeing to the customer's request.

4. If not approved, state what terms and conditions you would offer and what your reasons are for your decision.

5. State any alternate proposal that you would make if your customer and management rejected your initial decision.

6. What facts would you use to defend your decisions to management?

7. If overridden by management, what steps would you take to prevent a possible loss from this sale?

CREDIT REPORT

FILE #123456789   DATE PRINTED   SUMMARY
                         MAY 23, 1996   RATING   ---
SURE PROGRESS INC.   STARTED   1971
6201 BEHIND EIGHT BALL WAY WHOL INDUSTRIAL   EMPLOYS   110
RUNDOWNTOWN, TX 77630   SUPPLIES   HISTORY   CLEAR
TEL: 713 555-5000   SIC NO.
                              50 85

CHIEF EXECUTIVE: ARNOLD STOPGAP, PRES.

PAYMENTS (Amounts may be rounded to nearest figure in prescribed ranges)
REPORTED

	PAYING RECORD	HIGH CREDIT	NOW OWES	PAST DUE	SELLING TERMS	LAST SALE WITHIN
4/96	Ppt	200000	10000	-0-		1 Mo
	Ppt	50000	5000	-0-		
	Ppt	2500	2500	-0-	N15	2-3 Mos
	Ppt-Slow 15	7500	500	500	N30	
	Ppt-Slow 15	500	500	-0-	N30	
	Ppt-Slow 15	500	500	-0-		1 Mo
	Slow 15	1000	1000	-0-	N30	1 Mo
3/96	Ppt-Slow 15	200000	100000	-0-		1 Mo
	Slow 15	100000	-0-	-0-	N30	6-12 Mos
	Slow 30	50000	1000	-0-	N30	1 Mo
	Slow 30-60	10000	1000	-0-		1 Mo

* Payment experiences reflect how bills are met in relation to the terms granted. In some instances payment beyond terms can be the result of disputes over merchandise, skipped invoices, etc.

* Each experience shown represents a separate account reported by a supplier. Updated trade experiences replace those previously reported.

FINANCE
* Financial information is attached for your review. Sales for 1996 were forecasted to be $30,000,000.

PUBLIC FILINGS
UCC FILINGS
4/15/95
Financing statement #984345 filed 9/11/91 with Secretary, State of TX Debtor Sure Progress Inc., Rundowntown, TX Secured Party: All Secured Bank, NA, Watertown, TX

SURE PROGRESS INC.   May 23, 1996   PAGE 002

Collateral: Specified Inventory and Products - Specified Accounts Receivable and products - Specified Contract rights and products - Specified Vehicles and products - and Others

HISTORY
4/15/96
ARNOLD L. STOPGAP, PRES.
JACK L. STOPGAP, V. PRES.
BARRY R. STOPGAP, TREAS.
DIRECTOR(S): The officer(s)

INCORPORATED Texas May 20, 1971

Authorized capital consists of 50,000 shares Common Stock, no par value.

Business started 1971 by Arnold L. Stopgap. 100% stock is owned by Arnold L. Stopgap.

Arnold L. Stopgap born 1940, married. 1962 Graduated Slippery Rock College, Slippery Rock TX. 1962–1971 worked for Ace Distributor Inc., Massive, TX. 1971–present President and CEO here.

Jack L. Stopgap born 1964, single. Graduate Jackson University, Wheatland, NM 1986. 1986 started here. 1993–Present: Vice President here and continues.

Barry R. Stopgap born 1944. Brother of Jack. Active here since1971.

OPERATION
4/15/96
Wholesales industrial supplies (100%).

Terms Net 30 days. Has 500 accounts. Sells to industrial accounts. Territory: Texas. Non-seasonal.

EMPLOYEES: 110 including officers. 90 employed here.

FACILITIES: Leases 24,000 sq. ft. in 1-story concrete block building in good condition. Premises neat.

LOCATION: Suburban business section on side street.

FULL DISPLAY COMPLETE

New Deal Products Inc.
235 St. Patrick Drive
Rochester, TX 77653
FAX#: (716) 555-2932

BANK CREDIT INQUIRY

All Secured Bank NA
235 St. Patrick Drive
Watertown, TX 77632
(713) 555-2810

Ref: Sure Progress Inc.
6201 Behind Eight Ball Way
Rundowntown, TX 77630

The above-referenced company has given your concern's name as a credit reference.
Please provide us with your experience with them so that we may determine their credit
worthiness. Please fax this information back to us as soon as possible. Thank you in
advance for the information that you provide and be assured that it will be kept
confidential.

Sincerely,

I. M. Tracer
Credit Department

If business is not incorporated, please provide owners' name & address:

SAVINGS ACCOUNT   LOW __   MEDIUM __   HIGH __ $__ FIGURE

          OPEN ___   CLOSED ___

CHECKING ACCOUNT   LOW _X_   MEDIUM __   HIGH __ $ 6 _ FIGURE
          SATISFACTORY _X_   UNSATISFACTORY ___

CREDIT EXPERIENCE

Loans are granted: Frequently _X_ Occasionally ___ Seldom ___

Type: Working Capital _X_ Mortgage __ Installment __

Maximum Credit Extended $High 5 Figures Secured _X_ Unsecured ___

Present Outstandings: Secured $High 5 Figures Unsecured $

Relationship: SATISFACTORY _X_ UNSATISFACTORY ___

Have "NSF" checks been issued: Yes ___ No _X_

Prepared By: _B. A. Loanshark_____   Title: _Vice President_

New Deal Products Inc.
235 St. Patrick Drive
Rochester, TX 77653
PHONE (713) 555-2810
FAX   (713) 555-2932

CREDIT INQUIRY

*Sheet Material Company Inc.
*1235 Skyhigh Lane
*Runuptown, TX 77653

REF: Sure Progress Inc.
6201 Behind Eight Ball Way
Rundowntown, TX 77630

The above-referenced company has given your concern's name as a credit reference. Please provide us with your experience with them so that we may determine their credit worthiness. Please fax this information back to us as soon as possible. Thank you in advance for the information that you provide and be assured that it will be kept confidential.

Sincerely,

 I. M. Tracer
 Credit Department

Sold From 1985

Terms of Sales Net 30

Largest Amount Now Owing $200,000

Amount Past Due $25,000

Recent Trend Toward X Promptness
                    __ Slowness
Makes Unjust Claims (State) _____

_____
Credit Refused (State Cause)
_____
_____
Remarks: _____
_____
_____

MANNER OF PAYMENT
__ Discounts
__ Prompt & Satisfactory
 X Prompt to 30 Days Slow
__ Pays on Account
__ Asks for More Time
__ Slow but Collectible
__ Accepts COD's Promptly
__ Settles by Trade Acceptance
__ Notes Paid at Maturity
__ Account Secured

55 Average Days Paid

Information Given By: Jack A. Deadbeat, Credit Mgr. Date 05/26/96

WE REQUEST THE RETURN OF THIS FORM TO FACILITATE OUR
SYSTEM OF FILING REPORT.

New Deal Products Inc.
235 St. Patrick Drive
Rochester, TX 77653
PHONE (713) 555-2810
FAX   (713) 555-2932

CREDIT INQUIRY

*Gasket Maker Company Inc.
*1345 Giveup Street
*Runmedown, TX 77643

REF: Sure Progress Inc.
6201 Behind Eight Ball Way
Rundowntown, TX 77630

The above-referenced company has given your concern's name as a credit reference. Please provide us with your experience with them so that we may determine their credit worthiness. Please fax this information back to us as soon as possible. Thank you in advance for the information that you provide and be assured that it will be kept confidential.

Sincerely,

I. M. Tracer
Credit Department

Sold From 1978

Terms of Sales 1% 10 Net 30

Largest Amount Now Owing $100,000

Amount Past Due $50,000

Recent Trend Toward X Promptness
            _ Slowness
Makes Unjust Claims (State) _____
_____

Credit Refused (State Cause) _____
_____
_____

Remarks: _____
_____

MANNER OF PAYMENT
__ Discounts
__ Prompt & Satisfactory
 X Prompt to 30 Days Slow
__ Pays on Account
__ Asks for More Time
__ Slow but Collectible
__ Accepts COD's Promptly
__ Settles by Trade Acceptance
__ Notes Paid at Maturity
__ Account Secured

50 Average Days Paid

Information Given By: I. M. Mean, Credit Manager   Date 05/26/96

WE REQUEST THE RETURN OF THIS FORM TO FACILITATE OUR SYSTEM OF FILING REPORT.

New Deal Products Inc.
235 St. Patrick Drive
Rochester, TX 77653
PHONE (713) 555-2810
FAX   (713) 555-2932

CREDIT INQUIRY

*Rubber U.S.A. Inc.
*1569 Lowdown Varmit Highway
*Rolloverme, TX 77543

REF: Sure Progress Inc.
6201 Behind Eight Ball Way
Rundowntown, TX 77630

The above-referenced company has given your concern's name as a credit reference. Please provide us with your experience with them so that we may determine their credit worthiness. Please fax this information back to us as soon as possible. Thank you in advance for the information that you provide and be assured that it will be kept confidential.

Sincerely,

 I. M. Tracer
Credit Department

Sold From 1980

Terms of Sales _____ Net 30 _____

Largest Amount Now Owing $150,000

Amount Past Due $10,000

Recent Trend Toward X Promptness
              __ Slowness
Makes Unjust Claims (State) _____

Credit Refused (State Cause) _____

Remarks: _____

MANNER OF PAYMENT
__ Discounts
__ Prompt & Satisfactory
X Prompt to 30 Days Slow
__ Pays on Account
__ Asks for More Time
__ Slow but Collectible
__ Accepts COD's Promptly
__ Settles by Trade Acceptance
__ Notes Paid at Maturity
__ Account Secured

53 Average Days Paid

Information Given By: Rank Amateur, Credit Manager   Date 05/26/96

WE REQUEST THE RETURN OF THIS FORM TO FACILITATE OUR SYSTEM OF FILING REPORT.

Sure Progress Inc.
6201 Behind Eight Ball Way
Rundowntown, TX 77630

SIC 5085

ACCOUNT 123456

$2,435,642.00
$175,159.00

	12/31/95				12/31/94				12/31/93			
	$	% Change	% Assets	Ind % Assets	$	% Change	% Assets	Ind % Assets	$	% Change	% Assets	Ind % Assets
Cash	$10,601.00	-67.86	1.86	6.10	$32,979.00	181.41	5.55	5.80	$11,719.00	100.00	2.08	5.30
Accounts Receivable	$288,714.00	20.19	50.57	34.40	$240,220.00	10.11	40.41	33.40	$218,164.00	100.00	38.73	35.00
Inventory	$223,874.00	-24.75	39.21	37.60	$297,504.00	13.19	50.04	38.60	$262,825.00	100.00	46.65	39.50
Due from Shareholder	$0.00	0.00	0.00	---	$0.00	0.00	0.00	---	$0.00	0.00	0.00	---
Due From Affiliate	$0.00	0.00	0.00	---	$0.00	0.00	0.00	---	$0.00	0.00	0.00	---
Other Current	$6,000.00	2,243.75	1.05	1.30	$256.00	17.43	0.04	1.30	$218.00	100.00	0.04	1.30
Total Current	$529,189.00	-7.32	92.69	79.40	$570,959.00	15.83	96.04	79.10	$492,926.00	100.00	87.50	81.10
Fixed Assets	$33,781.00	128.51	5.92	14.10	$14,783.00	-57.72	2.49	13.50	$34,962.00	100.00	6.21	12.80
Notes Receivable	$0.00	0.00	0.00	---	$0.00	0.00	0.00	---	$0.00	0.00	0.00	---
Deposits	$0.00	0.00	0.00	---	$0.00	0.00	0.00	---	$0.00	0.00	0.00	---
Cash Value of Life Insur.	$7,949.00	-6.29	1.39	5.30	$8,483.00	1,596.60	1.43	6.30	$500.00	100.00	0.09	5.40
Intangible Assets	$0.00	-100.00	0.00	1.20	$250.00	-99.29	0.04	1.10	$34,969.00	100.00	6.21	0.70
Total Assets	$570,919.00	-3.96	100.00	100.00	$594,475.00	5.52	100.00	100.00	$563,357.00	100.00	100.00	100.00
Account Payable	$197,283.00	16.62	34.56	25.30	$169,161.00	-9.63	28.46	24.20	$187,190.00	100.00	33.23	24.70
Bank Loans + N.P.	$1,961.00	100.00	0.34	12.60	$0.00	-100.00	0.00	11.60	$79,000.00	100.00	14.02	14.60
Cur. Mat.-L.T.D.	$139,675.00	-23.05	24.46	4.20	$181,515.00	293.11	30.53	4.10	$46,174.00	100.00	8.20	3.40
Income Tax Payables	$4,327.00	-58.76	0.76	0.30	$10,492.00	-45.07	1.76	0.40	$19,100.00	100.00	3.39	0.50
Accrued Expenses	$43,519.00	-31.79	7.62	7.00	$63,800.00	66.06	10.73	5.60	$38,421.00	100.00	6.82	6.00
Total Current	$386,765.00	-8.99	67.74	49.40	$424,968.00	14.89	0.00	45.90	$369,885.00	100.00	65.66	49.20
Long Term Debt	$8,995.00	-79.39	1.58	11.90	$43,654.00	-55.17	7.34	11.60	$97,373.00	100.00	17.28	11.30
Deferred Taxes	$0.00	0.00	0.00	0.30	$0.00	0.00	0.00	0.20	$0.00	0.00	0.00	0.10
All Other L.T. Debt	$0.00	0.00	0.00	1.80	$0.00	0.00	0.00	2.30	$0.00	0.00	0.00	2.20
Net Worth	$175,159.00	39.18	30.68	36.60	$125,853.00	30.96	21.17	40.00	$96,099.00	100.00	17.06	37.20
Total Liab.& Equity	$570,919.00	-3.96	100.00	100.00	$594,475.00	5.52	28.51	100.00	$563,357.00	100.00	100.00	100.00
Net Sales	$2,435,642.00	19.93	100.00	100.00	$2,030,865.00	5.87	100.00	100.00	$1,918,294.00	100.00	100.00	100.00
Cost of Goods Sold	$1,581,201.00	17.72	64.92	67.90	$1,343,211.00	0.77	66.14	68.10	$1,332,982.00	100.00	69.49	69.00
Gross Profit	$854,441.00	24.25	35.08	32.10	$687,654.00	17.49	33.86	31.90	$585,312.00	100.00	30.51	31.00
Depreciation	$9,127.00	-11.19	0.37	---	$10,277.00	-48.42	0.51	---	$19,923.00	100.00	1.04	---
Lease Payments	$0.00	0.00	0.00	---	$0.00	0.00	0.00	---	$0.00	0.00	0.00	---
Other Operating Exps.	$768,861.00	21.42	31.57	29.40	$633,228.00	22.57	31.18	29.60	$516,633.00	100.00	26.93	28.20
Tot. Operating Exps.	$777,998.00	20.90	31.94	2.70	$643,505.00	19.93	31.69	2.30	$536,556.00	100.00	27.97	2.80
Operating Profit	$76,453.00	73.17	3.14	0.80	$44,149.00	-9.45	2.17	0.60	$48,756.00	100.00	2.54	1.00
Interest Inc./(Exp.)	$0.00	0.00	0.00	---	$0.00	0.00	0.00	---	$0.00	0.00	0.00	---
G/(L) on sale of Fxd Assets	$0.00	0.00	0.00	2.00	$0.00	0.00	0.00	1.70	$0.00	0.00	0.00	1.70
Profit Before Taxes	$76,453.00	73.17	3.14	2.00	$44,149.00	-9.45	2.17	1.70	$48,756.00	100.00	2.54	1.70
Taxes	$27,147.00	88.59	1.11	---	$14,395.00	-39.94	0.71	---	$23,967.00	100.00	1.25	---
Net Profit	$49,306.00	65.71	2.02	---	$29,754.00	20.03	1.47	---	$24,789.00	100.00	1.29	---
Other Data:												
Working Capital	$142,424.00	-2.44	24.95	30.00	$145,991.00	18.65	96.04	33.20	$123,041.00	100.00	21.84	31.90
Tangible Equity	$175,159.00	39.45	30.68	35.40	$125,603.00	105.47	21.13	38.90	$61,130.00	100.00	10.85	36.50
Recommended Credit Limit:	$23,471.31	73.03	---	---	$13,565.12	236.22	---	---	$4,034.58	---	---	---

Sure Progress Inc.
6201 Behind Eight Ball Way
Rundowntown, TX 77630

RATIOS	Unit	12/31/95	% Change	UQ	Med	LQ	12/31/94	% Change	UQ	Med	LQ	12/31/93	% Change	UQ	Med	LQ
SOLVENCY																
Current Ratio	($)	1.37	1.84	2.40	1.70	1.30	1.34	0.82	2.70	1.80	1.30	1.33	100.00	2.50	1.70	1.20
Quick Ratio	($)	0.77	99.93	1.20	0.80	0.60	0.64	3.44	1.40	0.90	0.60	0.62	100.00	1.20	0.80	0.60
Net Profit B4 Tax + Depr./Cur LTD	(X)	0.61	104.34	2.90	1.20	0.50	0.30	-79.84	2.80	1.30	0.20	1.49	100.00	5.00	1.80	0.70
Sales to Fixed Assets	(X)	72.10	79.30	62.70	31.80	14.50	40.21	-26.71	70.70	32.70	13.90	54.87	100.00	70.10	32.70	19.60
Sales to Total Assets	(X)	4.27	24.88	3.90	3.00	2.30	3.42	0.33	3.70	3.10	2.20	3.41	100.00	3.80	3.00	2.20
Total Liab. to NW	(X)	2.26	-39.32	0.90	1.80	4.30	3.72	-23.42	0.80	1.40	3.70	4.86	100.00	0.90	1.70	3.60
Fixed Assets to NW	(X)	0.19	64.19	0.10	0.30	0.80	0.12	-67.71	0.10	0.30	0.80	0.36	100.00	0.10	0.30	0.60
Tot. Liab. to Tot. Assets	(%)	69.32	-12.06	N/A	N/A	N/A	78.83	-4.96	N/A	N/A	N/A	82.94	0.00	N/A	N/A	N/A
Oper. Prof. to Int. Exp.	(X)	0.00	0.00	N/A	N/A	N/A	0.00	0.00	N/A	N/A	N/A	0.00	0.00	N/A	N/A	N/A
Oper Prof+Lease Py to Int Exp+LP	(X)	0.00	0.00	N/A	N/A	N/A	0.00	0.00	N/A	N/A	N/A	0.00	0.00	N/A	N/A	N/A
EFFICIENCY																
Sales to Receivables	(X)	8.44	-0.21	10.90	9.10	7.70	8.45	-3.85	11.60	9.10	7.90	8.79	100.00	11.00	9.20	7.10
Days Sales Outstanding	(D)	43	0.00	33	40	47	43	2.38	31	40	46	42	100.00	33	40	51
Cost of Sales to Inv.	(X)	7.06	56.43	9.10	5.10	3.60	4.51	-10.98	8.50	5.00	3.50	5.07	100.00	9.90	5.10	3.30
Days Sales in Inventory	(D)	52	-35.80	40	72	101	81	12.50	43	73	104	72	100.00	37	72	111
Sales to Net Working Cap.	(X)	17.10	22.93	5.90	9.30	21.40	13.91	-10.77	5.40	9.00	18.40	15.59	100.00	5.10	9.30	23.60
Cost of Sales/Payables	(X)	8.01	0.94	15.40	8.80	6.30	7.94	11.51	15.30	9.20	6.00	7.12	100.00	14.80	9.20	6.20
A/P Turnover	(D)	46	0.00	24	41	58	46	-9.80	24	40	61	51	100.00	25	40	59
PROFITABILITY																
Depreciation to Sales	(%)	0.37	-25.95	0.60	1.00	1.60	0.51	-51.28	0.50	0.80	1.60	1.04	100.00	0.60	0.90	1.40
Prof bef Tax to Tot Assets	(%)	13.39	80.32	10.70	4.30	0.40	7.43	-14.19	10.30	4.50	0.00	8.65	100.00	10.40	4.70	0.40
Profit before Taxes to TNW	(%)	43.65	24.42	32.40	14.70	2.60	35.08	-30.86	29.40	10.70	0.00	50.74	100.00	29.20	13.00	1.70

OTHER RATIOS NOT AVAILABLE WITH INDUSTRY STANDARDS

RATIOS	Unit	12/31/95	% Change	UQ	Med	LQ	12/31/94	% Change	UQ	Med	LQ	12/31/93	% Change	UQ	Med	LQ
SOLVENCY																
Inv. to Net Work. Capital	(X)	1.57	-22.86	N/A	N/A	N/A	2.04	-4.60	N/A	N/A	N/A	2.14	100.00	N/A	N/A	N/A
Current Liab. to NW	(X)	2.21	-34.61	N/A	N/A	N/A	3.38	-12.27	N/A	N/A	N/A	3.85	100.00	N/A	N/A	N/A
LT Debt to Tot. Debt & Capital	(%)	1.58	-78.47	N/A	N/A	N/A	7.34	-57.52	N/A	N/A	N/A	17.28	100.00	N/A	N/A	N/A
Fixed Assets to LT Debt	(X)	3.76	1,005.88	N/A	N/A	N/A	0.34	-5.56	N/A	N/A	N/A	0.36	100.00	N/A	N/A	N/A
EFFICIENCY																
Net Sales to NW	(X)	13.91	-13.82	N/A	N/A	N/A	16.14	-19.14	N/A	N/A	N/A	19.96	100.00	N/A	N/A	N/A
Net Sales to Inventory	(X)	10.88	59.30	N/A	N/A	N/A	6.83	-6.44	N/A	N/A	N/A	7.30	100.00	N/A	N/A	N/A
Cost of Sales/Working Capital	(X)	11.10	20.65	N/A	N/A	N/A	9.20	-15.05	N/A	N/A	N/A	10.83	100.00	N/A	N/A	N/A
Short Term Loan Turnover	(X)	0.00	0.00	N/A	N/A	N/A	0.00	-100.00	N/A	N/A	N/A	22.00	100.00	N/A	N/A	N/A
LT Liabilities Payback *	($)	($81.24)	-42.58	N/A	N/A	N/A	($141.48)	9,577.43	N/A	N/A	N/A	($1.46)	100.00	N/A	N/A	N/A
PROFITABILITY																
Gross Profit on Net Sales	(%)	35.08	3.60	--	32.10	--	33.86	10.98	--	31.90	--	30.51	100.00	--	31.00	--
Net Oper Inc on Net Sales	(%)	3.14	44.70	--	2.70	--	2.17	-14.57	--	2.30	--	2.54	100.00	--	2.80	--
Net Profit on Net Sales	(%)	2.02	37.41	N/A	N/A	N/A	1.47	13.95	N/A	N/A	N/A	1.29	100.00	N/A	N/A	N/A
Net Prof on Total Assets	(%)	8.64	72.46	N/A	N/A	N/A	5.01	13.86	N/A	N/A	N/A	4.40	100.00	N/A	N/A	N/A
Tot Assets to Equity	(X)	3.26	-31.00	N/A	N/A	N/A	4.72	-19.42	N/A	N/A	N/A	5.86	100.00	N/A	N/A	N/A
Net Prft on Stkhldrs Eqty	(%)	28.15	19.08	N/A	N/A	N/A	23.64	-8.37	N/A	N/A	N/A	25.80	100.00	N/A	N/A	N/A

(X) = TIMES   ($) = DOLLARS   (D) = DAYS   (%) = PERCENT

* IN THOUSANDS

OVERVIEW

First let us look at the questions, answer them, and then weigh the pros and cons of each decision recommended by my students. Question 1 requires a review of the financial data and the credit report and references provided. When analyzing the customer's three years of financial data, we can see an improvement in most numbers. The trend reflects a positive strengthening of liquidity and profitability as each is higher than the previous year. These, however, are still below industry average (negative). The customer's paying habits and collection effectiveness is also below average (both negative). Debt while dropping (positive) is also above the industry average (negative). The net worth, likewise, is also increasing and is above industry average (both positives).

As to the credit report and references, let us look at some basic facts. The company has been in business for 25 years and employs about 110 people (both positive). The high credit reflected by the credit report shows a $200,000 ceiling (positive) with some delinquency exhibited in paying habits (negative). The bank indeed has first lien on all assets (negative), and it is a family owned and operated firm (neither positive nor negative). It leases the building that houses the firm (negative), and the background of the individuals who own the company reflect a track record of experience in this particular type of business (positive).

The paying habits from the three trade references shows that it pays on an average of 53 days, which is 23 days past due (negative) and has had up to $200,000 for its high credit (positive). Their bank has extended a high five-figure (somewhere between $70,000 to $90,000) working capital line of credit (positive) that appears to be totally used up at this time (negative).

Question 2 asks the very direct question: Will you approve the deal as requested by the customer? All my students answered no to this question. Therefore, the answer to question 3 was not applicable so we move on to question 4. The answers to this question were widely varied and came from all different directions. At this time, I will introduce a few students who worked on this particular case, the industries they worked in and their decisions coupled with their reasoning behind their answers.

WHAT OTHER CREDIT MANAGERS THOUGHT

Student One

Joe B., a credit professional from a furniture-manufacturing firm, felt that the extended terms were acceptable but that raising the limit to $1,000,000 was out of the question. Extended terms were very commonplace in his industry, but limits of this magnitude for a firm of this size was not acceptable. He was willing to offer the firm the limit requested with security to cover a limit in excess of $250,000. He knew this was not possible since all the assets were tied up with the bank. He considered a purchase money security interest on the inventory but knew that the bank would not agree to giving up its rights to first interest in this inventory. His final offer was extending a line of credit of $250,000 with terms of 3% 10 days, 2% 30 days, 1% 60 days, net 90 days, but he would consider a higher limit with security. He based his decision on the fact that the company had been up to $200,000, its financial trends were generally up, and it had been in business for 25 years.

Student Two

Mary C., a credit professional from an architectural hardware manufacturing firm, was not willing to offer extended terms as she felt that if she did it for this firm she would be forced to offer it to all customers. This meant that in order to prove that her company offers the same terms to all customers under the Robinson-Patman Act, it would be forced to disclose the details of this order if sued. She did not want her competition to have access to information about a deal that represented a 55% profit margin and was for a total amount of $5,000,000 over a one-year period if a former customer took legal action.

Considering the company's limited net worth, the lack of access to assets to be used as collateral, and its recent trend toward delinquency, she would have been very uncomfortable in extending more than $200,000, the firm's high credit to date. Typical of her industry, she would not offer extended terms and was used to filing mechanic liens if a payment was late. Her company also deals in order-to-order terms if delinquency becomes a problem.

Student Three

Tom C. is from a computer circuit board manufacturer that sells to many small and minority-owed firms. He felt that in this case the customer's customer needed to have a minority supplier to keep its government contracts (supposition) intact. After confirming this fact with the customer, he suggested a meeting with the end user to discuss the size of the order and to request the end user's guarantee of payment in exchange for approving the necessary terms and limit needed by his customer to fill this order.

This type of arrangement is fairly commonplace in his industry as his clients sell to defense contractors that are required to hire minority-owned firms, which can be undercapitalized to meet the needs of huge government contractors. This was a very creative way to deal with the concerns of meeting the scheduled payments and to justify the credit limit his customer needs.

ALTERNATIVE RECOMMENDATIONS

Now it is time to ask the students for an alternate proposal if top management rejected their decisions.

Student One

Joe B. felt that if a business decision was required that meant extending credit in excess of $250,000 and 90-day terms, then he would reluctantly consider increasing the limit to $500,000. Any amount above that would require a signature by top management noting that he did not recommend the additional amount. He suggested that the multiple discount terms be offered and pushed heavily.

Student Two

Mary C. was not receptive to giving more than the $200,000 and stated that, if overruled, she would require top management to sign off on this one. She said that she would put this account on an immediate watch and would be prepared either to pull a shipment back or to file the necessary paperwork for reclamation at the first sign of trouble.

Student Three

Tom C. was willing to extend the amount needed if the end user was willing to guarantee the debt. Assuming that it was not, Tom felt that he would authorize up to $250,000 on 3% 15 days terms and have the end user speed up payments to our customer. This would allow the customer to meet the end user's needs but keep a tight rein on the customer. Tom also would require the customer to offer its customer terms of 2% 10 days, with payment via the automated clearinghouse (a form of electronic payment; ACH). This would give the end user the necessary incentive to pay the minority business faster.

ADVICE TO GIVE TOP MANAGEMENT

Student One

Joe B. felt that the company's small though increasing net worth was the biggest reason to convince top management to approve the transaction. He advised top management that the customer was starting to slow down on its paying habits and was pretty heavily laden with debt as compared to its industry. He would advise top management that he was being flexible by even offering to extend more credit than the total net worth. The reason for this was the level of margin made on the sale and the discounted-scaled terms that he had recommended.

Student Two

Mary C. concurred on all of Joe B.'s points but also added that the fact that the customer was totally leveraged out by the bank. Also, there was no security to be had other than a purchase money security interest that the bank would very likely react unfavorably to. She also reiterated that any extended terms would violate the Robinson-Patman Act and that it might end up in a suit filed against the firm by other customers if preferential terms were given.

Student Three

Tom C. noted that the maximum high credit that was currently extended was only $200,000 as referenced in the credit report. He also was concerned that the bank's working capital line of credit was all used up, allowing no wiggle room if money was needed to deal with an emergency situation connected to this order. The fact that the customer did not own its facility and that the best three trade references also were being paid slow meant that trouble might be on the horizon.

ACTION PLAN IF OVERRIDDEN BY MANAGEMENT

Student One

Joe B. said that he had always been a team player and would fully support top management's decision. He did state though that he would watch this one like a hawk. He planned to keep a sharp focus on his trade associations watch system to notify him immediately if any other vendor aged further past due than what had been experienced in recent times.

Student Two

Mary C. said that she would try to get top management to agree to put them on hold the minute the customer went past due. She would not allow any further product to be shipped until the past due was cleared up. She wanted the shipments to go out on an order-to-order basis, and when she got paid she would release the next one. She would also put the customer on watch with the credit-reporting agency. If any changes occurred she would be notified immediately.

Student Three

Tom C. was less worried but still very cautious. He felt that he needed to stay in touch with the salesperson who worked with both the customer and the end user to see if there were problems in meeting the end user's demands. He also would keep tabs on the end user's paying habits to see if it was slowing down payments to its suppliers. Considering its small size and easily disturbed financial status, the customer could run into serious trouble easily if the end user held it up for payment.

WHAT REALLY HAPPENED

Now that we have looked at how three of my students would handle the different aspects of this case, let us look at what really happened and how I dealt with this situation. This was not an easy case to deal with, and my decision in no way should be considered the only solution. There are many possible judgments in every case. Depending on the circumstances, any conclusion reached thus far would be just as valid as the one that actually happened. Any answer will be just as valid if readers take all aspects into consideration, make every effort to obtain the maximum amount of information, and are creative in their thinking. Never settling for just cash in advance or a flat-out no proves that you have earned your pay for the week. Those individuals who keep losses at an acceptable level while finding ways to make the maximum amount of sales happen earn their pay every week. So now on with the real events.

This order came to me at a time when my company was trying to expand our horizons yet keep our cash flow intact. When Joe, our salesman, approached me on this order, I decided that this order was not one that we wanted to turn down but it was going to be more difficult than the typical orders he had given me in the past. We had sold to this customer for a few years, and it had gone past due sometimes. This customer did have growing pains, which resulted in delinquency at times, but it usually paid up when told that this behavior would not be tolerated. We knew that they were a minority-owned business, which got it in a few doors, especially those of government agencies. We were pleased to pick up this type of business as the government usually preferred not to deal with large manufacturers direct but demanded that its contractors use minority-owned vendors instead.

Arnold Stopgap, the owner, was always reasonable and willing to work with us on ways to get the materials necessary to meet his orders. He did understand our concern when it came to the amount of credit that he was asking for as well as the terms needed. Joe and I met directly with Arnold to discuss how the deal could be structured so that his company, as a minority business, could get the order while keeping our concern over the amount needed to fill the order to a minimum. We discussed the paying habits of the government contractor as well as its desire to take advantage of cash discounts whenever possible. While Arnold did not wish to give up any of his firm's profit, he was willing to give the contractor a cash discount if that would help make the deal happen.

We also discussed the concern with the Robinson-Patman Act and the 90-day terms that he was requesting. Arnold needed these terms to have the time to take our raw materials and adjust them to meet the customer's order requirements. The process would take at least 60 days, and he would receive payment from the contractor 30 days thereafter.

When the topic of the bank arose, he confided that he had very little room left on his working capital line of credit and could not use this to pay us any faster. At this point, I requested that we reschedule the meeting with the loan officer. Before leaving, I suggested that the bank be presented with a request for a total financing package built around this order.

The package would require that all cash be paid to the bank and that the purchase order be used as collateral for the interim loans needed to cover the customer's needs. We would offer Arnold terms of 3% 15 days as a show of confidence in our customer; he in turn would offer his customer 2% 10 days via the ACH.

The bank would guarantee payment to us for materials of up to $500,000 under a standby letter of credit, which would allow Arnold to secure his credit line with us. Even though he would be getting the contractor to pay in 10 days, it still took him 60 days to turn the raw materials over. With this in mind, we understood that he needed a steady stream of our goods but would not have the funds to pay for the product until 70 days later. We also understood that the first shipment would be due in 60 days from date of contract signing and the last would be received by the 300th day thereafter.

This would allow us to ship him $250,000 at terms of 3% 15 days. Allowing for a few days mail time, we would have to ship him an additional $250,000 before being paid. This limited our exposure to no more than $500,000. The bank, in turn, would lend him $1,500,000 plus the standby letter of credit, which would give him the ability to borrow the necessary money to cover our initial five $250,000 shipments. At that point Arnold would be able to use the payments received from the contractor to pay us from then on.

When the presentation was held, we explained to the bank our relationship with the loan officer, the materials we would be selling, the type of contract Arnold had obtained, and the need for this specialized financial help from the bank. Arnold presented the bank with a copy of the contract and the facts covering his profit margins and the payment history that the contractor had with its suppliers. He also advised the bank on the terms that he would be offered by us and the terms that he would be selling the contractor on. He would give the bank the purchase order to use as collateral, and all payments from the contractor would come through the bank in the form of ACH transfers. After meeting with the loan committee, the financing package was approved, and we all moved forward a little more profitable than before.

CONCLUSION

At times personal meetings and presentations to the customer's bank are needed to put together a financing package that is outside the normal methods used in credit extension. In most situations the possibility of taking the order direct and having Arnold's firm withdraw its bid while paying his firm its profit would have been a solid solution. The only problem was that we would have not succeeded in our bid.

The government contractor awarded Arnold's firm the bid because he had not only the best proposal but, most important, he was the only minority firm submitting an offer. As this was the case, we could not have beaten Arnold out of the order, and we both would have lost out on the contract should that have been the company's decision. In the long run, it is better to be a team player than going after an order alone. This whole deal went smoothly. Arnold's firm has grown considerably since the sale and many more have taken place.

6

CASE STUDY 2: INTERNATIONAL EXPORTS, INC.

Creative Methods to Reestablish Open Account Credit with a Former Problem Customer

INTRODUCTION

This case provides new methods to employ when reestablishing former customers using negotiation techniques learned in Chapter 4. Looking at the customer from the point of view of making a sound business credit decision provides the student with new options in making a relatively safe sale. Skills in obtaining vital information may prove to be the key in the successful development of a sound business credit decision. Readers will learn how to deal with external factors that affect the ability to render a simple credit decision (i.e., international transactions, foreign parent companies, etc.).

By reviewing this real day in the life of a credit department, readers will learn to make effective use of data, facts, and alternative methods in reaching a decision. An appreciation for how other people in marketing or finance think will hone negotiating skills. Readers can use new insight into the creation of a sound business credit decision to prevent gaps or weaknesses in their decision-making processes.

THE FACTS

I.B. Strict, the division credit manager for Locktight Seals Company (a manufacturer), is discussing a problem account with I.M. Slick, the original equipment manufacturer's salesman. It seems that due to problems associated with getting currency out of Mexico by International's Mexican parent, International Export Haltto Ltd., the problem account was having extreme cash-flow problems. The account had become 60 to 90 days past due. Other divisions of Locktight's parent company, Openflow Industries, had been contacting Mr. Strict for status on the account. Their balances were farther past due but for significantly smaller dollars.

Locktight's exposure at the time was $165,000, and Openflow wanted to know what could be done on this account. Mr. Strict had been in constant contact with International's vice president of finance, Mr. Manny Promises, but no commitment had been made. He did indicate to Mr. Strict that he anticipated some small amounts of cash would be flowing across the border soon. The account finally was paid in full but not until it had gone six months past due. International now wished to reestablish open terms with Locktight. Mr. Slick reminded Mr. Strict that the margin on this business was very good (50%+ or 15% over average), total annual sales prior to the currency problem were $1,200,000, and Locktight had not lost any money. Mr. Strict had planned a visit to St. Louis, International's headquarters, to see other customers and decided to meet with Mr. Promises, Mr. Slick, and Mr. H.I. Powers, International's marketing director. An updated credit check and financial analysis is available for review.

INSTRUCTIONS

1. Analyze all data available on the case, summarizing findings using the following:
   A. Trend analysis, common-size analysis, ratio analysis, and comparison to industry standings
   B. Summarize the information available in the credit report, references, and information available above
2. What question(s) should Mr. Strict ask of Mr. Slick on this customer?
3. What question(s) should Mr. Strict ask of Mr. Promises and Mr. Power at International?

4. What terms, if any, should Mr. Strict offer while reestablishing business relations with International?

5. What facts would Mr. Strict use to defend his decision to management and to the customer?

6. If overridden by management, what steps should Mr. Strict take to prevent a possible loss?

CREDIT REPORT

FILE #123456789   DATE PRINTED   SUMMARY
      MAY 23, 1996   RATING   4A3

INTERNATIONAL EXPORT INC.   FORMERLY   3A2
(FOREIGN PARENT IS INTERNATIONAL EXPORT
HALTTO LTD., MEXICO CITY, MEXICO)   STARTED   1960
10TH AVE. AT 25TH STREET   MFR PUMPS &   SALES $27,831,118
BOUNCER, MO 94345   PUMPING EQUIP.   WORTH $10,853,762
   TEL: 515 555-9000   SIC NO.   HISTORY CLEAR
                           35 61   CONDITION FAIR

CHIEF EXECUTIVE: JACK L. STOPGAP, PRES.

PAYMENTS (Amounts may be rounded to nearest figure in prescribed ranges)
REPORTED

	PAYING RECORD	HIGH CREDIT	NOW OWES	PAST DUE	SELLING TERMS	LAST SALE WITHIN
4/96	Ppt-Slow 30	10000	-0-	-0-	N 30	2-3 Mos
	Slow 40	25000	15000	10000		1 Mo
3/96	Ppt	20000	-0-	-0-		6-12 Mos
	Ppt	500	50	-0-	N30	1 Mo
	Ppt-Slow 30	85000	55000	40000	N30	1 Mo
	Ppt-Slow 30	5000	5000	1000	N30	1 Mo
	Slow 60	25000	1000	1000		6-12 Mos
	Slow 30-60	10000	1000	1000		4-5 Mos
	Slow 60	25000	2500	2500		4-5 Mos
	Slow 60	50000	-0-	-0-	N30	4-5 Mos
	Slow 60	2500	2500	-0-	N30	
	Slow 90	10000	-0-	-0-		2-3 Mos
2/96	Slow 60	50000	10000	-0-	N15	1 Mo
	Slow 60	100000	50000	-0-		2-3 Mos
	Slow 90	20000	5000	1000	N30	1 Mo
	Slow 90	500	-0-	-0-	N30	4-5 Mos
1/96	Ppt-Slow 90	100000	10000	10000	N30	2-3 Mos
	Ppt-Slow 120	750000	75000	75000		1 Mo
	Slow 60	15000	2500	500		1 Mo
	Slow 60	100	-0-	-0-		6-12 Mos
	Slow 90-120	2500	2500	2500		
	Slow 90-120	100	-0-	-0-		1 Mo
	Slow 120	10000	1000	1000		
	Slow 120	10000	-0-	-0-		
	Slow 150	1000	-0-	-0-	N30	6-12 Mos
	Slow 150	750	-0-	-0-	N30	6-12 Mos

INTERNATIONAL EXPORT INC.   May 23, 1996   PAGE 002

* Payment experiences reflect how bills are met in relation to the terms granted. In some instances payment beyond terms can be the result of disputes over merchandise, skipped invoices, etc.
* Each experience shown represents a separate account reported by a supplier. Updated trade experiences replace those previously reported.

FINANCE

On 4/23/96, Jack L. Stopgap, Pres, deferred financial statement.

PUBLIC FILINGS

The following is for information purposes only, and is not the official record. Certified copies can be obtained from the official source.

*** UCC FILING(S) ***

COLLATERAL: Accounts receivable and products - All inventory and
        products - Specified equipment and products - Specified
        fixtures and products - Specified general intangible(s)
        and products.

FILING NO: 984345   DATE FILED: 9/11/91
TYPE: ORIGINAL   FILED WITH: Secretary of State/
                                 UCC Division, Mo.
Sec. Party: All Secured Bank, NA
                Watertown, Mo
DEBTOR: International Exports Inc.

The public record items reported above under "Pubic Filings" and "UCC Filings" may have been paid, terminated, vacated or released prior to the date this report was printed.

HISTORY
8/20/95

JACK L. STOPGAP, PRES.
BARRY R. STOPGAP, V.PRES.
BUSINESS TYPE: Corporation   DATE OF INCORPORATION: 1/20/63
                    Profit   STATE OF INCORPORATION: Missouri
Auth shares - Common: 500
Par Value - Common: $100.00

Business started 1960 by Arnold L. Stopgap. Present control succeeded1985. 100% capital stock is owned by the parent company.

INTERNATIONAL EXPORTS INC.   May 23, 1996   PAGE 003

Jack L. Stopgap born 1950 single. Graduate Jackson University, Wheatland, N.Y. 1972. 1972–1982 employed by father. 1982–1990 Vice President here. 1991 to present, President here and continues.
Barry R. Stopgap born 1951, brother of Jack. Active here since 1982. 1991 to Present, Vice President here and continues.

OPERATION
8/20/95

Foreign parent is International Export Haltto Ltd. of Mexico City, Mexico, File # 78956423. Reference is made to that report for background information on the parent and its management. The parent company owns 100% of the capital stock of the business.

Manufactures pumps and pumping equipment.

Terms are Net 30 days. Has 2,500 accounts. Sells to industrial accounts.
Territory: Worldwide Non-seasonal.

EMPLOYEES: 820 including officers; 800 employed here.

FACILITIES: Owns 10,000,000 sq. ft. in 3-story concrete block building in good condition. Premises neat.

LOCATION: Suburban business section on side street.

FULL DISPLAY COMPLETE

Locktight Seals Company
235 St. Patrick Drive
Rochester, NY 14623
FAX#: (716) 555-2932

BANK CREDIT INQUIRY

All Secured Bank, NA
235 St. Patrick Drive   Ref: International Exports Inc.
Watertown, MO 94355   10th Avenue At 25th Street
(515) 555-2810   Bouncer, MO 94345

The above-referenced company has given your concern's name as a credit reference.
Please provide us with your experience with them so that we may determine their credit
worthiness. Please fax this information back to us as soon as possible. Thank you in
advance for the information that you provide and be assured that it will be kept
confidential.

Sincerely,

I. B. Strict
Credit Department

If business is not incorporated, please provide owners' name & address:

SAVINGS ACCOUNT   LOW ___   MEDIUM ___   HIGH ___ $___ FIGURE
                   OPEN ___   CLOSED ___

CHECKING ACCOUNT   LOW ___   MEDIUM _X_   HIGH ___ $ 5 FIGURE
                    SATISFACTORY X___   UNSATISFACTORY ___

CREDIT EXPERIENCE

Loans are granted: Frequently ___   Occasionally ___   Seldom _X

Type: Working Capital _X_ Mortgage __   Installment __

Maximum Credit Extended $ High 7 Figures Secured _X_   Unsecured __

Present Outstandings: Secured $High 7 Figures   Unsecured $

Relationship: SATISFACTORY _X___   UNSATISFACTORY ___

Have "NSF" checks been issued: Yes ___   No _X_

Prepared By: I. M. Tight,   Title: Sr. Vice President

Locktight Seals Company
235 St. Patrick Drive
Rochester, NY 14623
PHONE (716) 555-2810
FAX   (716) 555-2932

CREDIT INQUIRY

*Pump Components U.S.A., Inc.   REF: <u>International Export Inc.</u>
*1136 Fallinarut Way   <u>10th Avenue At 25th Street</u>
*Skyhigh, ME 33659   <u>Bouncer, MO 94345</u>

The above-referenced company has given your concern's name as a credit reference.
Please provide us with your experience with them so that we may determine their credit
worthiness. Please fax this information back to us as soon as possible. Thank you in
advance for the information that you provide and be assured that it will be kept
confidential.

Sincerely,

  <u>I.B. Strict</u>
Credit Department

Sold From <u>1969</u>   <u>MANNER OF PAYMENT</u>
                                               ___ Discounts
Terms of Sales <u>Net 30</u>   ___ Prompt & Satisfactory
                                                X   Prompt to <u>60</u> Days Slow
Largest Amount Now Owing <u>$100,000</u>   ___ Pays on Account
                                               ___ Asks for More Time
Amount Past Due <u>$20,000</u>   ___ Slow but Collectible
                                               ___ Accepts COD's Promptly
Recent Trend Toward <u>X</u> Promptness   ___ Settles by Trade Acceptance
                    ___ Slowness   ___ Notes Paid at Maturity
Makes Unjust Claims (State) _____   ___ Account Secured
_____
Credit Refused (State Cause) _____
_____
_____
Remarks: _____   <u>55</u> Average Days Paid
_____
_____
Information Given By: <u>Ken I. Think, Credit Manager</u> Date <u>5/26/96</u>

WE REQUEST THE RETURN OF THIS FORM TO FACILITATE OUR SYSTEM OF
FILING REPORT.

Locktight Seals Company
235 St. Patrick Drive
Rochester, NY 14623
PHONE (716) 555-2810
FAX   (716) 555-2932

CREDIT INQUIRY

*Rubber Components Inc.
*2235 Fallonface Way
*Deadend, MI 55699

REF: International Export Inc.
10th Avenue At 25th Street
Bouncer, MO 94345

The above-referenced company has given your concern's name as a credit reference. Please provide us with your experience with them so that we may determine their credit worthiness. Please fax this information back to us as soon as possible. Thank you in advance for the information that you provide and be assured that it will be kept confidential.

Sincerely,

I.B. Strict
Credit Department

Sold From 1979

Terms of Sales   Net 30

Largest Amount Now Owing $200,000

Amount Past Due $50,000

Recent Trend Toward X Promptness
                    _ Slowness
Makes Unjust Claims (State) _____
_____
_____

Credit Refused (State Cause) _____
_____
_____

Remarks: _____
_____
_____

MANNER OF PAYMENT
___ Discounts
___ Prompt & Satisfactory
___ Prompt to __ Days Slow
___ Pays on Account
___ Asks for More Time
 X Slow but Collectible
___ Accepts COD's Promptly
___ Settles by Trade Acceptance
___ Notes Paid at Maturity
___ Account Secured

75 Average Days Paid

Information Given By: Ken I. Act, Credit Manager   Date 5/26/96

WE REQUEST THE RETURN OF THIS FORM TO FACILITATE OUR SYSTEM OF FILING REPORT.

Locktight Seals Company
235 St. Patrick Drive
Rochester, NY 14623
PHONE (716) 555-2810
FAX   (716) 555-2932

CREDIT INQUIRY

*Steel Parts Now Inc.   REF: International Export Inc.
*8935 Nowork Way   10th Avenue At 25th Street
*Lazyland, CA 99658   Bouncer, MO 94345

The above-referenced company has given your concern's name as a credit reference.
Please provide us with your experience with them so that we may determine their credit
worthiness. Please fax this information back to us as soon as possible. Thank you in
advance for the information that you provide and be assured that it will be kept
confidential.

Sincerely,

  I.B. Strict
Credit Department

Sold From 1989   MANNER OF PAYMENT
                                         ___ Discounts
Terms of Sales   Net 30   ___ Prompt & Satisfactory
                                         ___ Prompt to __ Days Slow
Largest Amount Now Owing $ 50,000   ___ Pays on Account
                                         ___ Asks for More Time
Amount Past Due $10,000   X Slow but Collectible
                                         ___ Accepts COD's Promptly
Recent Trend Toward __Promptness   ___ Settles by Trade Acceptance
              X Slowness   ___ Notes Paid at Maturity
Makes Unjust Claims (State) _____   ___ Account Secured
_____
_____
Credit Refused (State Cause) _____
_____
_____
Remarks: _____   85 Average Days Paid
_____
_____
Information Given By: Ken I. Decide, Credit Manager Date 5/26/96

WE REQUEST THE RETURN OF THIS FORM TO FACILITATE OUR SYSTEM OF
FILING REPORT.

International Exports Inc.
563 Slowpay Lane
Bouncer, MO 94345

SIC 3561 ACCOUNT # 123456

$27,831,118.00
$10,853,762.00

	12/31/95				12/31/94				12/31/93			
	$	% Change	% Assets	Ind % Assets	$	% Change	% Assets	Ind % Assets	$	% Change	% Assets	Ind % Assets
Cash	$1,280,712.00	91.35	5.87	8.00	$669,311.00	100.78	3.40	8.50	$333,356.00	100.00	1.46	5.60
Accounts Receivable	$3,346,047.00	-25.20	15.34	25.80	$4,473,355.00	-6.38	22.70	25.10	$4,778,276.00	100.00	20.98	25.80
Inventory	$5,925,578.00	6.70	27.17	23.00	$5,553,652.00	-38.33	28.18	26.70	$9,005,833.00	100.00	39.54	29.00
Due from Shareholder	$0.00	0.00	0.00		$0.00	0.00	0.00		$0.00	0.00	0.00	
Due From Affiliate	$0.00	0.00	0.00		$0.00	0.00	0.00		$0.00	0.00	0.00	
Other Current	$542,007.00	-33.56	2.48	3.70	$815,743.00	41.31	4.14	2.80	$577,257.00	100.00	2.53	2.50
Total Current	$11,094,344.00	-3.63	50.86	60.50	$11,512,061.00	-21.66	58.41	63.10	$14,694,722.00	100.00	64.51	62.90
Fixed Assets	$10,056,404.00	30.57	46.10	26.20	$7,702,134.00	1.11	39.08	26.10	$7,617,543.00	100.00	33.44	26.20
Notes Receivable	$0.00	0.00	0.00		$0.00	0.00	0.00		$0.00	0.00	0.00	
Deposits	$0.00	0.00	0.00		$0.00	0.00	0.00		$0.00	0.00	0.00	
Cash Value of Life Insur.	$662,037.00	34.12	3.04	8.50	$493,632.00	6.15	2.50	7.10	$465,013.00	100.00	2.04	7.30
Intangible Assets	$0.00	0.00	0.00	4.80	$0.00	0.00	0.00	3.70	$0.00	0.00	0.00	3.60
Total Assets	$21,812,785.00	10.68	100.00	100.00	$19,707,827.00	-13.48	100.00	100.00	$22,777,278.00	100.00	100.00	100.00
Account Payable	$6,123,984.00	6.13	28.08	10.90	$5,770,055.00	4.95	29.28	10.90	$5,497,699.00	100.00	24.14	10.90
Bank Loans + N.P.	$2,015,045.00	173.67	9.24	5.40	$736,314.00	-68.00	3.74	5.90	$2,301,045.00	100.00	10.10	6.50
Cur. Mat.–L.T.D.	$243,393.00	3.58	1.12	2.10	$234,976.00	667.72	1.19	2.60	$30,607.00	100.00	0.13	2.20
Income Tax Payables	$99,365.00	206.87	0.46	0.50	$32,380.00	100.00	0.16	0.90	$0.00		0.00	0.70
Accrued Expenses	$1,997,296.00	-9.31	9.16	13.30	$2,202,394.00	-50.81	11.18	13.20	$4,477,051.00	100.00	19.66	12.90
Total Current	$10,479,083.00	16.74	48.04	32.20	$8,976,119.00	-27.06	0.00	33.50	$12,306,402.00	100.00	54.03	33.20
Long Term Debt	$346,254.00	42.80	1.59	14.80	$242,481.00	-33.41	1.23	13.60	$364,118.00	100.00	1.60	14.80
Deferred Taxes	$133,686.00	31.12	0.61	1.10	$101,960.00	-10.05	0.52	1.60	$113,352.00	100.00	0.50	1.90
All Other L.T. Debt	$0.00	-100.00	0.00	5.20	$328,091.00	100.00	1.66	3.00	$0.00	0.00	0.00	3.00
Net Worth	$10,853,762.00	7.90	49.76	46.70	$10,059,176.00	0.66	51.04	48.30	$9,993,406.00	100.00	43.87	47.10
Total Liab & Equity	$21,812,785.00	10.68	100.00	100.00	$19,707,827.00	-13.48	54.45	100.00	$22,777,278.00	100.00	100.00	100.00
Net Sales	$27,831,118.00	2.21	100.00	100.00	$27,228,489.00	-0.01	100.00	100.00	$27,230,314.00	100.00	100.00	100.00
Cost of Goods Sold	$22,038,638.00	2.11	79.19	69.30	$21,582,564.00	9.92	79.26	69.70	$19,634,355.00	100.00	72.10	70.10
Gross Profit	$5,792,480.00	2.60	20.81	30.70	$5,645,925.00	-25.67	20.74	30.30	$7,595,959.00	100.00	27.90	29.90
Depreciation	$603,043.00	14.98	2.17		$524,478.00	30.92	1.93		$400,616.00	100.00	1.47	
Lease Payments	$0.00	0.00	0.00		$0.00	0.00	0.00		$0.00	0.00	0.00	
Other Operating Exps.	$3,924,880.00	-3.80	14.10	24.70	$4,080,119.00	-34.85	14.98	23.50	$6,262,729.00	100.00	23.00	23.70
Tot. Operating Exps.	$4,527,923.00	-1.67	16.27	6.00	$4,604,597.00	-30.90	16.91	6.80	$6,663,345.00	100.00	24.47	6.20
Operating Profit	$1,264,557.00	21.44	4.54	1.30	$1,041,328.00	11.66	3.82	1.30	$932,614.00	100.00	3.42	1.30
Interest Inc./(Exp.)	$53,976.00	-53.59	0.19		$116,312.00	-31.58	0.43		$169,996.00	100.00	0.62	
G/(L) on sale of Fxd Assets	$0.00	0.00	0.00		$0.00	0.00	0.00		$0.00	0.00	0.00	
Profit Before Taxes	$1,318,533.00	13.90	4.74	4.70	$1,157,640.00	4.99	4.25	5.50	$1,102,610.00	100.00	4.05	4.90
Taxes	$523,947.00	3.37	1.88		$506,870.00	123.64	1.86		$226,647.00	100.00	0.83	
Net Profit	$794,586.00	22.10	2.86		$650,770.00	-25.71	2.39		$875,963.00	100.00	3.22	
Other Data:												
Working Capital	$615,261.00	-75.74	2.82	28.30	$2,535,942.00	6.18	58.41	29.60	$2,388,320.00	100.00	10.49	29.70
Tangible Equity	$10,853,762.00	7.90	49.76	41.90	$10,059,176.00	0.66	51.04	44.60	$9,993,406.00	100.00	43.87	43.50
Recommended Credit Limit:	$955,131.06	24.94			$764,497.38	19.53			$639,577.98			

International Exports Inc.
563 Slowpay Lane
Bouncer, MO 94345

RATIOS

Ratio	Unit	12/31/95	% Change	UQ	Med	LQ	12/31/94	% Change	UQ	Med	LQ	12/31/93	% Change	UQ	Med	LQ
SOLVENCY																
Current Ratio	($)	1.06	-17.45	3.00	1.90	1.40	1.28	7.41	2.80	2.10	1.40	1.19	100.00	2.60	1.90	1.40
Quick Ratio	($)	0.44	-2.85	1.70	1.10	0.70	0.57	37.93	1.50	1.00	0.70	0.42	100.00	1.40	0.90	0.60
Net Profit B4 Tax + Depr./Cur LTD	(X)	7.89	10.29	18.40	6.10	1.50	7.16	-85.42	10.00	3.50	1.70	49.11	100.00	9.30	5.30	1.70
Sales to Fixed Assets	(X)	2.77	8.16	9.90	5.70	4.10	2.56	-28.42	10.10	6.20	4.00	3.57	100.00	9.30	5.80	4.20
Sales to Total Assets	(X)	1.28	-7.65	2.00	1.50	1.20	1.38	15.57	2.00	1.50	1.30	1.20	100.00	1.80	1.50	1.20
Total Liab. to NW	(X)	1.01	5.27	0.60	1.20	2.60	0.96	-25.02	0.60	1.00	2.50	1.28	100.00	0.70	1.20	2.40
Fixed Assets to NW	(X)	0.93	21.01	0.40	0.50	1.00	0.77	0.45	0.40	0.50	1.00	0.76	100.00	0.40	0.60	1.00
Tot. Liab. to Tot. Assets	(%)	50.24	2.62	N/A	N/A	N/A	48.96	-12.77	N/A	N/A	N/A	56.13	100.00	N/A	N/A	N/A
Oper. Prof. to Int. Exp.	(X)	23.43	161.68	N/A	N/A	N/A	8.95	63.19	N/A	N/A	N/A	5.49	100.00	N/A	N/A	N/A
Oper Prof+Lease Py to Int Exp+LP	(X)	23.43	161.68	N/A	N/A	N/A	8.95	63.19	N/A	N/A	N/A	5.49	100.00	N/A	N/A	N/A
EFFICIENCY																
Sales to Receivables	(X)	8.32	36.65	7.70	6.30	5.20	6.09	6.81	8.10	6.70	5.50	5.70	100.00	7.70	5.90	5.10
Days Sales Outstanding	(D)	44	-26.67	47	58	70	60	-6.25	45	54	66	64	100.00	47	62	72
Cost of Sales to Inv.	(X)	3.72	-4.30	7.00	4.40	3.10	3.89	78.25	6.10	4.10	3.00	2.18	100.00	5.90	3.60	2.60
Days' Sales in Inventory	(D)	98	4.26	52	83	118	94	-43.71	60	89	122	167	100.00	62	101	140
Sales to Net Working Cap.	(X)	45.23	321.30	3.40	4.80	12.00	10.74	-5.83	3.60	5.30	9.70	11.40	100.00	3.40	5.20	9.70
Cost of Sales/Payables	(X)	3.60	-3.79	15.20	10.90	8.10	3.74	4.73	15.50	10.70	8.70	3.57	100.00	14.20	11.20	7.50
A/P Turnover	(D)	101	3.06	24	33	45	98	-3.92	24	34	42	102	100.00	26	33	49
PROFITABILITY																
Depreciation to Sales	(%)	2.17	12.49	1.80	2.60	4.00	1.93	30.93	1.80	2.80	3.70	1.47	100.00	1.60	2.70	3.70
Prof bef Tax to Tot Assets	(%)	6.04	2.91	12.10	6.00	1.20	5.87	21.34	14.50	8.50	1.50	4.84	100.00	14.00	7.20	3.10
Profit before Taxes to TNW	(%)	12.15	5.56	24.80	15.80	5.80	11.51	4.30	34.50	17.10	4.90	11.03	100.00	30.50	16.80	7.60

OTHER RATIOS NOT AVAILABLE WITH INDUSTRY STANDARDS

Ratio	Unit	12/31/95	% Change	UQ	Med	LQ	12/31/94	% Change	UQ	Med	LQ	12/31/93	% Change	UQ	Med	LQ
SOLVENCY																
Inv. to Net Work. Capital	(X)	9.63	339.77	N/A	N/A	N/A	2.19	-41.92	N/A	N/A	N/A	3.77	100.00	N/A	N/A	N/A
Current Liab. to NW	(X)	0.97	8.20	N/A	N/A	N/A	0.89	-27.54	N/A	N/A	N/A	1.23	100.00	N/A	N/A	N/A
LT Debt to Tot. Debt & Capital	(%)	2.20	-35.48	N/A	N/A	N/A	3.41	62.38	N/A	N/A	N/A	2.10	100.00	N/A	N/A	N/A
Fixed Assets to LT Debt	(X)	29.04	-8.56	N/A	N/A	N/A	31.76	51.82	N/A	N/A	N/A	20.92	100.00	N/A	N/A	N/A
EFFICIENCY																
Net Sales to NW	(X)	2.56	-5.54	N/A	N/A	N/A	2.71	-0.37	N/A	N/A	N/A	2.72	100.00	N/A	N/A	N/A
Net Sales to Inventory	(X)	4.70	-4.08	N/A	N/A	N/A	4.90	62.25	N/A	N/A	N/A	3.02	100.00	N/A	N/A	N/A
Cost of Sales/Working Capital	(X)	35.82	320.92	N/A	N/A	N/A	8.51	3.53	N/A	N/A	N/A	8.22	100.00	N/A	N/A	N/A
Short Term Loan Turnover	(X)	33.00	175.00	N/A	N/A	N/A	12.00	-72.09	N/A	N/A	N/A	43.00	100.00	N/A	N/A	N/A
LT Liabilities Payback*	($)	$1,154.24	22.76	--	--	--	$940.27	-24.54	--	--	--	$1,245.97	100.00	--	--	--
PROFITABILITY																
Gross Profit on Net Sales	(%)	20.81	0.34	--	30.70	--	20.74	-25.66	--	30.30	--	27.90	100.00	--	29.90	--
Net Oper Inc on Net Sales	(%)	4.54	18.85	--	6.00	--	3.82	11.70	--	6.80	--	3.42	100.00	--	6.20	--
Net Profit on Net Sales	(%)	2.86	19.67	N/A	N/A	N/A	2.39	-25.78	N/A	N/A	N/A	3.22	100.00	N/A	N/A	N/A
Net Prof on Total Assets	(%)	3.64	10.30	N/A	N/A	N/A	3.30	-14.29	N/A	N/A	N/A	3.85	100.00	N/A	N/A	N/A
Tot Assets to Equity	(X)	2.01	2.58	N/A	N/A	N/A	1.96	-14.04	N/A	N/A	N/A	2.28	100.00	N/A	N/A	N/A
Net Prft on Stkhldrs Eqty	(%)	7.32	13.14	N/A	N/A	N/A	6.47	-26.23	N/A	N/A	N/A	8.77	100.00	N/A	N/A	N/A

(X) = TIMES (D) = DAYS ($) = DOLLARS ($) = PERCENT

* IN THOUSANDS

OVERVIEW

To save time, here we highlight some of the positives and negatives in the financial information and the credit references and report as requested in question 1. Because not all areas are improving, first we must break down the improvements and shortfalls, starting with the areas of improvement. Days sales outstanding (DSO) has vastly improved and is better than the best upper quartile number by three days. Debt to worth, although worsening slightly, is still better than industry average. Gross margin improved slightly while a greater improvement in operating income and profit before tax was reflected. Profit before taxes was the same as industry average. The net worth of the firm has improved each year and is better than industry average.

Now for the negative side of this case. Accounts payable turnover is a disastrous 101 days compared to an industry average of 33 days. Liquidity has dropped to $0.44 to $1.00, which is below the lowest quartile ($0.70 to $1.00). Inventory turnover is up to 98 days compared to an industry average of 83 days.

The credit report shows delinquencies as high as 150 days past due (negative). The more recent trend appears to be around 30 days slow (better but still negative). The bank currently holds first lien on all assets (negative but normal), and the stock of the company is 100% owned by a Mexican parent. This can make credit extension more difficult, so it is viewed as a negative.

The company owns its facility and employs 820 individuals (both positive aspects). There are no indications as to the qualifications of the management staff other than they used to own the firm and have been there a fairly long time (negative/positive). The highest credit extended shown is $750,000 (positive), but it was being paid prompt to 120 days slow (a definite negative). As to the three trade references, the high credit was $200,000 and the best rating received was prompt to 60 days slow (negative). The reference did say, though, that the trend was toward promptness (positive). The worst of the three reflected an average pay time of 85 days and still a trend toward slowness (major negative). The bank has extended them a high seven-figure credit line ($7 million to just under $10 million), and it is being paid satisfactorily.

Question 2 and 3 ask what additional information should be obtained from the sales rep, the vice president of finance, and the marketing director of International Exports. At this time, I will introduce a few of the students who reviewed this case.

WHAT OTHER CREDIT PROFESSIONALS THOUGHT

Student One

Jim S., a chief financial officer of a regional meatpacking firm, had some very unique questions for these three gentlemen. Jim was wondering what made the sales rep think that International would be able to pay any better now than when it went past due the last time. He also wanted to know where the sales rep was when the trouble broke out with this customer the first time and whether the rep would bet his commissions on the customer paying on time this go-round. From International's VP of finance and marketing director, he wanted to know what had changed within their company to enable them to pay on time now when they could not do so before. The answers to all these questions will have to be suppositions.

Student Two

Linda J., a corporate credit manager of a Fortune 500 multiline manufacturer, wanted to see if the sales rep had any information to prove that International again would want to buy $1.2 million annually from Locktight. Additional questions included whether it still had any of Locktight's product in inventory and where it got product from when it was shut off. She was going to ask the two men from International these questions to see if International really was trying to buy from Locktight or if the sales rep merely was trying to drum up business.

Student Three

Bruce W., from a manufacturer of bottled gas products, had no kind words to say about any of the three men. He did, however, have some questions. He would like to ask the sales rep if the product sold to International remained in the United States or if it was being shipped directly to Mexico. His main question for the two men from International was that if they were collecting the money so fast from their receivables, why were they paying so slowly? Bruce understood that their Mexican parent had problems getting U.S. dollars out of Mexico, but he wanted to know why it could not simply pay from the funds received from its receivables (an extremely good question).

RECOMMENDATIONS REGARDING TERMS

This question assumes that the company will be selling to the customer, which should be a safe assumption for all credit professionals to make. The question, however, also implies that some type of terms may be considered to sell to International. Always remember that certified cash in advance by wire transfer is a term of sale, albeit a very tough one. We can only hope that our panel of three will do better than that.

Student One

Jim S. stated that after looking over all the facts for this case, he would not sell on any real credit terms. The cash in advance sounded pretty good to him, but he knew that it would not fly. As an alternative, he recommended the use of a standby letter of credit equal to the amount of the credit line. International's paying habits, coupled with the fact that the bank had a first lien on all assets and that the bank was getting paid far better than industry average, made this the only reasonable decision.

With purchasing $1.2 million and a limit for using the standby letter of credit set at 45 days from invoice date, International would need a letter of credit for $150,000. It should be good for one year. At the end of that time a reevaluation of the credit would be conducted. If the investigation justified the limit and there were no problems in being paid over the past year, then the standby letter of credit requirement would be waived.

Student Two

Linda J. also was not impressed by what she had seen and heard on the issue of past payment performance. She felt that if the product were staying in the United States, then a purchase money security interest in the inventory sold to the customer would give Locktight some means of securing the new debt. Considering the size of International's inventory compared to what part of Locktight's product it would keep in inventory in the United States, the bank might be less adverse to Locktight taking the PMSI on its goods. She would not let International have a $150,000 limit to start. She would approve a limit of $50,000 and would allow an increase every three months if payments stayed steady and other trade references continued to improve.

Student Three

Bruce W. also was dissatisfied with the thought of doing business with a company that could so easily withhold payments as it had in the past. He also felt that Mr. Slick gave him no real comfort. Bruce was a true credit trooper and said that he would give International a chance, but only for a limit of $25,000, and would reconsider the limit again in six months. He liked the idea of the standby letter of credit but doubted International would be in the position to get one as it was probably tapped out on its line of credit with the bank. Considering its problems in paying others, he also doubted that the bank would be receptive to giving up any assets it currently held as collateral.

ADVICE TO TOP MANAGEMENT

Now the students must explain their decisions to top management.

Student One

Jim S. was not impressed with the way that International was paying its trade creditors. Since it went as much as 150 days past due only five months earlier, it is now doubtful that it can pay on time, no matter what International says. As proof, International's three "best" trade references showed the company anywhere between 55 to 85 days late. While two said the payment trend was improving, one said it was worsening. Jim felt that once International built up a sufficient inventory, it would return to its old tricks of paying slower and slower and blaming it on currency problems.

Student Two

Linda J. looked at the DSO at 44 days, which was three days under industry's best (47), and the A/P turnover at 101 days, which was 56 days higher than industry's worst (45), and felt that security was mandatory to entice this customer to pay on time. She knew that Locktight had not taken a loss on the credit extension but International had been close to being placed for collections and sued if the balance had not been paid soon. International was not a small, undercapitalized company having cash-flow problems but a sound midsize firm that used its ties to its parent company to control its cash management of its payables. (Besides that, she was not sold on all the broken promises given by Mr. Manny Promises.)

Student Three

Bruce W. felt the direct approach with top management was always the best. He simply showed them that even though the supposed profit margin on the product was 50%, it really would be far lower if Locktight were paid in 120 to 180 days. Bruce felt that it was unlikely for a firm that has run seriously delinquent in the past, due to currency problems, to improve in the future. This kind of turnaround can occur if some sort of leverage is obtained to keep the customer in line. Since the bank had all of the aces, there really was not any way to control International. Maintaining a low limit and watching the customer like a hawk to keep Locktight's exposure to a minimum was the only choice that Bruce felt comfortable with and was amenable to.

ACTION PLAN IF OVERRIDDEN BY MANAGEMENT

Student One

Jim S. said that he would be a team player and set up his defenses for handling any fallout that might occur as a result of selling to this customer on open account. Credit hold at 40 days from invoice date and immediate recall of product if payment were not received on time would be two procedures strictly followed. He also would consider shipping on an order-to-order basis if problems materialized.

Student Two

Linda J. was likewise unhappy but would follow the team objective to sell product to even marginal customers. She knew that the bread-and-butter customers covered the overhead but the marginal ones were where the profits came. To prevent problems, she required that Mr. Slick visit International's headquarters weekly to pick up a check if one were available. She kept Mr. Slick interested in the progress both by holding orders when necessary and by withholding his commissions until

International paid Locktight. She wanted International to know that it was being watched closely and that delinquency would not be tolerated.

Student Three

Bruce W. felt that management always has the right to make a business decision. (Right, wrong, or indifferent, they were still the bosses.) He did want to make sure that International knew in no uncertain terms that things were not going to be "business as usual." He would call on the company monthly, while Mr. Slick would make weekly calls to keep Locktight's physical presence always visible. His shipping department was given strict instructions that each order must be readily available to be recalled at a moment's notice and that no orders were to leave the dock until credit had given its approval. He did manage to obtain a concession from top management to require that all payments made by International be sent by ACH at Locktight's expense in order to keep promised payment times tight. He also had top management agree to shut International off at 35 days from invoice date.

WHAT REALLY HAPPENED

Now let us look at what really happened. Mr. Slick contacted me and asked me to meet with International's vice president of finance and marketing director. This company purchased materials for its Mexican parent and shipped them to Mexico City after doing some minor adjustments to the product. The Mexican parent company sold the product to the Mexican government, which in turn delayed payments by as much as 180 days. The parent company had the U.S. subsidiary transfer all of its U.S. dollars from its collection of receivables in the states to the parent and in turn transferred back some funds when they were available. At times the U.S. subsidiary had trouble even meeting payroll and the bank, let alone paying trade receivables.

This occurred at a time when the Mexican peso was being devalued greatly and hyperinflation was high. As times improved, the U.S. subsidiary was better prepared to make payments to trade creditors and eventually paid them to a more current status. When I met with the VP of finance and marketing director, I was quickly put into an adversarial position by the VP, who felt I did not understand what the problems of having a Mexican parent had caused International.

The marketing director was silent during the 40-minute discussion. I later found out that he was very closely tied to the parent company in Mexico and was a Mexican national. After getting literally nowhere during this time, Mr. Powers, the marketing director, stated that this was a waste of everyone's time. He asked what it would take to sell to International again. I had already approached the company with the idea of a standby letter of credit and a purchase money security interest. Both had been rejected by the VP of finance as not being something that the parent would agree to.

Our standard terms of sale to all of customers was 1% 10 days, net 30 days, and we sold a custom product that could not be sold to any other customer. At this point, I made the following proposal: For the next year, any materials sold would be paid for via wire transfer. For the first three months, International would wire transfer in advance with the order 75% down and 25% at 10 days from invoice date. We would allow the 1% cash discount for the entire amount. The next three months would go 50–50 as far as cash down and cash at 10 days. The next three months were 25–75, and finally the last three months would be 100% wired at 10 days. International would supply us with quarterly financials and an audited annual report at its year end. We would then do an updated credit review. If all was in order and there had been no problems with payments during this one-year period, normal terms would resume and we would determine a reasonable open credit line.

Expecting him to say no to this proposal, I was shocked when Mr. Powers asked the finance VP if there would be any logistical problems in doing the wire transfers. After recovering from the shock that his marketing director was considering this proposal, the VP answered that wire transfers were entirely possible.

At this point Mr. Powers announced that we had his personal commitment and that of the Mexican parent binding International to the agreement. His secretary, who had taken detailed notes at the meeting, would draft this into an agreement. He shook my hand, thanked me for my time, and asked if there was anything else that he could do for me. I left that day knowing who was really in charge of the U.S. subsidiary. International completed the plan as proposed and has been an excellent customer to this date.

7

CASE STUDY 3: SPECIAL MATERIALS, INC.

Business Issues and Costs That Affect a Sound Business Credit Decision

INTRODUCTION

This case provides experience and an understanding of external forces that influence the effectiveness of making a credit decision compared to making a sound business credit decision. The relevant factors are reviewed and studied in this case. This case tests and strengthens readers' abilities to weigh external factors against past history and other positive attributes.

By reviewing this real day in the life of a credit department, readers will learn to make effective use of data, facts, and alternative methods in reaching a decision. An appreciation for how other people in marketing or finance think will hone negotiating skills. Readers can use new insight into the creation of a sound business credit decision to prevent gaps or weaknesses in their decision-making processes.

In this case a top-flight potential customer has an unusual problem.

THE FACTS

I. B. Strict, the division credit manager for Locktight Seals Company (a manufacturer), is reviewing a new account with his credit analyst, Jane Dough. The customer, Special Materials, Inc., a subsidiary of Slidefast Enterprises, has been in business for about 14 years. It has strong financials for a company of its size. Special Materials is a market leader in its product lines and has had great success in areas that Locktight could not penetrate.

Anticipated additional sales for Locktight as reflected in the sales manager's report on Special Materials would be between $750,000 to $1,500,000 per year. Its paying habits are excellent, taking discounts when offered and paying at terms when only net is offered. The parent company has been in the news lately due to numerous lawsuits over asbestos sales. There have been rumors that if there is no letup in these suits, the parent could be forced to file bankruptcy. The parent's financial strength is also excellent with similar paying habits. The initial order placed by Special Materials is for $200,000 to be shipped in the next 30 days. Locktight's margin on the order is 35%, which is good to average for the industry. The standard terms of sale are net 30 days. A credit check and financial analysis are available for review.

INSTRUCTIONS

1. Analyze all data available on the case summarizing your findings using the following:
   A. Trend analysis, common-size analysis, ratio analysis, and comparison to industry standards
   B. Summarize the information available in the credit report, references, and information available above.
2. What is your credit decision?
3. If approved, will open account terms be offered? Is security needed? If so, what type? Or should the order be declined?
4. What facts would you use to defend your decision as listed on question 3 to management and to the customer?
5. If overridden by management, what steps would you take to prevent a possible loss?

CREDIT REPORT

FILE #123456789

SPECIAL MATERIALS INC.
1234 CREEK DRIVE
TAOS, NM 82345
　　TEL: 505 555-9000

DATE PRINTED
MAY 23, 1996

MFR GASKETS

SIC NO.
30 53

SUMMARY
RATING　　3A1
STARTED　　1982
SALES　　$33,197,566
WORTH　　$8,055,884
HISTORY　　CLEAR
CONDITION STRONG

CHIEF EXECUTIVE: ARNOLD STOPGAP, PRES.

PAYMENTS (Amounts may be rounded to nearest figure in prescribed ranges)
REPORTED

	PAYING RECORD	HIGH CREDIT	NOW OWES	PAST DUE	SELLING TERMS	LAST SALE WITHIN
4/96	Ppt	25000	250	-0-		1 Mo
3/96	Disc	10000	5000	-0-		
2/96	Ppt	250000	-0-	-0-	N15	2-3 Mos
	Ppt	75000			N30	
1/96	Disc	10000	-0-	-0-	1 Prox N30	
	Ppt	60000	10000	-0-		1 Mo
12/95	Disc	300000	10000	-0-	1 10 N30	1 Mo
8/95	Ppt	50000	2000	-0-		1 Mo
	Ppt	5000	-0-	-0-	N30	6-12 Mos
	Ppt	5000				
5/95	Ppt	10000	5000	-0-		1 Mo

　　* Payment experiences reflect how bills are met in relation to the terms granted.
In some instances payment beyond terms can be the result of disputes over
merchandise, skipped invoices, etc.

　　* Each experience shown represents a separate account reported by a supplier.
Updated trade experiences replace those previously reported.

FINANCE
* Financial information is attached for your review. Strong condition is indicated based
on debt to net worth. Sales for 1995 were forecasted to be $40,000,000.

PUBLIC FILINGS
UCC FILINGS
4/15/95
Financing statement #984345 filed 9/11/93 with Secretary, State of N.M. Debtor Special
Materials Inc., Talos, N.M., Secured Party: All Secured Bank, N.A., Watertown, N.M.

Collateral: Accounts receivable, inventory, all other fixed assets.

SPECIAL MATERIALS INC.   May 23, 1996   PAGE 002

HISTORY
4/15/96
    ARNOLD L. STOPGAP, PRES.
    JACK L. STOPGAP, V. PRES.
    BARRY R. STOPGAP, TREAS.
    DIRECTOR(S): The officer(s)

    INCORPORATED New Mexico January 20, 1982

    Authorized capital consists of 500,000 shares Common Stock, $100 par value.

    Business started 1982 by Slidefast Enterprises Inc. 100% of capital is owned by
    them.

    Arnold L. Stopgap born 1920, married. 1960 retired US Army. In 1982, he was a
    division president at parent company and with parent since 1960.

    Jack L. Stopgap born 1950, single. Graduate Jackson University, Wheatland, NM
    1972. 1972–1982 employed by parent company. 1982–Present: Vice President
    here and continues.

    Barry R. Stopgap born 1951. Brother of Jack. Active here since 1982.

OPERATION
4/15/96
    Manufactures gaskets (100%)

    Terms 1/10 Net 30 days. Has 25,000 accounts. Sells to industrial accounts.
    Territory: World-Wide. Non-seasonal.

    EMPLOYEES: 3,000 including officers. 2,300 employed here.

    FACILITIES: Owns 100,000 sq. ft. in 5-story concrete block building in good
    condition. Premises neat.

    LOCATION: Suburban business section on side street.

                        FULL DISPLAY COMPLETE

Locktight Seals Company
235 St. Patrick Drive
Rochester, NY 14623
FAX#: (716) 555-2932

BANK CREDIT INQUIRY

All Secured Bank, N.A.
235 St. Patrick Drive
Watertown, NM 94355   Ref: Special Materials Inc.
(515) 555-2810   1234 Creek Drive
                                                          Taos, NM 82345

The above-referenced company has given your concern's name as a credit reference.
Please provide us with your experience with them so that we may determine their credit
worthiness. Please fax this information back to us as soon as possible. Thank you in
advance for the information that you provide and be assured that it will be kept
confidential.

Sincerely,

I. B. Strict
Credit Department

If business is not incorporated, please provide owners' name & address:

SAVINGS ACCOUNT   LOW __ MEDIUM __ HIGH __ $__ FIGURE
              OPEN__   CLOSED ___

CHECKING ACCOUNT   LOW __ MEDIUM X HIGH __ $ 6 FIGURE
            SATISFACTORY X   UNSATISFACTORY ____

CREDIT EXPERIENCE

Loans are granted: Frequently ___ Occasionally ___ Seldom X

Type: Working Capital X Mortgage __ Installment __

Maximum Credit Extended $ High 7 Figures Secured X Unsecured ____

Present Outstandings: Secured $High 7 Figures Unsecured $

Relationship: SATISFACTORY X   UNSATISFACTORY ____

Have "NSF" checks been issued: Yes ___ No X

Prepared By: I. M. Loose   Title: Ex. Vice President

Locktight Seals Company
235 St. Patrick Drive
Rochester, N.Y. 14623
PHONE (716) 555-2810
FAX   (716) 555-2932

CREDIT INQUIRY

*Pump Components U.S.A., Inc.   REF: Special Materials Inc.
*1136 Fallinarut Way   1234 Creek Drive
*Skyhigh, ME 33659   Taos, NM 82345

The above-referenced company has given your concern's name as a credit reference. Please provide us with your experience with them so that we may determine their credit worthiness. Please fax this information back to us as soon as possible. Thank you in advance for the information that you provide and be assured that it will be kept confidential.

Sincerely,

  I.B. Strict
Credit Department

Sold From 1984   MANNER OF PAYMENT
                                          __ Discounts
Terms of Sales   Net 30   X Prompt & Satisfactory
                                          __ Prompt to __ Days Slow
Largest Amount Now Owing $300,000   __ Pays on Account
                                          __ Asks for More Time
Amount Past Due $0   __ Slow but Collectible
                                          __ Accepts COD's Promptly
Recent Trend Toward X_Promptness   __ Settles by Trade Acceptance
                     __ Slowness   __ Notes Paid at Maturity
Makes Unjust Claims (State) _____   __ Account Secured
_____
_____
Credit Refused (State Cause) _____
_____
_____
Remarks: _____   30 Average Days Paid
_____
_____
Information Given By: Ken I. Think, Credit Manager   Date 5/26/96

WE REQUEST THE RETURN OF THIS FORM TO FACILITATE OUR SYSTEM OF FILING REPORT.

Locktight Seals Company
235 St. Patrick Drive
Rochester, NY 14623
PHONE (716) 555-2810
FAX   (716) 555-2932

CREDIT INQUIRY

*Rubber Components Inc.   REF: Special Materials Inc.
*2235 Fallonface Way   1234 Creek Drive
*Deadend, MI 55699   Taos, NM 82345

The above-referenced company has given your concern's name as a credit reference.
Please provide us with your experience with them so that we may determine their credit
worthiness. Please fax this information back to us as soon as possible. Thank you in
advance for the information that you provide and be assured that it will be kept
confidential.

Sincerely,

  I.B. Strict
    Credit Department

Sold From __1988_____   MANNER OF PAYMENT
                                    ___ Discounts
Terms of Sales __Net 30_____   X Prompt & Satisfactory
                                    ___ Prompt to ___ Days Slow
Largest Amount Now Owing $500,000___ ___ Pays on Account
                                    ___ Asks for More Time
Amount Past Due $0_____   ___ Slow but Collectible
                                    ___ Accepts COD's Promptly
Recent Trend Toward X_Promptness   ___ Settles by Trade Acceptance
                    ___ Slowness   ___ Notes Paid at Maturity
Makes Unjust Claims (State) _____ ___ Account Secured
_____
_____
Credit Refused (State Cause) _____
_____
_____
Remarks: _____   30 Average Days Paid
_____

Information Given By: __Ken I. Act, Credit Manager__ Date 5/26/96

WE REQUEST THE RETURN OF THIS FORM TO FACILITATE OUR SYSTEM OF
FILING REPORT.

Locktight Seals Company
235 St. Patrick Drive
Rochester, NY 14623
PHONE (716) 555-2810
FAX   (716) 555-2932

CREDIT INQUIRY

*Steel Parts Now Inc.   REF: Special Materials Inc.
*8935 Nowork Way   1234 Creek Drive
*Lazyland, CA 99658   Taos, NM 82345

The above-referenced company has given your concern's name as a credit reference.
Please provide us with your experience with them so that we may determine their credit
worthiness. Please fax this information back to us as soon as possible. Thank you in
advance for the information that you provide and be assured that it will be kept
confidential.

Sincerely,

  I.B. Strict
  Credit Department

Sold From 1990   MANNER OF PAYMENT
                                         __ Discounts
Terms of Sales   Net 30   X Prompt & Satisfactory
                                         __ Prompt to __ Days Slow
Largest Amount Now Owing $600,000   __ Pays on Account
                                         __ Asks for More Time
Amount Past Due $0   __ Slow but Collectible
                                         __ Accepts COD's Promptly
Recent Trend Toward X Promptness   __ Settles by Trade Acceptance
               __ Slowness   __ Notes Paid at Maturity
Makes Unjust Claims (State) _____   __ Account Secured
_____
_____
Credit Refused (State Cause) _____
_____
_____
Remarks: _____   30 Average Days Paid
_____

Information Given By: Ken I. Decide, Credit Manager Date 5/26/96

WE REQUEST THE RETURN OF THIS FORM TO FACILITATE OUR SYSTEM OF
FILING REPORT.

Special Materials Inc.
1234 Creek Drive
Taos, NM 79258

SIC 5085   ACCOUNT # 123456

$33,197,566.00
$8,055,884.00

	12/31/95 $	12/31/95 % Change	12/31/95 % Assets	12/31/95 Ind % Assets	12/31/94 $	12/31/94 % Change	12/31/94 % Assets	12/31/94 Ind % Assets	12/31/93 $	12/31/93 % Change	12/31/93 % Assets	12/31/93 Ind % Assets
Cash	$298,623.00	-57.88	2.53	3.30	$708,909.00	790.98	5.82	2.40	$79,565.00	100.00	0.65	4.40
Accounts Receivable	$3,639,566.00	-21.59	30.80	31.80	$4,641,895.00	2.71	38.12	33.10	$4,519,284.00	100.00	37.15	34.80
Inventory	$3,450,005.00	6.02	29.20	41.30	$3,254,148.00	-11.27	26.73	39.90	$3,667,572.00	100.00	30.15	39.00
Due from Shareholder	$0.00	0.00	0.00	---	$0.00	0.00	0.00	---	$0.00	0.00	0.00	---
Due From Affiliate	$0.00	0.00	0.00	---	$0.00	0.00	0.00	---	$0.00	0.00	0.00	---
Other Current	$395,482.00	77.63	3.35	1.20	$222,648.00	-65.61	1.83	4.60	$647,465.00	100.00	5.32	1.90
Total Current	$7,783,676.00	-11.83	65.88	77.60	$8,827,600.00	-0.97	72.50	80.00	$8,913,896.00	100.00	73.27	80.10
Fixed Assets	$3,095,792.00	3.85	26.20	16.30	$2,981,068.00	-3.68	24.48	13.60	$3,095,080.00	100.00	25.44	14.30
Notes Receivable	$0.00	0.00	0.00	---	$0.00	0.00	0.00	---	$0.00	0.00	0.00	---
Deposits	$935,922.00	155.14	7.92	---	$366,829.00	134.53	3.01	---	$156,408.00	100.00	1.29	---
Cash Value of Life Insur.	$0.00	0.00	0.00	4.80	$0.00	0.00	0.00	4.10	$0.00	0.00	0.00	2.00
Intangible Assets	$0.00	0.00	0.00	1.30	$0.00	0.00	0.00	2.30	$0.00	0.00	0.00	3.60
Total Assets	$11,815,390.00	-2.96	100.00	100.00	$12,175,497.00	0.08	100.00	100.00	$12,165,374.00	100.00	100.00	100.00
Account Payable	$823,438.00	-37.17	6.97	19.30	$1,310,509.00	16.49	10.76	18.90	$1,124,961.00	100.00	9.25	20.50
Bank Loans + N.P.	$689,566.00	100.00	5.84	17.30	$0.00	0.00	0.00	11.70	$0.00	0.00	0.00	14.00
Cur. Mat.-L.T.D.	$1,730,000.00	282.14	14.64	2.30	$452,715.00	-52.48	3.72	1.80	$952,716.00	100.00	7.83	1.80
Income Tax Payables	$0.00	-100.00	0.00	0.60	$33,855.00	9.58	0.28	0.30	$30,894.00	100.00	0.25	0.90
Accrued Expenses	$384,969.00	-51.52	3.26	6.90	$794,112.00	-7.47	6.52	8.50	$858,184.00	100.00	7.05	7.70
Total Current	$3,627,973.00	40.01	30.71	46.40	$2,591,191.00	-12.66	0.00	41.20	$2,966,755.00	100.00	24.39	44.90
Long Term Debt	$131,533.00	-64.83	1.11	14.50	$374,041.00	-77.69	3.07	13.70	$1,676,322.00	100.00	13.78	10.00
Deferred Taxes	$0.00	0.00	0.00	0.40	$0.00	0.00	0.00	0.60	$0.00	0.00	0.00	0.80
All Other L.T. Debt	$0.00	0.00	0.00	3.40	$0.00	0.00	0.00	2.80	$0.00	0.00	0.00	2.50
Net Worth	$8,055,884.00	-12.53	68.18	35.30	$9,210,265.00	22.44	75.65	41.70	$7,522,297.00	100.00	61.83	41.80
Total Liab & Equity	$11,815,390.00	-2.96	100.00	100.00	$12,175,497.00	0.08	78.72	100.00	$12,165,374.00	100.00	100.00	100.00
Net Sales	$33,197,566.00	-4.50	100.00	100.00	$34,760,990.00	-1.48	100.00	100.00	$35,281,611.00	100.00	100.00	100.00
Cost of Goods Sold	$22,033,954.00	-4.45	66.37	74.80	$23,059,926.00	-2.78	66.34	73.80	$23,720,278.00	100.00	67.23	68.70
Gross Profit	$11,163,612.00	-4.59	33.63	25.20	$11,701,064.00	1.21	33.66	26.20	$11,561,333.00	100.00	32.77	31.30
Depreciation	$264,973.00	0.83	0.80	---	$262,787.00	0.91	0.76	---	$260,422.00	100.00	0.74	---
Lease Payments	$0.00	0.00	0.00	---	$0.00	0.00	0.00	---	$0.00	0.00	0.00	---
Other Operating Exps.	$9,276,909.00	6.99	27.94	---	$8,670,436.00	7.31	24.94	---	$8,080,005.00	100.00	22.90	---
Tot. Operating Exps.	$9,541,882.00	6.81	28.74	22.50	$8,933,223.00	7.11	25.70	22.30	$8,340,427.00	100.00	23.64	26.20
Operating Profit	$1,621,730.00	-41.41	4.89	2.80	$2,767,841.00	-14.07	7.96	3.90	$3,220,906.00	100.00	9.13	5.10
Interest Inc./(Exp.)	$0.00	0.00	0.00	1.10	($133,031.00)	-47.50	-0.38	0.80	($253,402.00)	100.00	-0.72	1.00
G/(L) on sale of Fxd Assets	$0.00	0.00	0.00	---	$0.00	0.00	0.00	---	$0.00	0.00	0.00	---
Profit Before Taxes	$1,621,730.00	-38.45	4.89	1.60	$2,634,810.00	-11.21	7.58	3.10	$2,967,504.00	100.00	8.41	4.00
Taxes	$524,627.00	-41.36	1.58	---	$894,661.00	-14.81	2.57	---	$1,050,142.00	100.00	2.98	---
Net Profit	$1,097,103.00	-36.95	3.30	---	$1,740,149.00	-9.24	5.01	---	$1,917,362.00	100.00	5.43	---
Other Data:												
Working Capital	$4,155,703.00	-33.36	35.17	31.20	$6,236,409.00	4.86	72.50	38.80	$5,947,131.00	100.00	48.89	35.20
Tangible Equity	$8,055,884.00	-12.53	68.18	34.00	$9,210,265.00	22.44	75.65	39.40	$7,522,297.00	100.00	61.83	38.20
Recommended Credit Limit:	$1,192,270.83	-7.54	---	---	$1,289,437.10	45.27	---	---	$887,631.05	---	---	---

Special Materials Inc.
1234 Creek Drive
Taos, NM 79258

RATIOS

Ratio	Unit	12/31/95 Value	12/31/95 % Change	12/31/95 UQ	12/31/95 Med	12/31/95 LQ	12/31/94 Value	12/31/94 % Change	12/31/94 UQ	12/31/94 Med	12/31/94 LQ	12/31/93 Value	12/31/93 % Change	12/31/93 UQ	12/31/93 Med	12/31/93 LQ
SOLVENCY																
Current Ratio	($)	2.15	-37.02	2.60	1.60	1.20	3.41	13.39	3.10	1.90	1.50	3.00	100.00	3.10	1.90	1.40
Quick Ratio	($)	1.09	-88.48	1.20	0.70	0.60	2.06	33.21	1.40	0.90	0.50	1.55	100.00	1.50	1.00	0.60
Net Profit B4 Tax + Depr./Cur LTD	(X)	1.09	-82.96	5.20	2.40	1.10	6.40	88.91	15.00	4.80	1.90	3.39	100.00	12.50	4.20	2.40
Sales to Fixed Assets	(X)	10.72	162.55	35.60	19.30	11.60	4.08	-64.17	53.40	25.30	14.60	11.40	100.00	45.60	21.10	13.40
Sales to Total Assets	(X)	2.81	-1.59	3.30	2.70	2.20	2.85	-1.56	3.60	2.80	2.40	2.90	100.00	3.50	2.90	2.30
Total Liab. to NW	(X)	0.47	44.95	0.90	2.50	5.10	0.32	-47.84	0.60	1.60	3.50	0.62	100.00	0.60	1.80	3.10
Fixed Assets to NW	(X)	0.38	18.73	0.30	0.40	0.90	0.32	-21.34	0.20	0.40	0.60	0.41	100.00	0.20	0.30	0.70
Tot. Liab. to Tot. Assets	(%)	31.82	30.65	N/A	N/A	N/A	24.35	-36.19	N/A	N/A	N/A	38.17	100.00	N/A	N/A	N/A
Oper. Prof. to Int. Exp.	(X)	0.00	-100.00	N/A	N/A	N/A	20.81	63.69	N/A	N/A	N/A	12.71	100.00	N/A	N/A	N/A
Oper Prof+Lease Py to Int Exp+LP	(X)	0.00	-100.00	N/A	N/A	N/A	20.81	63.69	N/A	N/A	N/A	12.71	100.00	N/A	N/A	N/A
EFFICIENCY																
Sales to Receivables	(X)	9.12	21.80	10.30	8.50	7.30	7.49	-4.08	10.30	9.00	7.60	7.81	100.00	9.20	8.40	7.00
Days Sales Outstanding	(D)	40	-18.37	35	43	50	49	4.26	35	41	48	47	100.00	40	43	52
Cost of Sales to Inv.	(X)	6.39	-9.87	7.30	4.90	3.80	7.09	9.57	7.30	5.40	3.60	6.47	100.00	7.00	5.10	3.20
Days' Sales in Inventory	(D)	57	9.62	50	74	96	52	-7.14	50	68	101	56	100.00	52	72	114
Sales to Net Working Cap.	(X)	7.99	43.32	5.20	8.20	22.90	5.57	-6.05	4.90	7.80	11.20	5.93	100.00	5.20	7.50	14.90
Cost of Sales/Payables	(X)	26.76	52.07	16.90	12.40	9.00	17.60	-16.55	19.10	11.90	7.80	21.09	100.00	14.50	12.10	7.60
A/P Turnover	(D)	14	-33.33	22	29	41	21	23.53	19	31	47	17	100.00	25	30	48
PROFITABILITY																
Depreciation to Sales	(%)	0.80	5.58	0.60	1.00	1.40	0.76	2.42	0.40	0.60	0.80	0.74	100.00	0.50	0.70	1.20
Prof bef Tax to Tot Assets	(%)	13.73	-36.57	7.30	4.30	0.90	21.64	-11.29	14.70	5.20	2.50	24.39	100.00	17.80	5.80	3.60
Profit before Taxes to TNW	(%)	20.13	-29.63	24.00	13.30	3.70	28.61	-27.48	24.70	16.40	8.30	39.45	100.00	29.60	19.10	10.00

OTHER RATIOS NOT AVAILABLE WITH INDUSTRY STANDARDS

Ratio	Unit	12/31/95 Value	12/31/95 % Change	12/31/95 UQ	12/31/95 Med	12/31/95 LQ	12/31/94 Value	12/31/94 % Change	12/31/94 UQ	12/31/94 Med	12/31/94 LQ	12/31/93 Value	12/31/93 % Change	12/31/93 UQ	12/31/93 Med	12/31/93 LQ
SOLVENCY																
Inv. to Net Work. Capital	(X)	0.83	59.10	N/A	N/A	N/A	0.52	-15.39	N/A	N/A	N/A	0.62	100.00	N/A	N/A	N/A
Current Liab. to NW	(X)	0.45	60.11	N/A	N/A	N/A	0.28	-28.68	N/A	N/A	N/A	0.39	100.00	N/A	N/A	N/A
LT Debt to Tot. Debt & Capital	(%)	1.11	-63.84	N/A	N/A	N/A	3.07	-77.72	N/A	N/A	N/A	13.78	100.00	N/A	N/A	N/A
Fixed Assets to LT Debt	(X)	23.54	195.36	N/A	N/A	N/A	7.97	330.81	N/A	N/A	N/A	1.85	100.00	N/A	N/A	N/A
EFFICIENCY																
Net Sales to NW	(X)	4.12	9.28	N/A	N/A	N/A	3.77	-19.62	N/A	N/A	N/A	4.69	100.00	N/A	N/A	N/A
Net Sales to Inventory	(X)	9.62	-9.93	N/A	N/A	N/A	10.68	11.02	N/A	N/A	N/A	9.62	100.00	N/A	N/A	N/A
Cost of Sales/Working Capital	(X)	5.30	43.24	N/A	N/A	N/A	3.70	-7.27	N/A	N/A	N/A	3.99	0.00	N/A	N/A	N/A
Short Term Loan Turnover	(X)	11.00	100.00	N/A	N/A	N/A	0.00	0.00	N/A	N/A	N/A			N/A	N/A	N/A
LT Liabilities Payback *	($)	($367.92)	-123.73	N/A	N/A	N/A	$1,550.22	26.54	N/A	N/A	N/A	$1,225.07	100.00	N/A	N/A	N/A
PROFITABILITY																
Gross Profit on Net Sales	(%)	33.63	-0.09	--	25.20	--	33.66	2.72	--	26.20	--	32.77	100.00	--	31.30	--
Net Oper Inc on Net Sales	(%)	4.89	-38.57	--	2.80	--	7.96	-12.81	--	3.90	--	9.13	100.00	--	5.10	--
Net Profit on Net Sales	(%)	3.30	-34.13	N/A	N/A	N/A	5.01	-7.73	N/A	N/A	N/A	5.43	100.00	N/A	N/A	N/A
Net Prof on Total Assets	(%)	9.29	-34.99	N/A	N/A	N/A	14.29	-9.33	N/A	N/A	N/A	15.76	100.00	N/A	N/A	N/A
Tot Assets to Equity	(X)	1.47	10.95	N/A	N/A	N/A	1.32	-18.26	N/A	N/A	N/A	1.62	100.00	N/A	N/A	N/A
Net Prft on Stkhldrs Eqty	(%)	13.62	-27.90	N/A	N/A	N/A	18.89	-25.89	N/A	N/A	N/A	25.49	100.00	N/A	N/A	N/A

(X)=TIMES   (D) = DAYS   (%) = PRECENT   ($) = DOLLARS

* IN THOUSANDS

OVERVIEW

Let us look at the numbers and the credit information to see just how top flight this customer really is. Liquidity is $1.09 to $1.00, which is far better than the average ($0.70 to $1.00) and almost as good as the upper quartile ($1.20 to $1.00). Debt to net worth is $0.47 to $1.00 compared to the industry best of $0.90 to $1.00. DSO is 40 days compared to the industry average of 43 days, and A/P turnover is 14 days versus the industry's best of 22 days. Gross and operating profits are far above the median, and even inventory turnover is great compared to industry average. Finally, net worth as a percent of total assets is almost twice as high as industry average. All financial information is extremely positive.

All references in the credit report are either prompt or discounted with a high credit of $300,000. The bank has first lien on all assets, and Special Materials has a high-seven-figure ($7 million to $9.9 million) line of credit. It owns its facilities, and the officers who run the firm have been in this business for about 36 years. The three trade references rate International as prompt and satisfactory with the highest credit being for $600,000. What is not to like?

WHAT OTHER CREDIT PROFESSIONALS THOUGHT

Now let us meet a few of the students who focused on this case.

Student One

Alex C. is a credit manager for a manufacturer of office writing supplies and was dismayed by the small "fly in the ointment" that this case referred to in its opening remarks. With an initial order of $200,000 and estimated total annual purchases at $1.5 million, after the first 30 days Special Materials would need a limit of about $140,000 monthly. While this is nowhere near its high credit and Special Materials' paying habits are 30 days except when discounts are offered, a loss of either $200,000 (first order) or $140,000 would be a nasty hit to the bottom line.

This loss would be due to the possibility of a bankruptcy resulting from lawsuits against the parent company. With a profit margin that is either at or only slightly above their average, a loss would not be easily offset. Knowing full well that there is no way to stop the customer from being pulled into a bankruptcy, Alex chose to sell this customer on a secured basis. Due to the rumor mill running wild over the possibility of a bankruptcy filing, he felt that taking at the very least a purchase money security interest filing in his inventory would give him a first position on it. This would put his firm in a better position as far as other creditors were concerned and would enable him to take product back and not have it appear as a preference. Since the inventory levels were quite high, he felt that the bank might not object to giving up its first on the inventory. He would extend a $200,000 line of credit with a purchase money security interest filing. After a year he would consider dropping the lien provided that the rumors had ceased.

Student Two

Marsha F., a credit manager with a computer equipment manufacturer, was very impressed with the fabulous numbers and golden reports in this case. The thought of the bankruptcy really set her teeth grinding as she had just been stung by a similar situation on a customer of her present employer. The big difference there was that her customer was not nearly as financially sound as this firm and the margins were much lower. She knew that her firm's loss was substantial. She had tried very hard to minimize the fallout but in the long run was overridden by top management. They now listen to her much more carefully.

She felt that credit for this customer should be approved but would be prepared to offer a cash discount to keep its credit line lower. Shipment of the initial order should be broken down into segments of no more than $65,000, and Special Materials should pay via ACH transfers. After the initial order had been filled and Special Materials' needs reduced to buying about $140,000 a month, her company could reduce the shipments and its exposure down to about $50,000 every 10 days. If things improved, then she would gradually increase the limit as needed.

Student Three

Thelma M., a credit manager with a major transportation firm, was dismayed at the circumstances of this particular case. Initially she was dead set against extending credit to Special Materials at all with the bankruptcy vulture circling overhead. After looking at the numbers and the credit references and report, she was torn by the very solid nature of the company and its paying habits. Typically she has dealt with the lack of security due to the type of service her firm offers. Thelma decided to approve this customer but would require a second lien behind the bank's first. She felt that there might be some equity left over behind what was locked up by the bank. With the lien intact, she would offer Special Materials an open account of $100,000 initially and request payment via ACH transfer. She also would consider increasing the line after three months if the rumors died down.

ADVICE TO TOP MANAGEMENT

Now comes the moment of truth: explaining the decision to top management and the customer.

Student One

Alex C. would explain to both top management and the customer that with the rumors going around, the possibility of a bankruptcy was greatly increased. A security interest might leave him in a better position to sell to Special Materials while in Chapter 11 bankruptcy as his firm's total exposure prior to the bankruptcy might be minimal. Locktight would be in the position to take goods back prior to the filing and, with court approval, even after filing.

He also wanted to explain to this new customer that Locktight did not want to take a loss if a bankruptcy did occur, so it had to cover its back with security. Despite the solid track record with other customers and the solid financials, both parties needed to understand that if the parent filed, the likelihood was that Special Materials would be pulled into bankruptcy. Alex would stay close to his sources of information (trade group, credit reporting agency, and the Internet) and would increase the limit if this problem disappeared. He also would release the lien at this same time if the clouds of bankruptcy departed from the otherwise extremely bright and sunny sky.

Student Two

Marsha F. felt by offering a cash discount she would be in a better position to sell the customer on a smaller unsecured limit than requiring it to provide collateral. She realized that Locktight could not offer discount terms to just Special Materials unless Locktight made custom product for them, which unfortunately was not the case. These terms would now have to be offered to all customers of similar status with Locktight (same product, same type of customer), and this would impact the bottom line. She also felt that if Locktight took a major hit from a bankruptcy, it would cost her firm more than the discount would and the discount could be added to the next price increase as a cost of doing business. These were her convincing arguments to top management.

Student Three

Thelma M. knew that it would be difficult to get top management to agree to push a new solid customer to allow them to take a second on all assets. This did not even take into consideration the fact that she also intended to keep the limit lower than what was requested. Considering the customer's excellent financial status and proven credit track record, it was going to take some hard facts to convince it not to just walk away from Locktight and go to a competitor. Thelma decided that after meeting personally with top management and presenting them with copies of newspaper reports (supposition) that showed indications that Special Materials Inc.'s parent, Slidefast Enterprises, was considering filing bankruptcy due to the asbestos lawsuits, their reaction would change. She likewise planned a personal visit to Special Materials to see if she could convince them that Locktight did want its business but did not want to get caught in the parent's possible bankruptcy action.

ACTION PLAN IF OVERRIDDEN BY MANAGEMENT

Let us see how the students intend to keep things tight when top management's door slams in their face and they are told to make the deal.

Student One

Alex C., a trooper, decided to push the idea of having the customer pay via ACH transfers. He also decided to put the customer on watch with his trade group and credit-reporting agency. He also would check the Internet daily to see if any news surfaced in connection with a possible filing or worsening of lawsuits against the parent company. He asked his local salesman to keep his ear to the ground when visiting this firm and to wander past their finance area to see if any trouble seemed on the horizon.

Student Two

Marsha F. agreed to the same steps as Alex, but also added that she would notify her shipping area to set up an emergency recall facility with the shipping firm used to deliver goods to this customer. She also had a reclamation letter prepared and undated along with a number of overnight envelopes to send to all parties needing notification for a reclamation claim filing.

Student Two

Thelma M. concurred with all recommendations. She added that she would subscribe to the local paper where the parent was headquartered to keep a closer watch on its activities. While she felt that all other sources were good, this would enable her to watch the firm's activities. She offered to have a listening device installed in the corporate boardroom but I thought that that might be a bit much.

WHAT REALLY HAPPENED

With all these excellent suggestions and careful considerations made by the three seasoned pros, I now have the pleasure to reveal what really happened in this case. Yes, the parent did file, taking the subsidiary down the tubes with it. Instead of being a new customer, the subsidiary had (even worse) a 30-year track record with our firm and had always paid on the 30th day after invoice date. Its financials were exquisite and its attitude exemplary. Every credit manager would give his or her right arm to have a customer like these folks. The limit was set at $250,000 and at the time of the filing, it had a balance of about $47,000.

Two days before Christmas top management of the parent company met with the largest bondholders to try to convince them to rewrite the bonds. Management was willing to offer any interest rate that the bondholders wanted as the parent was an LBO (leveraged buyout). Due to the lawsuits, the bondholders demanded instead payment in full of all out-standing junk bonds—$2 billion. Obviously, the company was not in the position to pay out this amount and two days after Christmas filed a Chapter 11 bankruptcy on behalf of itself and all its subsidiaries. The bank immediately froze its cash accounts. At the time my firm had deposited a check for $9,000, which was returned, and we filed a proof of claim for $56,000. We had no reclamation as the last shipment was made over 15 days earlier. After a month, DIP (debtor in possession) financing was arranged, and we continued to sell to the subsidiary on an open account basis with payments being made via an ACH transfer. My former firm anticipates that 100% plus interest will be paid out to all creditors and a similar type of settlement of the lawsuits will be arranged, as was done in the John Mansville bankruptcy case.

In this particular case, there were no real winners or losers but simply those who tried to do the best for their firms. All three students were justified in their decisions and their actions, but firms use business bankruptcy as a way to solve difficult business problems when nothing else will work. Credit managers cannot stop extending credit just because of rumors, but they must always be alert to the possibilities that a loss could occur. Losses are a cost of doing business. If losses do not occur, you may be passing up profitable business opportunities for your firm. With that said, let us move on to case study 4.

8

CASE STUDY 4: FAST ACTION SUPPLIERS, INC.

Preserving a Company's Reputation That Is Tarnished by a Customer's Slow Paying Practices

INTRODUCTION

This chapter provides experience in determining just how far to let customers control your company and your customer's ability to affect your appearance to the "ultimate customer." This case reviews how to deal with less-than-honorable customers and how to hedge your bets in extending credit to these types of firms. Topics such as reputation with the ultimate user, controlling the slow-paying habits of customers, and reducing the need to hold orders to these customers also are addressed.

By reviewing this real day in the life of a credit department, readers will learn to make effective use of data, facts, and alternative methods in reaching a decision. An appreciation for how other people in marketing or finance think will hone negotiating skills. Readers can use new insight into the creation of a sound business credit decision to prevent gaps or weaknesses in their decision-making processes.

THE FACTS

The quarter is ending with a rush of orders. Jack Slick, the regional sales manager of Tuff Manufacturing Co., calls the company's credit manager, I.B. Right, to obtain the status of the pending order for Fast Action Suppliers, Inc. Fast Action's history has been spotty at best with an average payment history of 65 days, many broken commitments for payment, and numerous messages left with no return calls. The recent history had improved because of a letter sent advising that if payment is received again in over 45 days from invoice date, all future orders would be shipped cash on delivery (COD).

In the last three months, payments have been averaging 44 days. Fast Action's purchases, still, are down about 30% over the same period. Tuff has a strict 45-day-from-invoice date hold order policy and uses 55 to 60 days as a guideline for putting a customer on COD. The order in question is for $50,000. If shipped, it would put Fast Action $25,000 over the $40,000 credit limit and $15,000 higher than it had ever been with Tuff. However, Tuff has wanted to sell to Fast Action for years, and has placed a strong effort to win Fast Action over to their product line. The potential for additional business with the end user is about $200,000 to $300,000 per year in new sales for Tuff at a gross margin of 40%, an excellent margin for the industry.

Mr. Right's biggest concern is that if he does approve the shipment and Fast Action cannot pay on time, the future orders to the end user will be sporadic until payment is received from Fast Action. This could jeopardize future orders, as he already knows from experience that delays in shipments will be blamed on Tuff and not on Fast Action's poor paying habits. Fast Action's updated credit check and a financial analysis are available for review.

INSTRUCTIONS

1. Analyze all data available on the case, summarizing your findings using the following:

   A. Trend analysis, common-size analysis, ratio analysis, and comparison to industry standards

   B. Summarize the information available in the credit report, references, and information available above

2. What questions, if any, should you ask Mr. Slick about this order?

3. What questions, if any, should you ask Fast Action about this order?

4. Should the order be shipped on an open account basis? Should security be obtained? Should it be rejected altogether? Why?

5. What facts would you use to defend your decision to management and to the customer?

6. If overridden by management, what steps would you take to prevent a possible loss?

CREDIT REPORT

FILE #123456789	DATE PRINTED MAY 23, 1996	SUMMARY RATING ---
FAST ACTION SUPPLIERS INC.		FORMERLY BA3
10TH AVE. AT 25TH STREET	MFR GASKETS	STARTED 1960
BOUNCER, MO 94345		SALES $100,000,000
TEL: 515 555-9000	SIC NO.	HISTORY CLEAR
	30 53	CONDITION FAIR

CHIEF EXECUTIVE: JACK L. STOPGAP, PRES.

PAYMENTS (Amounts may be rounded to nearest figure in prescribed ranges)
REPORTED

	PAYING RECORD	HIGH CREDIT	NOW OWES	PAST DUE	SELLING TERMS	LAST SALE WITHIN
4/96	Ppt	100	-0-	-0-	N 30	2-3 Mos
	Slow 40	25000	15000	10000		1 Mo
3/96	Ppt	250	-0-			6-12 Mos
	Ppt	50	50	-0-	N30	1 Mo
	Ppt-Slow 30	185000	55000	40000	N30	1 Mo
	Ppt-Slow 30	5000	5000	1000	N30	1 Mo
	Slow 60	2500	100			6-12 Mos
	Slow 30-60	1000	1000			4-5 Mos
	Slow 60	250	-0-			4-5 Mos
	Slow 15-120	5000	-0-	-0-	N30	4-5 Mos
	Ppt	2500	2500	-0-	N30	
	Ppt	250	-0-	-0-		2-3 Mos
2/96	Ppt	500	500	-0-	N15	1 Mo
	Ppt	250	250	-0-		2-3 Mos
	Ppt-Slow 30	2500	750	250	N30	1 Mo
	Ppt-Slow 60	500	-0-	-0-	N30	4-5 Mos
1/96	Ppt-Slow 90	250	250	250	N30	2-3 Mos
12/95	Ppt-Slow 60	500	500	500		1 Mo
	Slow 20	115000	2500	500		1 Mo
	Slow 60	100	-0-	-0-		6-12 Mos
	Slow 90-120	2500	2500	2500		
11/95	Ppt-Slow 30	100	-0-	-0-		1 Mo
7/95	Slow 30	50	50	50		
6/95	Disc	50	-0-	-0-		
5/95	Disc	1000	-0-	-0-	1 10 N30	6-12 Mos
4/95	Slow 25	750	-0-	-0-	N30	6-12 Mos

* Payment experiences reflect how bills are met in relation to the terms granted.
In some instances payment beyond terms can be the result of disputes over
merchandise, skipped invoices, etc.

FAST ACTION SUPPLIERS INC.   May 23, 1996   PAGE 002

   * Each experience shown represents a separate account reported by a supplier. Updated trade experiences replace those previously reported.

FINANCE

   On 4/23/96, Jack L. Stopgap, Pres., deferred financial statement.

PUBLIC FILINGS

   The following is for information purposes only, and is not the official record. Certified copies can be obtained from the official source.

*** UCC FILING(S) ***

COLLATERAL: Accounts receivable and products - All inventory and products - Specified equipment and products - Specified fixtures and products - Specified general intangible(s) and products.
FILING NO: 984345   DATE FILED: 9/11/91
TYPE: ORIGINAL   FILED WITH: Secretary of State/UCC Division, MO
Sec. Party: All Secured Bank, N.A. Watertown, MO
DEBTOR: Fast Action Suppliers Inc.

   The public record items reported above under "Public Filings" and "UCC Filings" may have been paid, terminated, vacated or released prior to the date this report was printed.

HISTORY
8/20/95

   JACK L. STOPGAP, PRES.
   BARRY R. STOPGAP, V. PRES.
   BUSINESS TYPE: Corporation   DATE OF INCORPORATION: 1/20/63
               Profit   STATE OF INCORPORATION: Missouri
   Auth shares - Common: 500,000
   Par Value - Common: $1.00

Business started 1960 by Arnold L. Stopgap. Present control succeeded 1991 by Jack L. Stopgap and Barry R. Stopgap. 50% of capital stock is owned by Jack L. Stopgap and 50% is owned by Barry R. Stopgap.

Jack L. Stopgap born 1950, single. Graduate Jackson University, Wheatland, NY 1972. 1972–1982 employed by father. 1982–1990 Vice President here. 1991 to present, President here and continues.

FAST ACTION SUPPLIERS INC.   May 23, 1996   PAGE 003

Barry R. Stopgap born 1951, brother of Jack. Active here since 1982. 1991 to Present, Vice President here and continues.

OPERATION
8/20/95
Manufactures gaskets.

Terms are 1% 10 Net 30 days. Has 250 accounts. Sells to industrial accounts. Territory: Missouri. Non-seasonal.

EMPLOYEES: 127 including officers; 23 employed here.

FACILITIES: Rents 100,000 sq. ft. in 1-story concrete block building in good condition. Premises neat.

LOCATION: Suburban business section on side street.

FULL DISPLAY COMPLETE

Tuff Manufacturing Co.
235 St. Patrick Drive
Rochester, PA 18723
FAX#:   (717) 555-2932

BANK CREDIT INQUIRY

All Secured Bank, N.A.
235 St. Patrick Drive
Watertown, MO 94355
(515) 555-2810

Ref: Fast Action Suppliers Inc.
10th Avenue At 25th Street
Bouncer, MO 94345

The above-referenced company has given your concern's name as a credit reference. Please provide us with your experience with them so that we may determine their credit worthiness. Please fax this information back to us as soon as possible. Thank you in advance for the information that you provide and be assured that it will be kept confidential.

Sincerely,

I. B. Right
Credit Department

If business is not incorporated, please provide owners' name & address:

SAVINGS ACCOUNT   LOW __   MEDIUM __   HIGH __ $__ FIGURE
                  OPEN ___   CLOSED ___

CHECKING ACCOUNT   LOW __   MEDIUM X_   HIGH __ $ 4_ FIGURE
                   SATISFACTORY X__   UNSATISFACTORY ___

CREDIT EXPERIENCE

Loans are granted: Frequently ___   Occasionally ___   Seldom _X

Type: Working Capital _X_ Mortgage __ Installment ____

Maximum Credit Extended $ High 5 Figures Secured _X_ Unsecured ____

Present Outstandings: Secured $ High 5 Figures Unsecured $ _____

Relationship: SATISFACTORY X__   UNSATISFACTORY ____

Have "NSF" checks been issued: Yes ___ No X

Prepared By: I. M. Loose_____   Title: Ex. Vice President

Tuff Manufacturing Company
235 St. Patrick Drive
Rochester, PA 18723
PHONE (716) 555-2810
FAX   (716) 555-2932

CREDIT INQUIRY

*Pump Components U.S.A., Inc.   REF: Fast Action Suppliers Inc.
*1136 Fallinarut Way   10th Avenue At 25th Street
*Skyhigh, ME 33659   Bouncer, MO 94345

The above-referenced company has given your concern's name as a credit reference.
Please provide us with your experience with them so that we may determine their credit
worthiness. Please fax this information back to us as soon as possible. Thank you in
advance for the information that you provide and be assured that it will be kept
confidential.

Sincerely,

 I.B. Right
Credit Department

Sold From 1984   MANNER OF PAYMENT
                                         ___ Discounts
Terms of Sales   Net 30   ___ Prompt & Satisfactory
                                         ___ Prompt to __ Days Slow
Largest Amount Now Owing $10,000   ___ Pays on Account
                                         ___ Asks for More Time
Amount Past Due $7,500   X Slow but Collectible
                                         ___ Accepts COD's Promptly
Recent Trend Toward __Promptness   ___ Settles by Trade Acceptance
                     X Slowness   ___ Notes Paid at Maturity
Makes Unjust Claims (State) _____   ___ Account Secured
_____
_____
Credit Refused (State Cause) _____
_____
_____

_____
Remarks: _____   75 Average Days Paid
_____

_____
Information Given By: Ken I. Think, Credit Manager Date 5/26/96

WE REQUEST THE RETURN OF THIS FORM TO FACILITATE OUR SYSTEM OF
FILING REPORT.

Tuff Manufacturing Company
235 St. Patrick Drive
Rochester, PA 18723
PHONE (717) 555-2810
FAX   (717) 555-2932

CREDIT INQUIRY

*Rubber Components Inc.
*2235 Fallonface Way
*Deadend, MI 55699

REF: Fast Action Suppliers Inc.
10th Avenue At 25th Street
Bouncer, MO 94345

The above-referenced company has given your concern's name as a credit reference. Please provide us with your experience with them so that we may determine their credit worthiness. Please fax this information back to us as soon as possible. Thank you in advance for the information that you provide and be assured that it will be kept confidential.

Sincerely,

I.B. Right
Credit Department

Sold From 1988

Terms of Sales   Net 30

Largest Amount Now Owing $25,000

Amount Past Due $15,000

Recent Trend Toward __Promptness
                     X Slowness
Makes Unjust Claims (State) _____
_____
_____

Credit Refused (State Cause) _____
_____
_____

Remarks: _____
_____

MANNER OF PAYMENT
___ Discounts
___ Prompt & Satisfactory
 X Prompt to 60 Days Slow
___ Pays on Account
___ Asks for More Time
___ Slow but Collectible
___ Accepts COD's Promptly
___ Settles by Trade Acceptance
___ Notes Paid at Maturity
___ Account Secured

55 Average Days Paid

Information Given By: Ken I. Act, Credit Manager   Date 5/26/96

WE REQUEST THE RETURN OF THIS FORM TO FACILITATE OUR SYSTEM OF FILING REPORT.

Tuff Manufacturing Company
235 St. Patrick Drive
Rochester, PA 18723
PHONE (717) 555-2810
FAX   (717) 555-2932

CREDIT INQUIRY

*Steel Parts Now Inc.
*8935 Nowork Way
*Lazyland, CA 99658

REF: Fast Action Suppliers Inc.
10th Avenue At 25th Street
Bouncer, MO 94345

The above-referenced company has given your concern's name as a credit reference. Please provide us with your experience with them so that we may determine their credit worthiness. Please fax this information back to us as soon as possible. Thank you in advance for the information that you provide and be assured that it will be kept confidential.

Sincerely,

I.B. Right
Credit Department

Sold From 1990

Terms of Sales Net 30

Largest Amount Now Owing $20,000

Amount Past Due $0

Recent Trend Toward __Promptness
                      X Slowness
Makes Unjust Claims (State) _____
_____
_____

Credit Refused (State Cause) _____
_____
_____

Remarks: _____
_____
_____

MANNER OF PAYMENT
___ Discounts
___ Prompt & Satisfactory
___ Prompt to ___ Days Slow
___ Pays on Account
 X Asks for More Time
___ Slow but Collectible
___ Accepts COD's Promptly
___ Settles by Trade Acceptance
___ Notes Paid at Maturity
___ Account Secured

90 Average Days Paid

Information Given By: Ken I. Decide, Credit Manager Date 5/26/96

WE REQUEST THE RETURN OF THIS FORM TO FACILITATE OUR SYSTEM OF FILING REPORT.

Fast Action Suppliers Inc.
10th Avenue at 25th Street
Bouncer, MO 60153

SIC 5085 $92,001,254.00   ACCOUNT # 123456
($1,903,397.00)

	12/31/95				12/31/94				12/31/93			
	$	% Change	% Assets	Ind % Assets	$	% Change	% Assets	Ind % Assets	$	% Change	% Assets	Ind % Assets
Cash	$782,755.00	180.23	2.97	3.30	$279,322.00	-50.48	1.15	2.40	$564,061.00	100.00	2.22	4.40
Accounts Receivable	$12,106,343.00	13.77	45.91	31.80	$10,640,662.00	-4.07	43.80	33.10	$11,091,636.00	100.00	43.71	34.80
Inventory	$8,868,077.00	-3.20	33.63	41.30	$9,160,879.00	-1.73	37.71	39.90	$9,321,757.00	100.00	36.73	39.00
Due from Shareholder	$0.00	0.00	0.00	---	$0.00	0.00	0.00	---	$0.00	0.00	0.00	---
Due From Affiliate	$0.00	0.00	0.00	---	$0.00	0.00	0.00	---	$0.00	0.00	0.00	---
Other Current	$649,518.00	168.36	2.46	1.20	$242,031.00	-36.42	1.00	4.60	$380,666.00	100.00	1.50	1.90
Total Current	$22,406,693.00	10.25	84.97	77.60	$20,322,894.00	-4.85	83.65	80.00	$21,358,120.00	100.00	84.17	80.10
Fixed Assets	$3,346,210.00	-4.40	12.69	16.30	$3,500,304.00	-0.08	14.41	13.60	$3,503,084.00	0.00	13.80	14.30
Notes Receivable	$0.00	0.00	0.00	---	$0.00	0.00	0.00	---	$0.00	0.00	0.00	---
Deposits	$199,722.00	46.59	0.76	---	$136,244.00	-14.53	0.56	---	$159,407.00	100.00	0.63	---
Cash Value of Life Insur.	$0.00	0.00	0.00	4.80	$0.00	0.00	0.00	4.10	$0.00	0.00	0.00	3.70
Intangible Assets	$417,064.00	24.35	1.58	1.30	$335,403.00	-5.62	1.38	2.30	$355,369.00	100.00	1.40	1.90
Total Assets	$26,369,689.00	8.54	100.00	100.00	$24,294,845.00	-4.26	100.00	100.00	$25,375,980.00	100.00	100.00	100.00
Account Payable	$13,342,173.00	11.16	50.60	19.30	$12,002,379.00	-4.73	49.40	18.90	$12,598,722.00	100.00	49.65	20.50
Bank Loans + N.P.	$0.00	0.00	0.00	17.30	$0.00	0.00	0.00	11.70	$0.00	0.00	0.00	14.00
Cur. Mat.-L.T.D.	$884,433.00	28.61	3.35	2.30	$687,689.00	-5.99	2.83	1.80	$731,476.00	100.00	2.88	1.80
Income Tax Payables	$0.00	0.00	0.00	0.60	$0.00	0.00	0.00	0.30	$0.00	0.00	0.00	0.90
Accrued Expenses	$966,209.00	10.93	3.66	6.90	$870,999.00	-10.62	3.59	8.50	$974,538.00	100.00	3.84	7.70
Total Current	$15,192,815.00	12.03	57.61	46.40	$13,561,067.00	-5.20	0.00	41.20	$14,304,736.00	100.00	56.37	44.90
Long Term Debt	$11,910,191.00	8.88	45.17	14.50	$10,938,572.00	0.01	45.02	13.70	$10,937,305.00	100.00	43.10	10.00
Deferred Taxes	$0.00	0.00	0.00	0.40	$0.00	0.00	0.00	0.60	$0.00	0.00	0.00	0.80
All Other L.T. Debt	$1,170,080.00	144.75	4.44	3.40	$478,074.00	0.82	1.97	2.80	$474,181.00	100.00	1.87	2.50
Net Worth	($1,903,397.00)	178.74	-7.22	35.30	($682,868.00)	100.70	-2.81	41.70	($340,242.00)	100.00	-1.34	41.80
Total Liab & Equity	$26,369,689.00	8.54	100.00	100.00	$24,294,845.00	-4.26	44.18	100.00	$25,375,980.00	100.00	100.00	100.00
Net Sales	$92,001,254.00	0.70	100.00	100.00	$91,362,205.00	-0.85	100.00	100.00	$92,149,804.00	100.00	100.00	100.00
Cost of Goods Sold	$71,483,832.00	2.64	77.70	74.80	$69,647,460.00	-1.03	76.23	73.80	$70,375,017.00	100.00	76.37	68.70
Gross Profit	$20,517,422.00	-5.51	22.30	25.20	$21,714,745.00	-0.28	23.77	26.20	$21,774,787.00	100.00	23.63	31.30
Depreciation	$392,009.00	3.31	0.43	---	$379,442.00	9.36	0.42	---	$346,970.00	100.00	0.38	---
Lease Payments	$0.00	0.00	0.00	---	$0.00	0.00	0.00	---	$0.00	0.00	0.00	---
Other Operating Exps.	$19,182,927.00	-3.16	20.85	22.50	$19,809,861.00	2.79	21.68	---	$19,271,549.00	100.00	20.91	26.20
Tot. Operating Exps.	$19,574,936.00	-3.04	21.28	2.80	$20,189,303.00	2.91	22.10	22.30	$19,618,519.00	100.00	21.29	5.10
Operating Profit	$942,486.00	-38.22	1.02	2.80	$1,525,442.00	-29.26	1.67	3.90	$2,156,268.00	100.00	2.34	1.00
Interest Inc./(Exp.)	($1,500,850.00)	-20.36	-1.63	1.10	($1,884,579.00)	-6.51	-2.06	0.80	($2,015,766.00)	100.00	-2.19	---
G/(L) on sale of Fxd Assets	$0.00	0.00	0.00	---	$0.00	0.00	0.00	---	$0.00	0.00	0.00	---
Profit Before Taxes	($558,364.00)	55.47	-0.61	1.60	($359,137.00)	-355.61	-0.39	3.10	$140,502.00	100.00	0.15	4.00
Taxes	$0.00	0.00	0.00	---	$0.00	-100.00	0.00	---	$62,383.00	100.00	0.07	---
Net Profit	($558,364.00)	55.47	-0.61	---	($359,137.00)	-559.73	-0.39	---	$78,119.00	100.00	0.08	---
Other Data:												
Working Capital	$7,213,878.00	6.69	27.36	31.20	$6,761,827.00	-4.13	83.65	38.80	$7,053,384.00	100.00	27.80	35.20
Tangible Equity	($2,320,461.00)	127.88	-8.80	34.00	($1,018,271.00)	46.39	-4.19	39.40	($695,611.00)	100.00	-2.74	39.90
Recommended Credit Limit:	$0.00	166.67	---	---	$0.00	67.81	---	---	$0.00	---	---	---

Fast Action Suppliers Inc.
10th Avenue at 25th Street
Bouncer, MO 60153

RATIOS

Ratio		12/31/95 Value	% Change	UQ	Med	LQ	12/31/94 Value	% Change	UQ	Med	LQ	12/31/93 Value	% Change	UQ	Med	LQ
SOLVENCY																
Current Ratio	($)	1.47	-1.59	2.60	1.60	1.20	1.50	0.37	3.10	1.90	1.50	1.49	100.00	3.10	1.90	1.40
Quick Ratio	($)	0.85	82.09	1.20	0.70	0.60	0.81	-1.17	1.40	0.90	0.50	0.81	100.00	1.50	1.00	0.60
Net Profit B4 Tax + Depr./Cur LTD	(X)	-0.19	-737.03	5.20	2.40	1.10	0.03	-95.57	15.00	4.80	1.90	0.67	100.00	12.50	4.20	2.40
Sales to Fixed Assets	(X)	27.49	296.12	35.60	19.30	11.60	6.94	-73.61	53.40	25.30	14.60	26.31	100.00	45.60	21.10	13.40
Sales to Total Assets	(X)	3.49	-7.22	3.30	2.70	2.20	3.76	3.56	3.60	2.80	2.40	3.63	100.00	3.50	2.90	2.30
Total Liab. to NW	(X)	-14.85	100.00	0.90	2.50	5.10	-36.58	-51.61	0.60	1.60	3.50	-75.58	100.00	0.60	1.80	3.10
Fixed Assets to NW	(X)	-1.76	-65.70	0.30	0.40	0.90	-5.13	-50.21	0.20	0.40	0.60	-10.30	100.00	0.20	0.30	0.70
Tot. Liab. to Tot. Assets	(%)	107.22	4.29	N/A	N/A	N/A	102.81	1.45	N/A	N/A	N/A	101.34	100.00	N/A	N/A	N/A
Oper. Prof. to Int. Exp.	(X)	0.63	-22.42	N/A	N/A	N/A	0.81	-24.33	N/A	N/A	N/A	1.07	100.00	N/A	N/A	N/A
Oper Prof+Lease Py to Int Exp+LP	(X)	0.63	-22.42	N/A	N/A	N/A	0.81	-24.33	N/A	N/A	N/A	1.07	100.00	N/A	N/A	N/A
EFFICIENCY																
Sales to Receivables	(X)	7.60	-11.49	10.30	8.50	7.30	8.59	3.35	10.30	9.00	7.60	8.31	100.00	9.20	8.40	7.00
Days Sales Outstanding	(D)	48	11.63	35	43	50	43	-2.27	35	41	48	44	100.00	40	43	52
Cost of Sales to Inv.	(X)	8.06	6.03	7.30	4.90	3.80	7.60	0.70	7.30	5.40	3.60	7.55	100.00	7.00	5.10	3.20
Days' Sales in Inventory	(D)	45	-6.25	50	74	96	48	0.00	50	68	101	48	100.00	52	72	114
Sales to Net Working Cap.	(X)	12.75	-5.61	5.20	8.20	22.90	13.51	3.42	4.90	7.80	11.20	13.06	100.00	5.20	7.50	14.90
Cost of Sales/Payables	(X)	5.36	-7.67	16.90	12.40	9.00	5.80	3.88	19.10	11.90	7.80	5.59	100.00	14.50	12.10	7.60
A/P Turnover	(D)	68	7.94	22	29	41	63	-3.08	19	31	47	65	100.00	25	30	48
PROFITABILITY																
Depreciation to Sales	(%)	0.43	2.59	0.60	1.00	1.40	0.42	10.30	0.40	0.60	0.80	0.38	100.00	0.50	0.70	1.20
Prof bef Tax to Tot Assets	(%)	-2.12	43.24	7.30	4.30	0.90	-1.48	-366.98	14.70	5.20	2.50	0.55	100.00	17.80	5.80	3.60
Profit before Taxes to TNW	(%)	29.34	-44.22	24.00	13.30	3.70	52.59	-227.36	24.70	16.40	8.30	-41.29	100.00	29.60	30.00	48.00

OTHER RATIOS NOT AVAILABLE WITH INDUSTRY STANDARDS

Ratio		12/31/95 Value	% Change	UQ	Med	LQ	12/31/94 Value	% Change	UQ	Med	LQ	12/31/93 Value	% Change	UQ	Med	LQ
SOLVENCY																
Inv. to Net Work. Capital	(X)	1.23	-9.26	N/A	N/A	N/A	1.35	2.51	N/A	N/A	N/A	1.32	100.00	N/A	N/A	N/A
Current Liab. to NW	(X)	-7.98	-59.81	N/A	N/A	N/A	-19.86	-52.76	N/A	N/A	N/A	-42.04	100.00	N/A	N/A	N/A
LT Debt to Tot. Debt & Capital	(%)	49.60	5.55	N/A	N/A	N/A	46.99	4.49	N/A	N/A	N/A	44.97	100.00	N/A	N/A	N/A
Fixed Assets to LT Debt	(X)	0.28	-12.50	N/A	N/A	N/A	0.32	0.00	N/A	N/A	N/A	0.32	100.00	N/A	N/A	N/A
EFFICIENCY																
Net Sales to NW	(X)	-48.34	-63.87	N/A	N/A	N/A	-133.79	-50.60	N/A	N/A	N/A	-270.84	100.00	N/A	N/A	N/A
Net Sales to Inventory	(X)	10.37	4.01	N/A	N/A	N/A	9.97	0.81	N/A	N/A	N/A	9.89	100.00	N/A	N/A	N/A
Cost of Sales/Working Capital	(X)	9.91	-3.79	N/A	N/A	N/A	10.30	3.21	N/A	N/A	N/A	9.98	0.00	N/A	N/A	N/A
Short Term Loan Turnover	(X)	0.00	0.00	N/A	N/A	N/A	0.00	0.00	N/A	N/A	N/A	0.00	100.00	N/A	N/A	N/A
LT Liabilities Payback *	($)	($1,050.79)	57.45	N/A	N/A	N/A	($667.38)	117.82	N/A	N/A	N/A	($306.39)	100.00	N/A	N/A	N/A
PROFITABILITY																
Gross Profit on Net Sales	(%)	22.30	-6.18	—	25.20	—	23.77	0.59	—	26.20	—	23.63	100.00	—	31.30	—
Net Oper Inc on Net Sales	(%)	1.02	-38.92	—	2.80	—	1.67	-28.63	—	3.90	—	2.34	100.00	—	5.10	—
Net Profit on Net Sales	(%)	-0.61	56.41	N/A	N/A	N/A	-0.39	-587.50	N/A	N/A	N/A	0.08	100.00	N/A	N/A	N/A
Net Prof on Total Assets	(%)	-2.12	43.24	N/A	N/A	N/A	-1.48	-577.42	N/A	N/A	N/A	0.31	100.00	N/A	N/A	N/A
Tot Assets to Equity	(%)	-13.85	-61.06	N/A	N/A	N/A	-35.58	-52.30	N/A	N/A	N/A	-74.58	100.00	N/A	N/A	N/A
Net Prft on Stkhldrs Eqty	(%)	29.34	-44.21	N/A	N/A	N/A	52.59	-329.05	N/A	N/A	N/A	-22.96	100.00	N/A	N/A	N/A

(X)=TIMES   (D) = DAYS   (%) = PRECENT   ($) = DOLLARS

* IN THOUSANDS

OVERVIEW

Let us review the numbers and credit information to see the positives and negatives that will affect the decision. Starting with the liquidity ratio, $0.85 to $1.00 is better than industry average ($0.70 to $1.00). To confirm that Fast Action is truly liquid, let us compare its DSO to the industry average. DSO is 48 days while industry average is 43 days. The lowest quartile is set at 50 days, which makes the 48 days results look even worse.

The quick ratio is computed by cash, marketable securities, and accounts receivables and divides them by the total current liabilities. Since the DSO is high, there is a good chance that some nonperforming receivables are part of the total outstanding. This means that the liquidity number is not as good as it would first appear, because the receivables are high not as a result of increased sales but rather to possible uncollectible accounts.

As to the accounts payable turnover, the 68 days is far worse than the lowest quartile (41 days). Having a negative net worth that is increasing with profits down and below the industry average bodes poorly for keeping the firm running. All debts, both current and long term, are up considerably, and after taxes the company has lost money for the last two years in a row. The only possible positive ratio is the inventory turnover, which is 45 days compared to industry best of 50 days, but this may mean that the company is "fire-selling" the inventory and losing money on it as well.

All three trade references have stated that the payment trend is toward slowness, with payments ranging from 55 to 90 days past due. The high credit on the three best references was only $25,000. The high credit on the credit report was up to $185,000 with ratings running anywhere from prompt to 120 days slow. Once again, the bank has first lien on everything and the company rents its facilities. Considering the size of the long-term debt as reflected on the financials and the balance reflected on the bank's credit rating (high 5 figure or $70,000 to $99,000), there must be other factors in this equation. Someone other than the bank must be holding a very large note on the firm.

WHAT OTHER CREDIT MANAGERS THOUGHT

Question 2 and 3 ask what additional information you should get from the salesperson and from Fast Action. Now let us see what my students thought about this case.

Student One

Aimee S. comes from an agricultural firm and typically runs into this kind of delinquency in dealings with some farm customers. The work, however, is seasonal, which along with weather problems can seriously affect paying habits. Since these problems do not affect Fast Action, she would like to know from the salesperson whether this business could be referred to another distributor. She also wanted to know if sales and marketing were thinking about canceling the distributor due to its previous slow paying habits and order reduction. After seeing Fast Action's financials and the slow ratings reflected in the three "best trade references," she wanted to know how it was going to pay for this and all future orders on time.

Student Two

Ernie A., a credit professional associated with a chemical manufacturer, has very tight terms of sale to his customers, so he is well acquainted with putting customers on credit hold. He would like to ask the salesperson if Tuff Manufacturing has had any record of complaints from end users concerning products not being delivered on time. This type of action usually is grounds for termination by the firm and may be an indication of what will happen to this customer if things go wrong and payments are slow.

Ernie would like to know if Fast Action would be willing to review its books and see if it has problems with its receivables and what it is selling its inventory at. This would give him an insight into the cash-flow and profitability difficulties.

Student Three

Mike P. is from an electronics manufacturer and tends to run into similar problems with his distributors. They bad-mouth his firm when, in fact, they are past due and on credit hold. After agreeing with the questions asked by his predecessors, Mike wanted to ask the salesperson if he had had any direct contact with the end user without Fast Action being present. He also wanted to know if the end user had a practice of checking out vendors that serviced its needs.

Mike felt that it would be important to know whom Fast Action owed this large amount of long-term debt to, the interest rate of the loan, the payment terms, and when it was due to be paid in full. Considering the size of the debt, if this note were called, Fast Action could be forced into bankruptcy.

RECOMMENDED TERMS

Student One

Aimee S. definitely would not sell to this customer on an open account basis an amount that was higher than they have ever had with Tuff. She would consider taking a standby letter of credit as collateral for the amount above the current limit. Tying questions 4 and 5 together (why security and defending your position to top management and the customer), she proceeded into a long list of reasons why she required a standby letter of credit. She felt reasons for demanding security included the financial information, previous payment history, problems with other creditors, and most important Fast Action's bad-mouthing of Tuff to end users. She would review in detail the reasons with Fast Action.

Student Two

Ernie A. felt that he would prefer to meet directly with the owners of Fast Action and discuss why his company should consider selling to them at all. He felt that the negative net worth, the slowness of the receivables, and the high turnover rate of the inventory left Tuff in a situation of not being paid for the goods that it does sell. With no cash flow, the likelihood of Tuff being paid was very poor. He would advise top management of these facts but would advise that a solution would be obtained from Fast Action.

Student Three

Mike P. said that he would require that Tuff take a first lien on its inventory, the receivables generated from sale of its products, and the cash received in payment for the receivables. He would require that the bank forgo its first on Tuff's inventory and receivables as its debt outstanding was small compared to the amount of assets owned by the firm. The reason behind this was the possibility of a bankruptcy occurring as a result of the heavy amount of debt that Fast Action carried and the poor cash flow generated from its receivables. This did not even take into account the negative net worth and the "fire-selling" of inventory. He would discuss the need to take security with top management, showing them that this would give Tuff a secured status in a bankruptcy up to the level of inventory on hand and open receivables for the sale of its product.

Fast Action had such a poor track record everywhere and such a shaky financial status that the requirement of a lien on the assets sold to it by Tuff should be a take-or-leave-it deal. Mike suspected that Tuff might have another distributor that could take over this order if Fast Action refused to cooperate. He did not feel it would take much to convince Fast Action.

RECOMMENDATIONS WHEN OVERRIDEN BY MANAGEMENT

Now comes the most difficult problem, being overridden by top management.

Student One

Aimee S. has decided that she will tighten the reins and require that no additional product be sold to Fast Action until the account is at 30 days. Then she will require payment receipt to be 35 days or orders will be held.

Since Jack Slick has been such a big advocate of getting this order filled, he should be the one to break the news to Fast Action about the order releases and hold time. He also will be designated as the person to pick up the check on the 35th day when invoices become due. Aimee felt that when top management knew how much of a problem Fast Action is and that it is very concerned with keeping the end user happy, they will readily agree to this measure of safety.

Student Two

Ernie A. was not happy about being overridden. After getting top management's signatures on approving this order release, he planned to tighten the thumbscrews on Fast Action. He would personally visit the company along with the director of sales and marketing (Jack Slick's boss's boss) and make it quite clear to Fast Action's president, Jack Stopgap, that delinquency would not be tolerated. He also wanted to let Jack Stopgap know that Tuff would not put up with any finger-pointing if Fast Action did go past due. If this were discovered, Tuff would terminate the distributor agreement effective immediately. He wanted Jack Stopgap to know that he wanted to be paid when due. Payment could be made either by ACH transfer or by check to Jack Slick.

Student Three

Mike P. got Jack Slick and Jack Stopgap on a conference call and told them that they would now be joined at the hip. He would be watching both of them and would be sitting on Jack Stopgap's desk when the payment became due. If payment were not delivered, the orders would be stopped immediately. He advised them both that he would do PR calls to the end user to make sure that they were happy with not only the product but with the service and delivery time. If any discouraging words were heard, he would present them in writing to the director of sales and marketing and the president and he would recommend immediate termination of Fast Action as a distributor.

Having a customer that undercuts your efforts to get new business for both you and them due to its delinquency makes it extremely difficult to keep the ultimate customer, the end user, satisfied and a continuous buyer of your products. Our three credit professionals were smart to inform the customer that nonsense would not be permitted.

WHAT REALLY HAPPENED

Now let us look at what really happened in this particular case. As Mike P. suspected, we did have another distributor in the shadows waiting to take over this order if Fast Action dropped the ball. In this particular case the regional sales manager, Jack Slick's boss, was called in to meet with the end user without Jack or Fast Action being present. He discussed the relationship of Fast Action with the end user's director of purchasing and learned that that company was not happy with Fast Action either.

It also came to light that Fast Action had asked to be paid in net 15 days terms instead of net 30 days. Typically the end user did not pay this way but made a concession after being told that Fast Action had been squeezed by its vendors and could not afford to sell if not paid in this manner. Jack Stopgap had said Fast Action was just a small privately held company and that the big vendors it bought from did not care about it or the end user but only wanted to be paid and quickly. While not happy to hear this, the director of purchasing realized that the product sold by Tuff was the best and that Tuff was its sole source. He could not afford to lose access to Tuff's materials so he agreed to help with the terms problem.

The end user considered going to another distributor but was promptly informed by Jack Stopgap that he had an exclusive contract for its location and that the end user must either buy from Fast Action or not at all. The director of purchasing suspected that the last part was nonsense after he checked the phone book and saw that there were six distributors of Tuff's product in his city. While he thought that the distributor may be getting beaten up on the terms of sale (as his firm did it to its small customers), he doubted that the sole-source distributorship was true.

He asked us for the name and address of another distributor for the product and was referred to one by the regional sales manager. The end user promptly canceled the order and placed it with the new distributor. Fast Action's contract with Tuff ran out a month later and a letter of nonrenewal was sent. Fast Action was given 30 days to make any purchases to complete orders and was told that the terms for the next 30 days were COD.

Later we had a problem collecting the balance and were told that Fast Action wished to return product. Typically we did not accept product in return but after a long discussion with the director of sales and marketing and the regional sales manager, I convinced them that it was in our best interest to take goods back to cover our outstanding balance. They had Jack Slick verify that all goods to be returned were in their original boxes and definitely were our product. Fast Action also had to present an invoice that showed the date of purchase for these particular goods. We took a 25% restocking fee for sending the goods back, which just broke us even for the balance. Four months later Fast Action filed bankruptcy (Chapter 7) and was liquidated.

CONCLUSION

This particular case was nasty and presented some of the least enjoyable situations for credit professionals. Negotiations sometimes, however, do come through and you can come out smelling like a rose. The director of purchasing's call to the regional sales manager was prompted by my call to the end user's credit manager, who happened to be an old friend. Sometimes it is not what you know but whom you know that can help save the day.

9

CASE STUDY 5:
TRUE DELIVERY SEALS, INC.

Minimizing Exposure to Loss Due to the Cancellation of a Distributor Contract

INTRODUCTION

This case provides expertise in how to minimize the potential for loss due to returns by a canceled contract with a customer. This case also reviews the ways to sell safely to a canceled customer on a short-term basis to complete its order needs and protect your firm's good reputation in the industry. The need to part company with a former partner (customer) yet still maintain its goodwill is critical to a firm's market presence. The ultimate customer is the end user, and bad publicity from a disgruntled ex-customer could tarnish your firm's reputation. This case reviews the art of negotiating a smooth and fair separation and explains preparing your approach, "selling" the separation, and parting on good terms.

By reviewing this real day in the life of a credit department, readers will learn to make effective use of data, facts, and alternative methods in reaching a decision. An appreciation for how other people in marketing or finance think will hone negotiating skills. Readers can use new insight into the creation of a sound business credit decision to prevent gaps or weaknesses in their decision-making processes.

Case study 5 is similar to case study 4 except that there is no order involved and no end user to offend. Once again we must deal with the problem of dropping a present customer but for something far more insidious that just slow payments or bad-mouthing of the supplier. This time it is for product substitution, which could really damage the manufacturer's reputation. Unlike the four previous case studies, this case was handled not by individual students but as a group effort. This case study, while shorter, can be far more difficult than making a credit decision.

THE FACTS

The credit manager of New Deal Products, I.M. "Skip" Tracer, received from the vice president of sales and marketing a notice of intent to cancel on a large distributor, True Delivery Seals, Inc. The reason for the cancellation was due to substitution of a competitor's product for New Deal's and slow payment habits. True Delivery had a current balance of $40,000. It was also granted 30 days to make purchases to complete present orders. This customer has approximately $55,000 in inventory that it wished to return. The distributor agreement reflects a 25% restocking charge for any returns that are not defective and must be in their original containers and sealed shut. The regional sales manager in charge of this customer does not feel that product should be allowed to be returned as this customer has substituted product. He blamed New Deal Products for defective merchandise and delays in delivery of goods to customers. The reason for the delay was due to being on credit hold for past-due invoices. Standard terms of sale are 1% 10 net 30 days and orders are held at 45 days. You have available an updated credit report and last year's annual statement analysis.

QUESTIONS

1. What terms of sale will you offer to True Delivery during the next 30 days?
2. What way will you handle your customer's request to return product?
3. How can you prevent a loss on this account?

CREDIT REPORT

FILE #123456789	DATE PRINTED	SUMMARY
	MAY 23, 1996	RATING ---
TRUE DELIVERY SEALS INC.		STARTED 1960
123 EASY STREET	DIST. GASKETS	SALES $4,000,000 Est
OVER THE HILL, MS 54923	& SEALS	HISTORY CLEAR
TEL: 504 555-9000	SIC NO.	CONDITION FAIR
	5085	

CHIEF EXECUTIVE: ARNOLD STOPGAP, PRES.

PAYMENTS (Amounts may be rounded to nearest figure in prescribed ranges)
REPORTED

	PAYING RECORD	HIGH CREDIT	NOW OWES	PAST DUE	SELLING TERMS	LAST SALE WITHIN
4/96	Slow 30	2500	250	-0-		1 Mo
	Slow 30	10000	5000	-0-		
	Slow 30	25000	-0-	-0-	N15	2-3 Mos
	Slow 30-60	5000			N30	
	Slow 30-60	1000	-0-	-0-	N30	
	Slow 30-60	6000	1000	-0-		1 Mo
	Slow 30-90	30000	10000	-0-	N30	1 Mo
3/96	Slow 30	5000	2000	-0-		1 Mo
	Slow 30	5000	-0-	-0-	N30	6-12 Mos
	Slow 30-60	5000				
	Slow 30-60	10000	5000	-0-		1 Mo

* Payment experiences reflect how bills are met in relation to the terms granted. In some instances payment beyond terms can be the result of disputes over merchandise, skipped invoices, etc.

* Each experience shown represents a separate account reported by a supplier. Updated trade experiences replace those previously reported.

FINANCE
* Financial information refused by Arnold Stopgap. Sales for 1996 were forecasted to be $5,000,000.

PUBLIC FILINGS
UCC FILINGS
4/15/92
   Financing statement #984345 filed 9/11/91 with Secretary, State of La. Debtor True Delivery Seals Inc., Over The Hill, MS. Secured Party: All Secured Bank, N.A., Watertown, MS. Collateral: Specific leased equipment

TRUE DELIVERY SEALS INC.   May 23, 1996   PAGE 002

HISTORY
4/15/96
      ARNOLD L. STOPGAP, PRES.
      JACK L. STOPGAP, V. PRES.
      BARRY R. STOPGAP, TREAS.
      DIRECTOR(S): The officer(s)

      INCORPORATED Mississippi January 20, 1962

      Authorized capital consists of 50,000 shares Common Stock, $1 par value.

      Business started 1960 by Joseph Stopgap.

      Arnold L. Stopgap born 1928, married. 1960 started with company as a clerk and
      held various positions. 1975–1982 he was a Vice-President. 1982–Present President
      and CEO.

      Jack L. Stopgap born 1950, single. Graduate Jackson University, Wheatland, NM
      1972. 1970 started here. 1982–Present: Vice President here and continues.

      Barry R. Stopgap born 1951. Brother of Jack. Active here since 1982.

OPERATION
4/15/96
      Distributor of Seals and Gaskets (100%)

      Terms Net 30 days. Has 2,500 accounts. Sells to industrial accounts. Territory:
      Mississippi.

      EMPLOYEES: 30 including officers. 23 employed here.

      FACILITIES: Owns 10,000 sq. ft. in 1-story concrete block building in good
      condition. Premises neat.

      LOCATION: Suburban business section on side street.

                        FULL DISPLAY COMPLETE

New Deal Products Inc.
235 St. Patrick Drive
Rochester, TX 77653
FAX#: (716) 555-2932

BANK CREDIT INQUIRY

All Secured Bank N.A.
235 St. Patrick Drive   Ref: True Delivery Seals Inc.
Watertown, MS 54932   123 Easy Street
(504) 555-2810   Over The Hill, MS 54923

The above-referenced company has given your concern's name as a credit reference.
Please provide us with your experience with them so that we may determine their credit
worthiness. Please fax this information back to us as soon as possible. Thank you in
advance for the information that you provide and be assured that it will be kept
confidential.

Sincerely,

I. M. Tracer
Credit Department

If business is not incorporated, please provide owners' name & address:

SAVINGS ACCOUNT   LOW ___ MEDIUM ___ HIGH ___ $___ FIGURE
                  OPEN ___   CLOSED ____

CHECKING ACCOUNT   LOW ___ MEDIUM _X_ HIGH ___ $_5_ FIGURE
                   SATISFACTORY _X___ UNSATISFACTORY ____

CREDIT EXPERIENCE

Loans are granted: Frequently _X_ Occasionally ___ Seldom _____

Type: Working Capital _X_ Mortgage ___ Installment ___

Maximum Credit Extended $Low 6 Figures Secured _X_ Unsecured ____

Present Outstandings: Secured $Low 6 Figures Unsecured $ _____

Relationship: SATISFACTORY _X___ UNSATISFACTORY _____

Have "NSF" checks been issued: Yes ___ No _X_

Prepared By: B. A. Loanshark _____ Title: Vice President

New Deal Products Inc.
235 St. Patrick Drive
Rochester, TX 77653
PHONE (713) 555-2810
FAX   (713) 555-2932

CREDIT INQUIRY

*Sheet Material Company Inc.
*1235 Skyhigh Lane
*Runuptown, TX 77653

REF: True Delivery Seals Inc.
123 Easy Street
Over The Hill, MS 54923

The above-referenced company has given your concern's name as a credit reference. Please provide us with your experience with them so that we may determine their credit worthiness. Please fax this information back to us as soon as possible. Thank you in advance for the information that you provide and be assured that it will be kept confidential.

Sincerely,

 I. M. Tracer
   Credit Department

Sold From 1985

Terms of Sales Net 30

Largest Amount Now Owing $20,000

Amount Past Due $10,000

Recent Trend Toward X Promptness
                 __ Slowness
Makes Unjust Claims (State) _____
_____
_____

Credit Refused (State Cause) _____
_____
_____

Remarks: _____
_____
_____

MANNER OF PAYMENT
__ Discounts
__ Prompt & Satisfactory
 X Prompt to 15 Days Slow
__ Pays on Account
__ Asks for More Time
__ Slow but Collectible
__ Accepts COD's Promptly
__ Settles by Trade Acceptance
__ Notes Paid at Maturity
__ Account Secured

45 Average Days Paid

Information Given By: Jack A. Deadbeat, Credit Mgr. Date 05/26/96

WE REQUEST THE RETURN OF THIS FORM TO FACILITATE OUR SYSTEM OF FILING REPORT.

New Deal Products Inc.
235 St. Patrick Drive
Rochester, TX 77653
PHONE (713) 555-2810
FAX   (713) 555-2932

CREDIT INQUIRY

*Gasket Maker Company Inc.
*1345 Giveup Street
*Runmedown, TX 77643

REF: True Delivery Seals Inc.
123 Easy Street
Over The Hill, MS 54923

The above-referenced company has given your concern's name as a credit reference. Please provide us with your experience with them so that we may determine their credit worthiness. Please fax this information back to us as soon as possible. Thank you in advance for the information that you provide and be assured that it will be kept confidential.

Sincerely,

I. M. Tracer
Credit Department

Sold From 1978

Terms of Sales 1% 10 Net 30

Largest Amount Now Owing $30,000

Amount Past Due $20,000

Recent Trend Toward X Promptness
                                      __ Slowness
Makes Unjust Claims (State) _____
_____
_____
Credit Refused (State Cause) _____
_____
_____
Remarks: _____
_____
_____
Information Given By: I. M. Mean, Credit Manager   Date 05/26/96

MANNER OF PAYMENT
___ Discounts
___ Prompt & Satisfactory
 X Prompt to 30 Days Slow
___ Pays on Account
___ Asks for More Time
___ Slow but Collectible
___ Accepts COD's Promptly
___ Settles by Trade Acceptance
___ Notes Paid at Maturity
___ Account Secured

50 Average Days Paid

WE REQUEST THE RETURN OF THIS FORM TO FACILITATE OUR SYSTEM OF FILING REPORT.

New Deal Products Inc.
235 St. Patrick Drive
Rochester, TX 77653
PHONE (713) 555-2810
FAX   (713) 555-2932

CREDIT INQUIRY

*Rubber U.S.A. Inc.   REF: True Delivery Seals Inc.
*1569 Lowdown Varmit Highway   123 Easy Street
*Rolloverme, TX 77543   Over The Hill, MS 54923

The above-referenced company has given your concern's name as a credit reference.
Please provide us with your experience with them so that we may determine their credit
worthiness. Please fax this information back to us as soon as possible. Thank you in
advance for the information that you provide and be assured that it will be kept
confidential.

Sincerely,

 I. M. Tracer
   Credit Department

Sold From 1980   MANNER OF PAYMENT
                                         ___ Discounts
Terms of Sales _____ Net 30 _____   ___ Prompt & Satisfactory
                                          X Prompt to 30 Days Slow
Largest Amount Now Owing $15,000   ___ Pays on Account
                                         ___ Asks for More Time
Amount Past Due $10,000   ___ Slow but Collectible
                                         ___ Accepts COD's Promptly
Recent Trend Toward X Promptness   ___ Settles by Trade Acceptance
                    ___ Slowness   ___ Notes Paid at Maturity
Makes Unjust Claims (State) _____   ___ Account Secured
_____
_____
Credit Refused (State Cause) _____
_____
_____
Remarks: _____   53 Average Days Paid
_____

Information Given By: Rank Amateur, Credit Manager   Date 05/26/96

WE REQUEST THE RETURN OF THIS FORM TO FACILITATE OUR SYSTEM OF
FILING REPORT.

True Delivery Seals Inc.
123 Easy Street
Over The Hill, MS 54923

SIC 3621   ACCOUNT # 123456

$6,122,845.96
$1,311,123.03

	12/31/95				12/31/94				12/31/93			
	$	% Change	% Assets	Ind % Assets	$	% Change	% Assets	Ind % Assets	$	% Change	% Assets	Ind % Assets
Cash	$153,685.44	129.62	6.76	8.00	$66,931.10	-49.81	3.42	8.50	$133,342.40	100.00	6.43	5.60
Accounts Receivable	$706,613.62	2.05	31.08	25.80	$692,406.60	-0.50	35.34	25.10	$695,911.30	100.00	33.55	25.80
Inventory	$592,557.80	6.70	26.07	23.00	$555,365.20	-11.90	28.35	26.70	$630,408.31	100.00	30.39	29.00
Due from Shareholder	$0.00	0.00	0.00	---	$0.00	0.00	0.00	---	$0.00	0.00	0.00	---
Due From Affiliate	$0.00	0.00	0.00	---	$0.00	0.00	0.00	---	$0.00	0.00	0.00	---
Other Current	$108,401.40	32.89	4.77	3.70	$81,574.30	-29.34	4.16	2.80	$115,451.40	100.00	5.57	2.50
Total Current	$1,561,258.26	11.82	68.68	60.50	$1,396,277.20	-11.35	71.27	63.10	$1,575,113.41	100.00	75.93	62.90
Fixed Assets	$678,807.27	32.20	29.86	26.20	$513,475.60	26.39	26.21	26.10	$406,268.96	100.00	19.59	26.20
Notes Receivable	$0.00	0.00	0.00	---	$0.00	0.00	0.00	---	$0.00	0.00	0.00	---
Deposits	$33,101.85	-32.94	1.46	---	$49,363.20	-46.92	2.52	---	$93,002.60	100.00	4.48	---
Cash Value of Life Insur.	$0.00	0.00	0.00	8.50	$0.00	0.00	0.00	7.10	$0.00	0.00	0.00	7.30
Intangible Assets	$0.00	0.00	0.00	4.80	$0.00	0.00	0.00	3.70	$0.00	0.00	0.00	3.60
Total Assets	$2,273,167.38	16.03	100.00	100.00	$1,959,116.00	-5.56	100.00	100.00	$2,074,384.97	100.00	100.00	100.00
Account Payable	$526,139.60	17.62	23.15	10.90	$447,335.50	-6.38	22.83	10.90	$477,827.64	100.00	23.03	10.90
Bank Loans + N.P.	$100,752.25	36.83	4.43	5.40	$73,631.40	60.00	3.76	5.90	$46,020.90	100.00	2.22	6.50
Cur. Mat.-L.T.D.	$24,339.30	3.58	1.07	2.10	$23,497.60	667.72	1.20	2.60	$3,060.70	100.00	0.15	2.00
Income Tax Payables	$9,936.50	206.87	0.44	0.50	$3,238.00	100.00	0.17	0.90	$0.00	0.00	0.00	0.70
Accrued Expenses	$252,882.70	129.64	11.12	13.30	$110,119.70	-64.86	5.62	13.20	$313,393.57	100.00	15.11	12.90
Total Current	$914,050.35	38.95	40.21	32.20	$657,822.20	-21.72	0.00	33.50	$840,302.81	100.00	40.51	33.20
Long Term Debt	$34,625.40	42.80	1.52	14.80	$24,248.10	-33.41	1.24	13.60	$36,411.80	100.00	1.76	14.80
Deferred Taxes	$13,368.60	31.12	0.59	1.10	$10,196.00	-10.05	0.52	1.60	$11,335.20	100.00	0.55	1.90
All Other L.T. Debt	$0.00	-100.00	0.00	5.20	$32,809.10	100.00	1.67	3.00	$0.00	0.00	0.00	3.00
Net Worth	$1,311,123.03	6.25	57.68	46.70	$1,234,040.60	4.02	62.99	48.30	$1,186,335.16	100.00	57.19	47.10
Total Liab & Equity	$2,273,167.38	16.03	100.00	100.00	$1,959,116.00	-5.56	66.42	100.00	$2,074,384.97	100.00	100.00	100.00
Net Sales	$6,122,845.96	12.43	100.00	100.00	$5,445,697.80	-0.01	100.00	100.00	$5,446,062.80	100.00	100.00	100.00
Cost of Goods Sold	$3,342,455.56	17.34	54.59	69.30	$2,848,572.30	-10.06	52.31	69.70	$3,167,275.10	100.00	58.16	70.10
Gross Profit	$2,780,390.40	7.06	45.41	30.70	$2,597,125.50	13.97	47.69	30.30	$2,278,787.70	100.00	41.84	29.90
Depreciation	$60,304.30	14.98	0.98	---	$52,447.80	30.92	0.96	---	$40,061.60	100.00	0.74	---
Lease Payments	$0.00	0.00	0.00	---	$0.00	0.00	0.00	---	$0.00	0.00	0.00	---
Other Operating Exps.	$2,611,170.27	4.21	42.65	24.70	$2,505,661.70	17.27	46.01	23.50	$2,136,631.10	100.00	39.23	23.70
Tot. Operating Exps.	$2,671,474.57	4.43	43.63	6.00	$2,558,109.50	17.52	46.97	6.80	$2,176,692.70	100.00	39.97	6.20
Operating Profit	$108,915.83	179.16	1.78	1.30	$39,016.00	-61.78	0.72	1.30	$102,095.00	100.00	1.87	1.30
Interest Inc./(Exp.)	$16,192.80	-53.59	0.26	---	$34,893.60	105.26	0.64	---	$16,999.60	100.00	0.31	---
G/(L) on sale of Fxd Assets	$0.00	0.00	0.00	---	$0.00	0.00	0.00	---	$0.00	0.00	0.00	---
Profit Before Taxes	$125,108.63	69.27	2.04	4.70	$73,909.60	-37.94	1.36	5.50	$119,094.60	100.00	2.19	4.90
Taxes	$48,026.20	83.28	0.78	---	$26,204.16	-58.22	0.48	---	$62,715.40	100.00	1.15	---
Net Profit	$77,082.43	61.58	1.26	---	$47,705.44	-15.38	0.88	---	$56,379.20	100.00	1.04	---
Other Data:												
Working Capital	$647,207.91	-12.36	28.47	28.30	$738,455.00	0.50	71.27	29.60	$734,810.60	100.00	35.42	29.70
Tangible Equity	$1,311,123.03	6.25	57.68	41.90	$1,234,040.60	4.02	62.99	44.60	$1,186,335.16	100.00	57.19	43.50
Recommended Credit Limit:	$157,334.76	6.25	---	---	$148,084.87	9.50	---	---	$135,242.21	---	---	---

True Delivery Seals Inc.
123 Easy Street
Over The Hill, MS 54923

RATIOS

Ratio	Unit	12/31/95	% Change	UQ	Med	LQ	12/31/94	% Change	UQ	Med	LQ	12/31/93	% Change	UQ	Med	LQ
SOLVENCY																
Current Ratio	($)	1.71	-19.53	3.00	1.90	1.40	2.12	13.24	2.80	2.10	1.40	1.87	100.00	2.60	1.90	1.40
Quick Ratio	($)	0.94	-666.32	1.70	1.10	0.70	1.15	16.97	1.50	1.00	0.70	0.99	100.00	1.40	0.90	0.60
Net Profit B4 Tax + Depr./Cur LTD	(X)	7.62	41.66	18.40	6.10	1.50	5.38	-89.66	10.00	3.50	1.70	52.00	100.00	9.30	5.30	1.70
Sales to Fixed Assets	(X)	9.02	136.41	9.90	5.70	4.10	3.82	-71.54	10.10	6.20	4.00	13.41	100.00	9.30	5.80	4.20
Sales to Total Assets	(X)	2.69	-3.10	2.00	1.50	1.20	2.78	5.88	2.00	1.50	1.30	2.63	100.00	1.80	1.50	1.20
Total Liab. to NW	(X)	0.73	24.88	0.60	1.00	2.60	0.59	-21.51	0.60	1.00	2.50	0.75	100.00	0.70	1.20	2.40
Fixed Assets to NW	(X)	0.52	24.43	0.40	0.50	1.00	0.42	21.50	0.40	0.50	1.00	0.34	100.00	0.40	0.60	1.00
Tot. Liab. to Tot. Assets	(%)	42.32	14.35	N/A	N/A	N/A	37.01	-13.55	N/A	N/A	N/A	42.81	100.00	N/A	N/A	N/A
Oper. Prof. to Int. Exp.	(X)	6.73	501.55	N/A	N/A	N/A	1.12	-81.38	N/A	N/A	N/A	6.01	100.00	N/A	N/A	N/A
Oper Prof+Lease Py to Int Exp+LP	(X)	6.73	501.55	N/A	N/A	N/A	1.12	-81.38	N/A	N/A	N/A	6.01	100.00	N/A	N/A	N/A
EFFICIENCY																
Sales to Receivables	(X)	8.67	10.17	7.70	6.30	5.20	7.86	0.50	8.10	6.70	5.50	7.83	100.00	7.70	5.90	5.10
Days Sales Outstanding	(D)	42	-8.70	47	58	70	46	-2.13	45	54	66	47	100.00	47	62	72
Cost of Sales to Inv.	(X)	5.64	9.97	7.00	4.40	3.10	5.13	2.09	6.10	4.10	3.00	5.02	100.00	5.90	3.60	2.60
Days' Sales in Inventory	(D)	65	-8.45	52	83	118	71	-2.74	60	89	122	73	100.00	62	101	140
Sales to Net Working Cap.	(X)	9.46	28.29	3.40	4.80	12.00	7.37	-0.50	3.60	5.30	9.70	7.41	100.00	3.40	5.20	9.70
Cost of Sales/Payables	(X)	6.35	-0.24	15.20	10.90	8.10	6.37	-3.93	15.50	10.70	8.70	6.63	100.00	14.20	11.20	7.50
A/P Turnover	(D)	57	0.00	24	33	45	57	3.64	24	34	42	55	100.00	26	33	49
PROFITABILITY																
Depreciation to Sales	(%)	0.98	2.26	1.80	2.60	4.00	0.96	30.93	1.80	2.80	3.70	0.74	100.00	1.60	2.70	3.70
Prof bef Tax to Tot Assets	(%)	5.50	45.89	12.10	6.00	1.20	3.77	-34.29	14.50	8.50	1.50	5.74	100.00	14.00	7.20	3.10
Profit before Taxes to TNW	(%)	9.54	59.32	24.80	15.80	5.80	5.99	-40.34	34.50	17.10	4.90	10.04	100.00	30.50	16.80	7.60

OTHER RATIOS NOT AVAILABLE WITH INDUSTRY STANDARDS

Ratio	Unit	12/31/95	% Change	UQ	Med	LQ	12/31/94	% Change	UQ	Med	LQ	12/31/93	% Change	UQ	Med	LQ
SOLVENCY																
Inv. to Net. Work. Capital	(X)	0.92	21.74	N/A	N/A	N/A	0.75	-12.33	N/A	N/A	N/A	0.86	100.00	N/A	N/A	N/A
Current Liab. to NW	(X)	0.70	30.78	N/A	N/A	N/A	0.53	-24.74	N/A	N/A	N/A	0.71	100.00	N/A	N/A	N/A
LT Debt to Tot. Debt & Capital	(%)	2.11	-38.48	N/A	N/A	N/A	3.43	49.13	N/A	N/A	N/A	2.30	100.00	N/A	N/A	N/A
Fixed Assets to LT Debt	(X)	19.60	-7.46	N/A	N/A	N/A	21.18	89.78	N/A	N/A	N/A	11.16	100.00	N/A	N/A	N/A
EFFICIENCY																
Net Sales to NW	(X)	4.67	5.90	N/A	N/A	N/A	4.41	-3.92	N/A	N/A	N/A	4.59	100.00	N/A	N/A	N/A
Net Sales to Inventory	(X)	10.33	5.30	N/A	N/A	N/A	9.81	13.54	N/A	N/A	N/A	8.64	100.00	N/A	N/A	N/A
Cost of Sales/Working Capital	(X)	5.16	33.68	N/A	N/A	N/A	3.86	-10.44	N/A	N/A	N/A	4.31	100.00	N/A	N/A	N/A
Short Term Loan Turnover	(X)	11.00	22.22	N/A	N/A	N/A	9.00	80.00	N/A	N/A	N/A	5.00	100.00	N/A	N/A	N/A
LT Liabilities Payback*	($)	$113.05	47.47	N/A	N/A	N/A	$76.66	-17.91	N/A	N/A	N/A	$93.38	100.00	N/A	N/A	N/A
PROFITABILITY																
Gross Profit on Net Sales	(%)	45.41	-4.78	--	30.70	--	47.69	13.98	--	30.30	--	41.84	100.00	--	29.90	--
Net Oper Inc on Net Sales	(%)	1.78	147.22	--	6.00	--	0.72	-61.50	--	6.80	--	1.87	100.00	--	6.20	--
Net Profit on Net Sales	(%)	1.26	43.18	N/A	N/A	N/A	0.88	-15.38	N/A	N/A	N/A	1.04	100.00	N/A	N/A	N/A
Net Prof on Total Assets	(%)	3.39	38.93	N/A	N/A	N/A	2.44	-10.29	N/A	N/A	N/A	2.72	100.00	N/A	N/A	N/A
Tot Assets to Equity	(X)	1.73	9.21	N/A	N/A	N/A	1.59	-9.21	N/A	N/A	N/A	1.75	100.00	N/A	N/A	N/A
Net Prft on Stkhldrs Eqty	(%)	5.88	51.94	N/A	N/A	N/A	3.87	-18.53	N/A	N/A	N/A	4.75	100.00	N/A	N/A	N/A

(X)=TIMES   (D)=DAYS   (%)=PRECENT   ($)=DOLLARS

* IN THOUSANDS

OVERVIEW

In considering what to do about the balance and how to sell to True Delivery during the next 30 days, we need to review its financial and credit position to determine how we might fare in the days to come. Starting with liquidity, True Delivery appears to be below the average ($0.94 to $1.00 compared to $1.10 to $1.00 on average and $0.70 to $1.00 for lowest quartile). DSO, however, is better than the highest quartile (42 days compared to 47 days). Debt to net worth is above average ($0.73 to $1.00 compared to $1.20 to $1.00) and inventory turnover is also better that average (65 days compared to 83 days).

The real killer is the A/P turnover, which is 57 days compared to 33 days on average and 45 days at the lowest quartile. This indicates that even though the company has the money to pay earlier, it has chosen to live off its suppliers. Gross profit is far above industry average (45.4% compared 30.7%) while operating profit is way below industry average (1.8% compared to 6.0%). This means that True Delivery spends a lot on salaries, bonuses, and benefits rather than pouring the money back into the firm.

The three trade references show ranges in payments from 15 to 23 days, slow with a trend toward promptness. The highest credit established was $30,000 with no real derogatory remarks. The credit report reflects a much higher delinquency range of slow 30 days to 90 days past due. Once again the bank has a lien on all assets, but the company does own the building where it runs its operation. The firm has been in business for 34 years and has been a family-owned and operated company. The bank currently has a working capital line of credit open to the company for a low six-figure amount ($100,000 to $200,000), and it might be fully used at this time.

WHAT OTHER CREDIT PROFESSIONALS THOUGHT

Once again, past students answer the questions using their background and expertise and also drawing on the knowledge and experience of their credit committee.

Student One

Elaine B., a seasoned pro from a jewelry manufacturer, was quite excited about this case. She had been placed in this position many times in the past and now had a chance to deal with it in a less volatile setting. When asked about the terms she would offer during the next 30 days, Elaine indicated that she felt that the sales and marketing area had dropped the bomb on the customer and once again she must pick up the debris. She felt she should minimize her risk by selling on terms of certified cash in advance. If the reason for nonrenewal was not meeting sales quotas or the customer had minor delinquency problems, then it would have been reasonable to sell to it on an open account basis. To Elaine, the fact that True Delivery had been caught substituting product and had a track record of high delinquency makes this the only possible decision.

Student Two

Barb V., from a clothing manufacturer, was not quite so tough on True Delivery. Given its low debt position and high DSO turnover, she was willing to sell on an open account basis. She would restrict purchases to a much smaller amount and would demand that payment be made on a timely basis. She was not happy about the switching of product and the past delinquency that had occurred but felt that the margins were sufficient to take a chance on open account terms.

Student Three

Ray C. was from a glass manufacturing firm. He was sure that if we sold on anything but open account, True Delivery would be bad-mouthing New Deal to everyone as a "David vs. Goliath" test of wills. He sees True Delivery coming out the winner, as it is a small company compared to his multinational firm. While he would not give away the house and the farm, he would sell on open account up to a reasonable amount (about half of the normal monthly purchases). Assuming that New Deal would not be getting any new orders for its products and would be just completing current orders, half the normal monthly purchases should be sufficient to meet obligations. As for terms, it would be "business as usual" or 1% 10 days, net 30 days from invoice date.

HANDLING RETURNED GOODS

Student One

Elaine B. was all in favor of goods being returned to reduce True Delivery's outstanding balance. She would make it mandatory that the local salesperson inspect all goods and that True Delivery references an invoice in which it had purchased the goods from New Deal. (This prevents the customer from trying to substitute other goods and also would eliminate taking back product never purchased from New Deal.) The inspection should occur when the goods were being picked up by the trucking firm and the salesperson should remain guard over these goods until they were picked up. Assuming that all items returned were valid, she would agree to cover the debt in full and not issue any credit beyond that of the balance.

She knew that she would have to sell this idea to the regional sales manager, who was totally against taking any product back. She would explain that if this account were turned over to a collection agency or to an attorney and went to court, the judge would ask us if we had accepted product in return. When the judge was advised that we had not, likely he or she would require that we take the goods back under our normal terms and conditions. The agency or the attorney would get its percentage of the credit for the returned goods. We would be forced to give True Delivery any part that would be over the normal credit less restocking fee plus court costs and attorney's fees, assuming that we had that in our distributor agreement. It would be much better for New Deal to take product back now rather than later.

Student Two

Barb V. agreed with Elaine on taking the product back as soon as possible. She, however, did not feel that it was necessary to have the salesperson ride shotgun over the return. When the goods hit New Deal's dock, they could be inspected. If they did not qualify for credit due to no sale being made on the product or if substituted product were returned, then no credit would be issued for those goods. A much more thorough examination of the returns could be made at the factory and the source of substitute product might be determined. This would help our position if we had to take True Delivery to court. Photos could be taken, if necessary, and all facts would be documented to support our case. Convincing the sales manager to take the goods back would not be too difficult, as New Deal would charge back both the salesperson and the regional sales manager's commission if it had to turn this over to a collection agency.

Student Three

Ray C. was sure that True Delivery would not be stupid enough to return goods that it had substituted to New Deal. It would be comparable to signing a confession of guilt. He did feel that it might try to return goods that were purchased from another New Deal distributor at a time when True Delivery was on credit hold. Considering the long shelf life of the goods that New Deal sold, it would not be unusual that they may been have bought somewhere else and also purchased from New Deal. This meant that True Delivery might have to do some thorough research to find the "original invoice," but to get additional credit it might be worth its while to do so. As to the regional sales manager, Ray felt that it would be in the best interests of New Deal to take the product back rather than deal with a firm that would besmirch its reputation. Knowing that True Delivery was quite capable of substituting goods in New Deal's boxes indicates that True Delivery would stop at nothing to make New Deal look worse in the eyes of its customers (end users).

PREVENTING A LOSS

Student One

Elaine B. felt that the only way to prevent a loss was to follow her recommendation. All sales should be certified cash in advance for the next 30 days and the goods should be returned after New Deal's salesperson had ridden shotgun over it. She also felt that some type of damage control would need to be done with the end users. True Delivery could and probably would do much damage to hurt New Deal's reputation.

Student Two

Barb V. felt that trying to work with New Deal during the transition time and by eliminating it as a distributor would help keep the bad feelings

from getting out of hand. While getting the balance resolved was important, it was more important that New Deal's reputation not be torn up by a
firm that was capable of doing anything to make money, including substituting of inferior product. The steps she outlined in her two earlier
answers laid the groundwork for keeping the risk of a loss to a minimum.

Student Three

Ray C. likewise felt that New Deal's reputation needed to be protected at
all costs but refused to take any steps to jeopardize his balance. He would
keep the amount he would sell to True Delivery at a minimum in line with
its normal purchases and would be thorough in reviewing goods returned
by True Delivery. He was sure that True Delivery would take advantage of
the situation to try to undercut New Deal but felt that normal procedures
had to be followed in dealing with the return.

WHAT REALLY HAPPENED

What really happened shows that sometimes the best interests of the company are also in the best interests of the public. In this case, the materials
were used to make gaskets for nuclear power plants and had to be of the
finest materials possible. By substituting inferior materials, True Delivery
was jeopardizing not only the reputation of New Deal but also public
safety. If these pipes were to leak radioactive water, then an entire area
could be put at risk as well as the lives of those who work at the plants
where the material was used.

When one gasket did show signs of leakage, the power plant called
New Deal to discuss the materials used. After examining the gasket in
question, New Deal determined that substituted materials had been used.
The power plant requested an immediate examination of all gaskets put in
by True Delivery. New Deal sent in its best engineers and determined that
at least 30% of all "its" gaskets had been substituted and needed to be
replaced. New Deal offered to do this at no charge and would take steps to
prevent substitutions from recurring. The power plant was notified that
True Delivery was no longer an approved New Deal distributor and that
all further purchases could be made from a different distributor in their
area. True Delivery was immediately canceled and the balance in full
demanded. True Delivery returned its inventory without a return autho-

rization and no further orders were released. After inspecting the goods received, it was determined that there was enough after a 25% restocking fee to cover New Deal's balance. New Deal had no more dealings with True Delivery, which was investigated by the FBI and indited for fraud and endangering the public. The case is still pending in court.

CONCLUSION

This case had a very unusual twist at the end that could have caused even greater "fallout" (no pun intended) than what really occurred. All firms that sell products to the public or sell to those areas that will ultimately affect the public must be concerned not only about their reputation but about public safety.

10

CASE STUDY 6: FIRST CHOICE COMPANY, INC.

Dealing with a Last-Minute Credit Decision

INTRODUCTION

This case provides practical methods to deal with those last-minute "surprises" by the boss and the marketing manager—the ones where they need an instant decision on a large sale. Seeing why it is important to determine the real reasons behind the "last-minute order" revealed in the final events of the actual case. The three students give their ways to prevent these scenarios from occurring. Readers can develop a final strategy from these insights that will help eliminate this problem in their organization.

By reviewing this real day in the life of a credit department, readers will learn to make effective use of data, facts, and alternative methods in reaching a decision. An appreciation for how other people in marketing or finance think will hone negotiating skills. Readers can use new insight into the creation of a sound business credit decision to prevent gaps or weaknesses in their decision-making processes.

This case study is quite different from the earlier ones. It is a credit professional's worst nightmare.

THE FACTS

It is Friday at 4:55 P.M. on the beginning of a three-day holiday weekend. It is also the closing day for the quarter, and you have been working frantically all day trying to get all the orders safely out the door. Just when you think you are free, your boss and the director of sales walk into your office to discuss the possibility of shipping a $200,000 truckload shipment out to First Choice today to make the quarter numbers. The margin on this sale would be 45% and the customer is asking for terms of 3% 10 days, net 90 for this large shipment. Your normal margin is 30%. The inflation rate currently is at 5% per annum.

Since 1987, First Choice has paid 33 days from invoice date, and your normal (and only) terms of sale are 1% 10 days, net 30. Your high credit with First Choice has been $84,000; its limit is $70,000, and its balance is $25,000. Sales have been slow due to the recession.

INSTRUCTIONS

1. Analyze all data available on the case, summarizing your findings using the following:
   A. Trend analysis, common-size analysis, ratio analysis, and comparison to industry standards
   B. Summarize the information available in the credit report, references, and information available above
2. Do you make the sale and accept the customer's terms? If not, what counteroffer could be made? Secured?
3. If approved, do you increase the credit limit?
4. What facts would you use to defend your decision to management and to the customer?
5. If overridden by management, what steps would you take to prevent a possible loss?
6. What steps can you take in the future to prevent being put in this situation again?

CREDIT REPORT

File #: 12698654   DATE PRINTED   SUMMARY
FIRST CHOICE COMPANY INC.   MAY 30, 1996   RATING   -----
BOX 4163   STARTED   1985
BLOCKAGE, IL 60606   WHOL HOSES &   PAYMENTS SEE BELOW
RT 99 NORTH   ACCESSORIES   SALES $4,000,000
BLOCKAGE, IL 60606   (PROJ)
 TEL: 312 555-1259   SIC NO.   EMPLOYS   20
                                   50 85   HISTORY   CLEAR

CHIEF EXECUTIVE: BIFF BLOCK, PRES

PAYMENTS   (Amounts may be rounded to nearest figure in prescribed ranges)
REPORTED

	PAYING RECORD	HIGH CREDIT	NOW OWES	PAST DUE	SELLING TERMS	LAST SALE WITHIN
04/96	Ppt	150000	10000		Regular Terms	1 Mo
	Ppt	50000	40000	5000	N30	6-12 Mos
	Ppt	5000	-0-	-0-	N30	1 Mo
	Ppt	2500	1000	-0-	N30	6-12 Mos
	Ppt	2500	1000	-0-	N30	
	Ppt	1000	250	-0-	N15	1 Mo
	Ppt	1000	1000	-0-		1 Mo
	Ppt	100	100	-0-	N30	1 Mo
	Ppt-Slow 15	7500	5000	2500		1 Mo
	Slow 30	750	-0-	-0-	1/10 N30	2-3 Mos
	Slow 30	100	-0-	-0-		6-12 Mos
	Slow 30	50	50	50	N30	1 Mo
	Slow 60	2500	-0-	-0-		4-5 Mos
03/96	Ppt	2500	1000	-0-	N30	1 Mo
	Ppt	250	50	-0-		1 Mo
	Ppt	100	100	-0-	N30	2-3 Mos
02/96	Slow 30	250	-0-	-0-		2-3 Mos
	Ppt-Slow 30	2500	750	50		1 Mo
	Ppt	100	-0-	-0-		6-12 Mos
	Lease Agreement					
	Slow 60	250	250		1/10 N30	
	Ppt	100	-0-	-0-	N30	6-12 Mos

* Payment experiences reflect how bills are met in relation to the terms granted. In some instances payment beyond terms can be the result of disputes over merchandise, skipped invoices, etc.

* Each experience shown represents a separate account reported by a supplier. Updated trade experience replace those previously reported.

FIRST CHOICE COMPANY INC.   May 30, 1995   PAGE 002

FINANCE
05/21/96

   Monthly rent $2,500. Lease expires Dec. 1995.
   On Oct 21, 1995, Biff Block, President, deferred financial statement.

   He submitted the following partial estimates dated May 21, 1995:
   Projected annual sales are $4,000,000.

PUBLIC FILINGS

   The following data is for information purposes only and is not the official record.
   Certified copies can only be obtained from the official source.

                         * * * UCC FILING(S) * * *

COLLATERAL: Negotiable instruments - Specified accounts receivable -
        Chattel paper - Contract rights - General intangibles and proceeds
   FILING NO: 41382436   DATE FILED: 05/04/1990
   TYPE: Original   FILED WITH: Secretary of State
Sec. PARTY: Continental Bank, Chicago, IL.
   DEBTOR: First Choice Company Inc.

COLLATERAL: Leased business machinery/equipment and proceeds
   FILING NO: 49683216   DATE FILED: 03/04/1992
   TYPE: Original   FILED WITH: Secretary of State
Sec. PARTY: Square Deal Credit Inc., Chicago, IL.
   DEBTOR: First Choice Company Inc.

   FILING NO: 9061234   DATE FILED: 09/02/1993
   TYPE: Amendment   Received By A&R : 10/25/1993
   Sec. PARTY: Continental Bank, Chicago ORIG. UCC FILED: 09/12/1988
              IL.   ORIG. FILING NO. 43813941
   DEBTOR: First Choice Company Inc. FILED WITH: Secretary of State/
                                         UCC Division, IL.

        The public record items contained in this report may have been paid,
        terminated, vacated or released prior to the date this report was printed.
BANKING
01/96   Account open over 3 years. Borrowing account.

HISTORY
10/21/95 Biff Block, Pres.   Butch Brick, V. Pres-Operations Sec-Treas

FIRST CHOICE COMPANY INC.   May 30, 1996   PAGE 003

Jack Rocks, V. Pres-Sales
Director(s): The Officer(s)

Corporate and business registrations reported by the Secretary of State or other official source as of 01/06/1996:

Business Type: Corporation - Date Incorporated: 07/10/1985
                    Profit   State of Incorp: Illinois

Auth Shares - Common: 10,000,000
Par Value - Common: No par value

Business started 1985 by Biff Block, Butch Brick and Jack Rocks. Relocated Jan 1990 from Chicago, IL. $33\frac{1}{3}$% of capital stock is owned by Biff Block. $33\frac{1}{3}$% of capital stock is owned by Butch Brick. $33\frac{1}{3}$% of capital stock is owned by Jack Rocks.

Biff Block born 1946. 1971-1974 attended Slippery Rock University, Rockford, IL. 1974-85 Nordick Gasket Co., Rockford, IL as sales manager. 1985 to present active here.

Butch Brick born 1948. 1971-1974 attended Jackson Business College, Blockage, IL. 1971-85 Nordick Gasket Co., Rockford, IL as business manager. 1985 to present active here.

Jack Rocks born 1951. 1973-85 Nordick Gasket Co., Rockford, IL as salesman. 1985 to present active here.

OPERATION
10/21/95 Wholesales hoses and accessories.
        Terms: 1% 10, Net 30 days. Has 300 Accounts. Sells to paper industry.
        Territory: Illinois and Michigan.
        Non-seasonal.
        Employees: 20 including officers.
        Facilities: Leases 30,000-sq. ft. in a one-story steel building in good condition.
        Location: Suburban business section on a well-traveled street.

FULL DISPLAY COMPLETE

New Deal Products Inc.
235 St. Patrick Drive
Rochester, TX 77653
FAX#: (716) 555-2932

BANK CREDIT INQUIRY

Continental Bank N.A.
235 St. Patrick Drive   Ref: First Choice Company Inc.
Chicago, IL 60606   Rt. 99 North
(312) 555-2810   Blockage, IL 60606

The above-referenced company has given your concern's name as a credit reference.
Please provide us with your experience with them so that we may determine their credit
worthiness. Please fax this information back to us as soon as possible. Thank you in
advance for the information that you provide and be assured that it will be kept
confidential.

Sincerely,

I. M. Tracer
Credit Department

If business is not incorporated, please provide owners' name & address:

SAVINGS ACCOUNT   LOW ___ MEDIUM ___ HIGH ___ $__ FIGURE ___
                  OPEN ___   CLOSED ___

CHECKING ACCOUNT   LOW _X_ MEDIUM ___ HIGH ___ $_5_ FIGURE
                   SATISFACTORY _X___ UNSATISFACTORY ____

CREDIT EXPERIENCE

Loans are granted: Frequently _X_ Occasionally ___ Seldom ___

Type: Working Capital _X_ Mortgage __ Installment ___

Maximum Credit Extended $Med 5 Figures Secured _X_ Unsecured ____

Present Outstandings: Secured $Med 5 Figures Unsecured $ _____

Relationship: SATISFACTORY _X__ UNSATISFACTORY _____

Have "NSF" checks been issued: Yes ___ No _X_

Prepared By: B. A. Loanshark _____ Title: Vice President

New Deal Products Inc.
235 St. Patrick Drive
Rochester, TX 77653
PHONE (713) 555-2810
FAX   (713) 555-2932

CREDIT INQUIRY

*Sheet Material Company Inc.
*1235 Skyhigh Lane
*Runuptown, TX 77653

REF: First Choice Company Inc.
Rt. 99 North
Blockage, IL 60606

The above-referenced company has given your concern's name as a credit reference. Please provide us with your experience with them so that we may determine their credit worthiness. Please fax this information back to us as soon as possible. Thank you in advance for the information that you provide and be assured that it will be kept confidential.

Sincerely,

 I. M. Tracer
Credit Department

Sold From 1989

Terms of Sales Net 30

Largest Amount Now Owing $20,000

Amount Past Due $200

Recent Trend Toward X Promptness
                    __ Slowness
Makes Unjust Claims (State) _____
_____
_____

Credit Refused (State Cause) _____
_____
_____

Remarks: _____
_____
_____

MANNER OF PAYMENT
__ Discounts
__ Prompt & Satisfactory
 X Prompt to 10 Days Slow
__ Pays on Account
__ Asks for More Time
__ Slow but Collectible
__ Accepts COD's Promptly
__ Settles by Trade Acceptance
__ Notes Paid at Maturity
__ Account Secured

35 Average Days Paid

Information Given By: Jack A. Deadbeat, Credit Mgr. Date 05/26/96

WE REQUEST THE RETURN OF THIS FORM TO FACILITATE OUR SYSTEM OF FILING REPORT.

New Deal Products Inc.
235 St. Patrick Drive
Rochester, TX 77653
PHONE (713) 555-2810
FAX   (713) 555-2932

CREDIT INQUIRY

*Gasket Maker Company Inc.   REF: First Choice Company Inc.
*1345 Giveup Street   Rt. 99 North
*Runmedown, TX 77643   Blockage, IL 60606

The above-referenced company has given your concern's name as a credit reference.
Please provide us with your experience with them so that we may determine their credit
worthiness. Please fax this information back to us as soon as possible. Thank you in
advance for the information that you provide and be assured that it will be kept
confidential.

Sincerely,

 I. M. Tracer
Credit Department

Sold From 1990   MANNER OF PAYMENT
                                              X Discounts
Terms of Sales 1% 10 Net 30   ___ Prompt & Satisfactory
                                             ___ Prompt to __ Days Slow
Largest Amount Now Owing $30,000   ___ Pays on Account
                                             ___ Asks for More Time
Amount Past Due $500   ___ Slow but Collectible
                                             ___ Accepts COD's Promptly
Recent Trend Toward X Promptness   ___ Settles by Trade Acceptance
                    __ Slowness   ___ Notes Paid at Maturity
Makes Unjust Claims (State) _____   ___ Account Secured
_____
_____
Credit Refused (State Cause) _____
_____
_____
Remarks: _____   10 Average Days Paid
_____

Information Given By: I. M. Mean, Credit Manager   Date 05/26/96

WE REQUEST THE RETURN OF THIS FORM TO FACILITATE OUR SYSTEM OF
FILING REPORT.

New Deal Products Inc.
235 St. Patrick Drive
Rochester, TX 77653
PHONE (713) 555-2810
FAX   (713) 555-2932

CREDIT INQUIRY

*Rubber U.S.A. Inc.   REF: First Choice Company Inc.
*1569 Lowdown Varmit Highway   Rt. 99 North
*Rolloverme, TX 77543   Blockage, IL 60606

The above-referenced company has given your concern's name as a credit reference.
Please provide us with your experience with them so that we may determine their credit
worthiness. Please fax this information back to us as soon as possible. Thank you in
advance for the information that you provide and be assured that it will be kept
confidential.

Sincerely,

I. M. Tracer
Credit Department

Sold From 1993   MANNER OF PAYMENT
                                             ___ Discounts
Terms of Sales _____ Net 30 _____   ___ Prompt & Satisfactory
                                             _X_ Prompt to 10 Days Slow
Largest Amount Now Owing $75,000   ___ Pays on Account
                                             ___ Asks for More Time
Amount Past Due $1,000   ___ Slow but Collectible
                                             ___ Accepts COD's Promptly
Recent Trend Toward X Promptness   ___ Settles by Trade Acceptance
                    __ Slowness   ___ Notes Paid at Maturity
Makes Unjust Claims (State) _____   ___ Account Secured
_____
_____

Credit Refused (State Cause) _____
_____
_____

Remarks: _____   40 Average Days Paid
_____

Information Given By: Rank Amateur, Credit Manager   Date 05/26/96

WE REQUEST THE RETURN OF THIS FORM TO FACILITATE OUR SYSTEM OF
FILING REPORT.

First Choice Company Inc.
Rt. 99 North
Blockage, IL 60606

SIC 5085

$3,868,310.00
$605,673.00

ACCOUNT # 123456

	12/31/95				12/31/94				12/31/93			
	$	% Change	% Assets	Ind % Assets	$	% Change	% Assets	Ind % Assets	$	% Change	% Assets	Ind % Assets
Cash	$247,675.00	6.77	19.03	4.70	$231,971.00	23.12	18.04	5.10	$188,406.00	100.00	16.24	8.80
Accounts Receivable	$427,247.00	32.69	32.83	34.30	$321,980.00	0.98	25.04	31.80	$318,866.00	100.00	27.49	30.80
Inventory	$501,425.00	-17.92	38.53	30.10	$610,917.00	17.30	47.52	29.00	$520,823.00	100.00	44.89	28.00
Due from Shareholder	$0.00	0.00	0.00	---	$0.00	0.00	0.00	---	$0.00	0.00	0.00	---
Due From Affiliate	$0.00	0.00	0.00	---	$0.00	0.00	0.00	---	$0.00	0.00	0.00	---
Other Current	$4,834.00	67.44	0.37	1.00	$2,887.00	-93.66	0.22	1.20	$45,571.00	100.00	3.93	0.80
Total Current	$1,181,181.00	1.15	90.77	70.10	$1,167,755.00	8.76	90.83	67.10	$1,073,666.00	100.00	92.55	68.40
Fixed Assets	$72,033.00	-19.56	5.54	21.10	$89,546.00	35.70	6.97	24.20	$65,987.00	100.00	5.69	24.50
Notes Receivable	$0.00	0.00	0.00	---	$0.00	0.00	0.00	---	$0.00	0.00	0.00	---
Deposits	$0.00	0.00	0.00	---	$0.00	0.00	0.00	---	$0.00	0.00	0.00	---
Cash Value of Life Insur.	$48,069.00	69.65	3.69	7.90	$28,335.00	38.28	2.20	6.50	$20,491.00	100.00	1.77	4.70
Intangible Assets	$0.00	0.00	0.00	0.90	$0.00	0.00	0.00	2.20	$0.00	0.00	0.00	2.40
Total Assets	$1,301,283.00	1.22	100.00	100.00	$1,285,636.00	10.82	100.00	100.00	$1,160,144.00	100.00	100.00	100.00
Account Payable	$321,325.00	-7.43	24.69	18.20	$347,109.00	43.65	27.00	17.90	$241,640.00	100.00	20.83	15.20
Bank Loans + N.P.	$119,000.00	14.08	9.14	10.80	$104,311.00	-19.87	8.11	11.00	$130,177.00	100.00	11.22	9.10
Cur. Mat.-L.T.D.	$24,176.00	-4.66	1.86	5.20	$25,357.00	86.39	1.97	6.20	$13,604.00	100.00	1.17	6.70
Income Tax Payables	$1,414.00	-63.17	0.11	0.10	$3,839.00	-10.35	0.30	0.90	$4,282.00	100.00	0.37	0.50
Accrued Expenses	$9,033.00	1.06	0.69	6.40	$8,938.00	-27.33	0.70	4.70	$12,299.00	100.00	1.06	8.30
Total Current	$474,948.00	-2.98	36.50	40.70	$489,554.00	21.78	0.00	40.70	$402,002.00	100.00	34.65	39.80
Long Term Debt	$220,662.00	3.53	16.96	12.30	$213,145.00	5.66	16.58	12.20	$201,725.00	100.00	17.39	11.10
Deferred Taxes	$0.00	0.00	0.00	0.10	$0.00	0.00	0.00	0.60	$0.00	0.00	0.00	0.40
All Other L.T. Debt	$0.00	0.00	0.00	0.00	$0.00	0.00	0.00	0.90	$0.00	0.00	0.00	2.70
Net Worth	$605,673.00	3.90	46.54	46.90	$582,937.00	4.77	45.34	45.60	$556,417.00	100.00	47.96	46.00
Total Liab & Equity	$1,301,283.00	1.22	100.00	100.00	$1,285,636.00	10.82	61.92	100.00	$1,160,144.00	100.00	100.00	100.00
Net Sales	$3,868,310.00	3.20	100.00	100.00	$3,748,239.00	13.10	100.00	100.00	$3,313,955.00	100.00	100.00	100.00
Cost of Goods Sold	$2,887,467.00	3.33	74.64	70.00	$2,794,406.00	13.70	74.55	68.10	$2,457,705.00	100.00	74.16	66.70
Gross Profit	$980,843.00	2.83	25.36	30.00	$953,833.00	11.40	25.45	31.90	$856,250.00	100.00	25.84	33.30
Depreciation	$22,970.00	-0.09	0.59	---	$22,991.00	6.94	0.61	---	$21,498.00	100.00	0.65	---
Lease Payments	$0.00	0.00	0.00	---	$0.00	0.00	0.00	---	$0.00	0.00	0.00	---
Other Operating Exps.	$914,970.00	4.10	23.65	29.00	$878,961.00	12.12	23.45	---	$783,928.00	100.00	23.66	---
Tot. Operating Exps.	$937,940.00	3.99	24.25	---	$901,952.00	11.98	24.06	28.10	$805,426.00	100.00	24.30	25.10
Operating Profit	$42,903.00	-17.30	1.11	1.00	$51,881.00	2.08	1.38	3.70	$50,824.00	100.00	1.53	8.20
Interest Inc./(Exp.)	($3,877.00)	-71.42	-0.10	0.00	($13,567.00)	-41.83	-0.36	0.70	($23,323.00)	100.00	-0.70	1.50
G/(L) on sale of Fxd Assets	$0.00	0.00	0.00	---	$0.00	0.00	0.00	---	$0.00	0.00	0.00	---
Profit Before Taxes	$39,026.00	1.86	1.01	0.90	$38,314.00	39.32	1.02	3.00	$27,501.00	100.00	0.83	6.70
Taxes	$16,290.00	38.12	0.42	---	$11,794.00	10.59	0.31	---	$10,665.00	100.00	0.32	---
Net Profit	$22,736.00	-14.27	0.59	---	$26,520.00	57.52	0.71	---	$16,836.00	100.00	0.51	---
Other Data:												
Working Capital	$706,233.00	4.13	54.27	29.40	$678,201.00	0.97	90.83	26.40	$671,664.00	100.00	57.89	28.60
Tangible Equity	$605,673.00	3.90	46.54	46.00	$582,937.00	4.77	45.34	43.40	$556,417.00	100.00	47.96	43.60
Recommended Credit Limit:	$81,160.18	14.12	---	---	$71,118.31	22.90	---	---	$57,867.37	---	---	---

First Choice Company Inc.
Rt. 99 North
Blockage, IL 60606

RATIOS

Ratio	Unit	12/31/95 Value	12/31/95 % Change	12/31/95 UQ	12/31/95 Med	12/31/95 LQ	12/31/94 Value	12/31/94 % Change	12/31/94 UQ	12/31/94 Med	12/31/94 LQ	12/31/93 Value	12/31/93 % Change	12/31/93 UQ	12/31/93 Med	12/31/93 LQ
SOLVENCY																
Current Ratio	($)	2.49	4.26	2.40	1.70	1.20	2.39	-10.69	2.40	1.80	1.30	2.67	100.00	2.30	1.80	1.30
Quick Ratio	($)	1.42	-17.89	1.50	0.80	0.50	1.13	-10.33	1.30	0.90	0.80	1.26	100.00	1.50	1.00	0.60
Net Profit B4 Tax + Depr./Cur LTD	(X)	2.56	6.07	2.60	1.00	0.00	2.42	-32.88	3.80	2.10	0.50	3.60	100.00	7.30	3.30	1.30
Sales to Fixed Assets	(X)	53.70	274.04	35.30	16.90	10.20	14.36	-71.41	17.50	11.10	7.80	50.22	100.00	38.80	14.30	4.80
Sales to Total Assets	(X)	2.97	1.96	3.50	2.80	2.60	2.92	2.06	3.00	2.60	1.90	2.86	100.00	2.90	2.40	1.50
Total Liab. to NW	(X)	1.15	-4.72	0.70	1.00	2.20	1.21	11.10	0.80	1.20	2.20	1.09	100.00	0.60	1.80	3.30
Fixed Assets to NW	(%)	0.12	-22.58	0.20	0.50	1.10	0.15	29.53	0.30	0.50	0.90	0.12	100.00	0.20	0.50	1.10
Tot. Liab. to Tot. Assets	(%)	53.46	-2.20	N/A	N/A	N/A	54.66	5.03	N/A	N/A	N/A	52.04	100.00	N/A	N/A	N/A
Oper. Prof. to Int. Exp.	(X)	11.07	189.38	N/A	N/A	N/A	3.82	75.49	N/A	N/A	N/A	2.18	100.00	N/A	N/A	N/A
Oper Prof+Lease Py to Int Exp+LP	(X)	11.07	189.38	N/A	N/A	N/A	3.82	75.49	N/A	N/A	N/A	2.18	100.00	N/A	N/A	N/A
EFFICIENCY																
Sales to Receivables	(X)	9.05	-22.22	10.30	8.40	7.50	11.64	12.01	9.80	8.20	6.20	10.39	100.00	9.20	7.40	6.40
Days Sales Outstanding	(D)	40	29.03	35	43	49	31	-11.43	37	45	59	35	100.00	40	49	57
Cost of Sales to Inv.	(X)	5.76	25.89	9.30	6.20	5.10	4.57	-3.07	9.30	6.00	3.90	4.72	100.00	9.60	5.50	4.00
Days' Sales in Inventory	(D)	63	-21.25	39	59	72	80	3.90	38	66	91	77	100.00	38	66	91
Sales to Net Working Cap.	(X)	5.48	-0.89	6.30	10.70	30.10	5.53	12.01	5.70	9.70	16.60	4.93	100.00	5.40	8.80	18.00
Cost of Sales/Payables	(X)	8.99	11.62	22.00	10.20	7.20	8.05	-20.85	19.30	9.90	7.00	10.17	100.00	15.10	12.00	9.20
A/P Turnover	(D)	41	-8.89	17	36	51	45	25.00	24	30	40	36	100.00	24	30	40
PROFITABILITY																
Depreciation to Sales	(%)	0.59	-3.19	0.70	1.60	3.10	0.61	-5.45	1.10	2.30	3.10	0.65	100.00	1.30	2.00	3.70
Prof bef Tax to Tot Assets	(%)	3.00	0.63	12.40	7.50	0.00	2.98	25.72	15.70	7.00	0.30	2.37	100.00	19.30	13.70	7.00
Profit before Taxes to TNW	(%)	6.44	-1.97	23.90	16.10	0.00	6.57	32.98	29.80	15.70	2.50	4.94	100.00	65.10	35.40	21.00
OTHER RATIOS NOT AVAILABLE WITH INDUSTRY STANDARDS																
SOLVENCY																
Inv. to Net Work. Capital	(X)	0.71	-21.18	N/A	N/A	N/A	0.90	16.17	N/A	N/A	N/A	0.78	100.00	N/A	N/A	N/A
Current Liab. to NW	(X)	0.78	-6.62	N/A	N/A	N/A	0.84	16.24	N/A	N/A	N/A	0.72	100.00	N/A	N/A	N/A
LT Debt to Tot. Debt & Capital	(%)	16.96	2.29	N/A	N/A	N/A	16.58	-4.66	N/A	N/A	N/A	17.39	100.00	N/A	N/A	N/A
Fixed Assets to LT Debt	(X)	0.33	-21.43	N/A	N/A	N/A	0.42	27.27	N/A	N/A	N/A	0.33	100.00	N/A	N/A	N/A
EFFICIENCY																
Net Sales to NW	(X)	6.39	-0.62	N/A	N/A	N/A	6.43	7.89	N/A	N/A	N/A	5.96	100.00	N/A	N/A	N/A
Net Sales to Inventory	(X)	7.71	25.57	N/A	N/A	N/A	6.14	-3.46	N/A	N/A	N/A	6.36	100.00	N/A	N/A	N/A
Cost of Sales/Working Capital	(X)	4.09	-0.73	N/A	N/A	N/A	4.12	12.57	N/A	N/A	N/A	3.66	100.00	N/A	N/A	N/A
Short Term Loan Turnover	(X)	15.00	7.14	N/A	N/A	N/A	14.00	-26.32	N/A	N/A	N/A	19.00	100.00	N/A	N/A	N/A
LT Liabilities Payback *	($)	$21.53	-10.86	N/A	N/A	N/A	$24.15	-2.33	N/A	N/A	N/A	$24.73	100.00	N/A	N/A	N/A
PROFITABILITY																
Gross Profit on Net Sales	(%)	25.36	-0.35	--	30.00	--	25.45	-1.51	--	31.90	--	25.84	100.00	--	33.30	--
Net Oper Inc on Net Sales	(%)	1.11	-19.57	--	1.00	--	1.38	-9.80	--	3.70	--	1.53	100.00	--	8.20	--
Net Profit on Net Sales	(%)	0.59	-16.90	N/A	N/A	N/A	0.71	39.22	N/A	N/A	N/A	0.51	100.00	N/A	N/A	N/A
Net Prof on Total Assets	(%)	1.75	-15.05	N/A	N/A	N/A	2.06	42.07	N/A	N/A	N/A	1.45	100.00	N/A	N/A	N/A
Tot Assets to Equity	(X)	2.15	-2.58	N/A	N/A	N/A	2.21	5.77	N/A	N/A	N/A	2.09	100.00	N/A	N/A	N/A
Net Prft on Stkhldrs Eqty	(%)	3.75	-17.58	N/A	N/A	N/A	4.55	50.17	N/A	N/A	N/A	3.03	100.00	N/A	N/A	N/A

(X)=TIMES   (D) = DAYS   (%) = PRECENT   ($) = DOLLARS

* IN THOUSANDS

OVERVIEW

The first piece of bright news deals with the liquidity, which is almost as good as the top quartile ($1.42 to $1.00 compared to $1.50 to $1.00 upper quartile and $0.80 to $1.00 to the average). Debt to equity is slightly better than average ($1.15 to $1.00 compared to $1.20 to $1.00) as is DSO (40 days compared to 43 days). A/P turnover is worse than industry average (41 days compared to 36 days), as is inventory turnover (63 days compared to 59 days). All trends are improving except for DSO, which worsened by 5 days. The gross margin is up slightly but worse than industry average; operating profit is down but better than industry average. Net worth also increased slightly.

As for the credit references and report, the three trade references reflect no worse than 10 days slow, and they do discount. High credit was $75,000 with all three trade references reflecting a trend toward promptness. The credit report had high credit up to $150,000 with a lot of prompts but a few 30 and two 60 days past due. The bank has a first lien on everything, and the firm leases the premises. The principals' backgrounds are in line with the work they do for the company. The business was started and has been managed for 11 years by the same three owners. The company has a small working capital line of credit for a medium five-figure balance ($40,000 to $60,000), and the balance is somewhere near the limit.

WHAT OTHER CREDIT PROFESSIONALS THOUGHT

Student One

Now that you have the basics to work with, let us meet the first of our players to this case. Grace C., who works for a pool systems firm, is not happy at being forced to rush a decision. The order is not only higher than the customer has ever had with the firm, but it is higher than any reference that has appeared on the credit report, bank, or trade references. The fact that the margin is high is a major positive. Extending the terms requested would be a direct violation of the Robinson-Patman Act. A truckload shipment such as this one is rarely for a specific order, which eliminates any exemption that could be gained from the act. Since it would be a violation of the law to extend special terms in connection with this order, Grace shot down the special terms.

She is more likely to approve the sale on 30 days terms. The counteroffer that she would propose would be to break up the shipment into three and send one at the end of the next three months. Each would be at terms of 1% 10 days, net 30 days. If this was not acceptable, she would require that a purchase money security interest be taken to secure the shipment. The documents would need to be signed before this could happen, which would mean that the goods would not go out for month end.

Student Two

Robert H. is with a computer software firm. He thought that this order was not doable as is. He concurred with Grace's analysis and added that the time to get an order of this magnitude through was at the beginning of the month. He felt that some additional information would be needed before he could make even a reasonable decision. He would like to know why the bank only gave First Choice a median five-figure working capital line of credit. He also was disturbed by the fact that, even though it was minor, some delinquency did exist. Why had First Choice never approached the company before for an order of this magnitude? While higher discounts are offered for this size shipment, it was not clear why First Choice would want so much product all at once.

He felt that in all likelihood First Choice could not get a standby letter of credit to use as collateral to offer as additional security. He based this assumption on the fact that the bank's working capital line of credit was for an amount far smaller than this order. A personal guarantee from the three owners, while improving the customer's position, would not provide the degree of security needed for this size of credit extension. Without answers to these questions, he felt that he would not be in a position to render a decision.

Student Three

Jo-Ann D. was from an industrial handling equipment manufacturer. She was also not comfortable with this deal. Despite the margin, the financial statistics warranted consideration of the order. The terms that were requested told her that First Choice was looking for a price break on the next three months' worth of orders rather than just filling a particular need of a customer. Even asking for 3% 10 days terms shows that the company does have access to some cash needed to clinch the deal. First Choice's inventory would increase drastically if this amount of goods all went out at once. Jo-Ann decided that she would be receptive to the order after month end if a sufficient down payment was made. She would require 30% down and would give a 2% cash discount for that portion, as it is offered to all customers who are willing to pay cash in advance and 1% 10 days, net 30 for the other 70%. She felt that due to First Choice's fine paying habits and strong financials, security was not needed.

THE FINAL DECISION

Student One

Since Grace C. was willing to approve this only via a third, third, and a third, increasing the credit line was not as big of an issue for her. First Choice currently had a credit limit of $75,000; this would require three shipments of about $67,000 each month, so a limit of about $141,000 would be needed. This was only slightly higher than the highest balance currently extended to the company so approving this limit increase would be reasonable. She would, however, wait until the first third was paid before she made it official.

Student Two

Robert H. felt that he was not in the position to make a decision. When reminded that he was allowed to make suppositions, he decided to do just that. He decided that First Choice's bank extension of the low working capital was due to the lack of a need in the past. Knowing that the company paid us so well, he felt that the reason for the delinquency with others was probably related to a dispute of some kind and the reporting firms had no way to separate out the difference between delinquency and the disputed items.

As to why First Choice never approached us before with such a large order, he felt that it had never wanted to take on that amount of inventory in the past. Now the company must have a very large order that would require it to maintain a larger quantity of stock in hand. Some firms buy on a just-in-time basis, which makes dealing with them more difficult but also more profitable. The potential customer may even request First

Choice to maintain an on-site warehouse that would be readily available to meet its every need. As to First Choice's inability to obtain a standby letter of credit due to the low bank working capital line of credit, this concern could be changed quickly if the bank had always been interested in increasing the line. Getting an increase in its bank line or a letter of credit would take time and would not allow for the shipment to leave at month end. Robert would not release the order until a standby letter of credit for $100,000 was received and would then raise First Choice's limit to $175,000.

Student Three

Jo-Ann D. would not raise the credit limit to $215,000 immediately. She would increase it in three-month intervals of about $50,000 increments to confirm that the company would be in the position to make payments of this size. She believed that if this order went well, First Choice probably would be back for another order of this amount sooner rather than later. While she was receptive to its needs, she was not going to increase the line to a level that could not be handled.

ADVICE TO TOP MANAGEMENT

Now it is time to explain your decision to top management and the customer.

Student One

Grace C. discussed this matter in detail with her boss when he came trotting down with the director of sales on Friday at 4:55 P.M. First she made sure that she indicated that she was very annoyed that sales had never approached her about this order before today. She also emphasized the fact that sales went to her boss and not her, which added insult to injury.

Next she told management about the current high credit with all companies and the bank. While there was a great margin on the deal and First Choice had always paid her company on time, it might have difficulty coming up with so much cash all at once. As to the terms requested, they would violate a federal statute unless we offered them to all customers, which she felt might cause panic buying. She felt that her proposal was the best possible scenario for all concerned, as it kept our balance reasonable. We still get the order and could even offer First Choice the same discount if it committed to taking the three shipments, provided that we offered the same deal to all similar customers.

As to the purchase money security interest, since we would become the largest trade creditor with a balance in excess of the bank's, it is in our best interest to secure the position with at least the inventory that we are selling them. These reasons would also be used to settle any concerns that the customer might have in getting this order approved.

Student Two

Robert H. also was not happy with the director of sales' approach to this order, and he was not happy with his boss for entertaining the idea without referring the director of sales to him directly. Having similar concerns as Grace C., Robert explained that he would not consider shipping the goods until the standby letter of credit was in place. This certainly would not take place until next week, as First Choice would have to get bank approval. He was willing to meet the company halfway by upping the credit limit by $100,000 and asking for only a $100,000 standby letter of credit. Robert advised his boss that without some from of security, we would be taking on a greater risk than the bank and would literally make up over 30% to 40% of First Choice's total inventory. His concern over disputes showing up as delinquency and the worsening of the DSO made it even more important to have some form of collateral available to cover this exposure. Robert would use the same arguments when discussing his decision with the customer.

Student Three

Jo-Ann D.'s attitude was also soured by the way both her boss and the director of sales had acted. She planned to have a private meeting on Tuesday with her boss on the credit manager's role in the firm. She was prepared to settle the deal but would need to receive the 30% in advance of releasing the order. Since she doubted that the customer needed all of that material at that particular minute, it would be easy to convince First Choice that the order would not go out until after she had received the down payment. Jo-Ann's greatest concern was the fact that we were extending credit far in excess of everyone else, including the fully secured bank. She was willing to ship the goods out on an unsecured basis but felt that at least a token payment of 30% was in order.

ACTION PLAN WHEN OVERRIDEN BY MANAGEMENT

How did our group of credit professionals deal with management overriding their decisions?

Student One

Grace C. was not surprised that she had been overridden as it was quarter closing and this order would let her company meet its sales goals for the quarter. Fortunately, it had at least picked a customer that was decent instead of one that was marginal at best. Since this was an unusually high amount of goods to be shipped, she decided to contact the customer some seven days after the shipment went out to remind First Choice of the 3% cash discount that was available on the 10th day after invoice date. She explained that it would be in its best interest to save this amount, as the compounded return on a 3% cash discount was about 54% on an annual basis. This would make it worth the customer's while to increase its line of credit with the bank to cover this discount savings. If this didn't work, she planned to be on the phone at the 85th day from invoice date to make sure that the customer knew that the invoice was due in 5 days. She would even offer to pay the overnight fee to get it there on time.

Student Two

Robert H. was not too concerned about being overridden. He felt that he had made a credit decision; if a business decision needed to be made, it was up to top management to do so and sign off on the approval. He likewise would follow up on the discount and the final due date. In his month-end reports, he would state that one reason why his DSO went up was due to this sale and the 90-day terms that were approved by top management. During the 90 days, he would keep a close watch on his industrial trade credit group report to make sure that no one else was experiencing difficulties in collecting from this customer.

Student Three

Jo-Ann D. was upset not about being overridden but by the way that it was done. She felt that her boss had not supported her by allowing the director of sales to circumvent her by going to him first. It would have been different if the director had gone to her first and she had refused his request and she then decided to meet with both her boss and the director, after briefing her boss prior to the meeting. She was not given the respect she was due. Without her boss's support and backing, there would be no need of a credit department, only a collections department. She said that she would meet with her boss to discuss the problem; if the situation did not improve, she would take it up with his boss. If this had no effect, she would tender her resignation. Assuming that things did improve, she likewise would push the discount and follow up on the 85th day. The industrial trade group was also a solid idea, and she would notify First Choice that she wanted to get quarterly financials as well as year-end ones. She also would put it on watch with her credit-reporting agency to keep tabs on any major changes to its report or rating.

AVOIDING THE SITUATION IN THE FUTURE

How would the three students avoid being stuck in this situation again?

Student One

Grace C. said she would leave at 4:30 P.M. on Friday. I quickly told her that nothing would have changed, they simply would have approved and shipped the order as if she did not even exist. She stated that when the deal blew up, she knew whom she would go to point the finger at. After she stopped laughing, she decided that it would be worth her while to set up a meeting with her boss and the director of sales. The topic of discussion would be order etiquette, how to get orders approved without upsetting the apple cart.

   She would plan on a premeeting with her boss to clarify that his support was critical if they were to control the habitual "end-around" plays of the director of sales and marketing. After they met with that director, she requested that her boss meet with the president and advise him that they would be instituting controls to prevent problems like this from occurring again. At month end, noon would be the cut-off time for processing orders for shipments. This would allow credit to make any last-minute negotiations to prevent problems in the future with collecting the receivable. Regardless of whether month-end numbers were reached or not, no further deals could be run through the system after noon. Her boss should also request that the president insist that sales be pushed more at the beginning of the month rather than the end, as it would improve cash flow and allow more time for the company to prevent mistakes that cause deductions from returns due to defective product. The boss should explain to the president that it is rare that all customers who place orders place them at their month end; so why should they ship all orders at month end?

Student Two

Robert H. suggested that he would simply take the day off and go golfing. After this, he felt it would help to determine just how much business is done on both the last week and the last day. He would then chart the time for receipt of cash compared to how the average customer pays. The chart would show how the company could improve both cash flow and DSO results if a policy were instituted requiring the balancing of shipment of orders over the entire month rather than just during the last few days. Computing this for a period covering the previous year, he would show that by changing the dates goods went out the door, a major drop in DSO and increase in cash flow would have occurred if that policy had already been in effect.

The additional cash flow that would have resulted could have been invested and obtained higher profits or interest savings by paying down debt for that year. He would send this information to his boss with a recommendation that he and the president institute a policy that all orders become uniform with the needs of the customers, and that sales does not try to score a touchdown at month end on a "Hail Mary" pass.

Student Three

Having had problems with this very issue in the past, Jo-Ann D. said she would arrange a meeting of the sales and marketing staff and the credit staff and open a brainstorming session to smooth out problems between their respective departments. She would ask her boss and the director of sales and marketing to attend so that they could help to enforce the end results of this meeting. The topics of discussion would include order timing, new orders, processing new customers, delinquent customers, deduction problems, and communication between departments.

The minutes of the meeting would be recorded and any policy decided upon would be forwarded to the president for his or her approval. These meetings would be held every two weeks in order to prevent problems of month-end shipments from recurring.

WHAT REALLY HAPPENED

Now we get to see how events really did play out. It was quarter closing and it was 4:30 P.M. when the crowd arrived in my office. I listened in amusement to the long story of how this great deal had been in the works for months but finally broke just a few minutes ago.

I had spoken to Biff Block, the president of First Choice, recently, trying to get him to overnight a check to help us meet our month-end cash forecast. At that time, he did not mention that any order of this size existed, and Biff never held anything back. Hearing about this great coup of the sales department made me just a tad suspicious. At that very moment, Biff chose to call me to discuss this order. When I asked him how long ago had he been approached about this order, he said 10, maybe 15 minutes earlier. I asked him to hold for a minute, quickly put him on the speakerphone, and asked him to repeat that for the benefit of my boss and the director of sales.

Biff repeated what he had told me and asked if I knew anything about it. After my boss turned bright red and the director of sales shrank to about the size of an ant, I advised Biff that this was the first time that I had heard of it. Biff stated that he would like to work out the deal as it was a good price for the goods but would probably not be ordering much over the next three months. I asked Biff if I could call him back in about five minutes to work out the final details.

Turning to my boss, I smiled and stated that this whole thing did not surprise me at all and that if the director of sales had approached me first, I would have tried to make the deal a little doable. My boss turned to the director of sales and advised him that he had every intention of meeting with the president to discuss the debacle. I knew that this was not what the director of sales wanted to hear and was worried that he might be fired. I interrupted my boss's verbal thrashing to say that we might still save the sale if they needed it for month end.

The one point I wanted to make clear was that by shipping this order now, they would be making today's goal by robbing from future sales, which would mean that they would have to find another source to replace this order. With that dealt with, I advised my boss to table his actions against the director of sales until after I spoke with Biff and him later. My boss, still enraged, agreed but wanted this settled by 5:00 P.M. that day in his office. The director of sales, still very nervous, asked what he should do. I advised him that I would meet with him in my boss's office at 5:30.

He left rather downtrodden and I started to gear up. I immediately called Biff and advised him that we could not give him the 3% 10 days, net 90 days terms that he requested. I could, however, offer him a 2% cash discount on any part that he could come up with now by wire transfer and 1% 10 days, net 30 days on the remaining balance. The special price would remain in effect, and we would pass on the savings we got on shipping the goods out in by truckload rather than smaller shipments over the next three months. I also advised him that we would pay the wire fee for sending the money. He stated that he could wire $100,000 and pay the balance in 10 days.

This was acceptable and I provided all the necessary information for him to send the wire transfer to our bank. I asked that he call my assistant back when the transfer was complete. (Note that he was on Central Time and was able to still do the wire transfer.) This gave us early cash flow on half the order, a better DSO, and we still met our sales goals for the month. Before hanging up, I asked Biff if he really intended not to buy anything in the next three months. He said that he had these goods already sold but did not want to have the director of sales trying to push even more goods down his throat.

When I left my office to meet with my boss, I decided that it was time to get the sales department and the credit department working together rather than against each other. My boss was still fuming over the whole incident. After I told him what had transpired, he appeared quite pleased. Despite all of this, he was not through with the director of sales. I told him that if he got that director of sales fired, we would just start all over again with another salesperson and end up going three steps backward. I proposed that we give the director of sales an ultimatum that each week sales and credit would meet, discuss new and pending orders, delinquency and deduction problems, and ways to resolve them.

The credit manager would be present at all sales meetings and a more consistent shipping schedule would be worked out for orders. The outflow of shipments should be spaced out evenly each week so the company could benefit from an improved cash flow and DSO as well as meeting sales objectives. The director of sales would be the force behind keeping this level of cooperation intact and would be responsible for dealing with anyone who did not work well with the credit staff. My boss, obviously pleased with this suggestion, asked when we would break the news to the director of sales. At that point there was a knock at my boss's door.

After the proposal was laid out and the director of sales balked, my boss promptly reminded him that I had saved his job. Not only did I get him his precious order but I gave the company better cash flow and DSO, enabled us to meet our sales goal, and requested that my boss not go to the president over this incident. The director of sales was floored by this and asked why I had helped him. I replied that cooperation and communication made companies successful and if he promoted those attributes from his side, we both could do well in the company. The director of sales shook my hand, thanked me for my help, and said that the first meeting would be held next Friday.

CONCLUSION

The moral of this story is that you get more cooperation by saving a drowning person than by holding his head under water. With this in mind, let us move on to case study 7.

11

CASE STUDY 7: PERFECT IMAGE SUPPLIES, INC.

Addressing a Customer with an Overbearing Attitude

INTRODUCTION

This case provides techniques for handling difficult customers. Readers will learn how to deal with many types of personalities and dispositions and compare and match up countermethods in dealing with difficult behavioral problems. The students discuss the art of negotiating with difficult, egotistical individuals in the case. The goal is to minimize the potential for loss while still confirming the sale. The case has students play devil's advocate to hone their ability to bring home a done deal.

By reviewing this real day in the life of a credit department, readers will learn to make effective use of data, facts, and alternative methods in reaching a decision. An appreciation for how other people in marketing or finance think will hone negotiating skills. Readers can use new insight into the creation of a sound business credit decision to prevent gaps or weaknesses in their decision-making processes.

Case study 7 uses the five "C's" of credit to direct answers to questions. Unlike the past cases, this one delves into the people aspect of those who run the company rather than just the financial and credit issues that surround every credit decision. Our group of three will have to address issues that deal with getting along with unruly customers as well as how attitude can affect a firm's profitability.

THE FACTS

I.B. Strict, the corporate credit manager for Locktight Seals Company, the world's leader in rubber gasket manufacturing, is reviewing a new account with his credit analyst, Jane Dough. The customer, Perfect Images Supplies Inc. (a Subchapter "S" corporation), has been in business since 1955. It has good financials for a company of its size. Perfect Images is a top distributor in its region, controlling nearly 75% of the market, and has had great success in areas that Locktight could not penetrate.

Locktight's product would replace Perfect Image's largest current supplier of rubber gaskets and Locktight's number-two competitor in the industry. If Locktight agrees to sign them on, it would become one of Perfect Images' top 15 suppliers. Anticipated additional sales for Locktight as reflected in the sales manager's report on Perfect Images would be between $3.5 million and $5 million per year, which would be a 3.5 to 5% overall increase. Large sales increases in this very competitive and narrow market are critical to the growth and survival of all of the industry players. Perfect Image's paying habits are good, taking some larger discounts when offered and paying nearly at terms when only net is offered. The initial order placed by Perfect Images is for $1 million to be shipped complete in the next 30 days. Locktight's margin on the order is 35%, which is good to average for the industry. Terms of 2% 30 net 60 for the first purchase are being asked. Locktight's standard terms of sale are 1% 10 net 30 days. A check with some members of their national industry credit trade group reveals that Perfect Image's owner, Arnold Stopgap, has a demanding, sometimes overbearing, attitude toward suppliers and employees. As a result the company has just lost its two top salespeople, and there is a rumor that they took some business with them. Perfect Image has a large contract with a Fortune 50 company that will be up for renewal in two months, and one of the salespeople who left was the Fortune 50's account rep. This customer represents some 30% of the total sales. A credit report and financial analysis are available for review.

INSTRUCTIONS

1. Analyze capital: Discuss the firm's creditworthiness based on the above information, credit report, references, and the financial analyses report provided. Use trend analysis, common-size analysis, ratio analysis, and comparison to industry standards to help justify your decision.

2. Analyze market conditions: Discuss the facts available on the condition of the market, profitability, and other factors that could affect a credit decision.

3. Analyze character and management capacity: How does the company's background and management style affect the credit decision? What factors do you consider important? Is more investigation needed and if so what?

4. Analyze collateral: Is this a factor to be considered? Will you need it? If so, how do you justify it to the customer, its bank, and your company's officials?

5. Summarize your findings; use these to formulate and justify a course of action. Be complete, creative, and specific.

6. What facts would you use to defend your decision to management and to the customer?

7. If overridden by management, what steps would you take to prevent a possible loss?

CREDIT REPORT

FILE #123456789   DATE PRINTED   SUMMARY
                                   MAY 23, 1996   RATING   3A2
PERFECT IMAGE SUPPLIES INC.   STARTED   1955
640 DOWNHILL ROAD   DIST GASKETS   SALES $141,286,300
STIFF CITY, NY 14609   WORTH $8,841,900
  TEL: 716 555-9000   SIC NO.   HISTORY CLEAR
                                   50 84   CONDITION GOOD

CHIEF EXECUTIVE: ARNOLD STOPGAP, PRES.

PAYMENTS (Amounts may be rounded to nearest figure in prescribed ranges)
REPORTED

	PAYING RECORD	HIGH CREDIT	NOW OWES	PAST DUE	SELLING TERMS	LAST SALE WITHIN
4/96	Ppt	25000	250	-0-		1 Mo
	Slow 15	25000	15000	10000		1 Mo
3/96	Disc	10000	5000	-0-		
	Ppt	250	-0-			6-12 Mos
	Ppt	50	50	-0-	N30	1 Mo
	Ppt-Slow 10	85000	55000	40000	N30	1 Mo
	Ppt-Slow 10	5000	5000	1000	N30	1 Mo
	Slow 15	2500	100			6-12 Mos
	Slow 15	1000	1000			4-5 Mos
	Slow 15	250	-0-			4-5 Mos
	Slow 15	5000	-0-	-0-	N30	4-5 Mos
	Ppt	2500	2500	-0-	N30	
	Ppt	250	-0-	-0-		2-3 Mos
2/96	Ppt	250000	-0-	-0-	N15	2-3 Mos
	Ppt	75000			N30	
	Ppt	500	500	-0-	N15	1 Mo
	Ppt	250	250	-0-		2-3 Mos
	Ppt-Slow 10	2500	750	250	N30	1 Mo
	Ppt-Slow 15	500	-0-	-0-	N30	4-5 Mos
1/96	Disc	10000	-0-	-0-	1 Prox N30	
	Ppt	60000	10000	-0-		1 Mo
	Ppt-Slow 10	250	250	250	N30	2-3 Mos
12/95	Disc	300000	10000	-0-	1 10 N30	1 Mo
	Ppt-Slow 15	500	500	500		1 Mo
	Slow 15	15000	2500	500		1 Mo
	Slow 15	100	-0-	-0-		6-12 Mos
	Slow 10-15	2500	2500	2500		
11/95	Ppt	50000	2000	-0-		1 Mo
	Ppt	5000	-0-	-0-	N30	6-12 Mos
	Ppt	5000				

	Ppt-Slow 10	100	-0-	-0-	1 Mo
10/95	Ppt	10000	5000	-0-	1 Mo

* Payment experiences reflect how bills are met in relation to the terms granted. In some instances payment beyond terms can be the result of disputes over merchandise, skipped invoices, etc.

* Each experience shown represents a separate account reported by a supplier. Updated trade experiences replace those previously reported.

FINANCE
* Financial information is attached for your review. Good condition is indicated based on debt to net worth. Sales for 1996 were forecasted to be $150,000,000.

PUBLIC FILINGS
UCC FILINGS
4/15/95
   Financing statement #984345 filed 9/11/93 with Secretary, State of N.Y. Debtor Perfect Image Supplies Inc., Stiff City, NY, Secured Party: All Secured Bank, NA, Watertown, NY.

Collateral: Accounts receivable, inventory, all other fixed assets.

HISTORY
4/15/96
   ARNOLD L. STOPGAP, PRES.
   JACK L. STOPGAP, V. PRES.
   BARRY R. STOPGAP, TREAS.
   DIRECTOR(S): The officer(s)

INCORPORATED New York January 20, 1955

Authorized capital consists of 500,000 shares Common Stock, $100 par value.

Business started 1955 by Arnold G. Stopgap 100% of capital is owned by Arnold L. Stopgap.

Arnold L. Stopgap born 1935, married 1960. started here in 1962. He is the son of founder and is now president

PERFECT IMAGE SUPPLIES INC.   May 23, 1996   PAGE 003

    Jack L. Stopgap born 1961, single. Graduate Jackson University, Wheatland, NY 1983. 1983–Present: Vice President here and continues.

    Barry R. Stopgap born 1961. Brother of Jack. Active here since 1985.

OPERATION
4/15/96
    Distributes gaskets (100%)

    Terms 1/10 Net 30 days. Has 25,000 accounts. Sells to industrial accounts. Territory: New York, Pennsylvania, and international. Nonseasonal.

    EMPLOYEES: 300 including officers. 275 employed here.

    FACILITIES: Owns 100,000 sq. ft. in 1-story concrete block building in good condition. Premises neat.

    LOCATION: Suburban business section on side street.

FULL DISPLAY COMPLETE

Locktight Seals Company
235 St. Patrick Drive
Rochester, NY 14623
FAX#: (716) 555-2932

BANK CREDIT INQUIRY

All Secured Bank, NA
235 St. Patrick Drive
Watertown, NY 14623
(716) 555-2810

Ref: Perfect Image Supplies Inc.
640 Downhill Road
Stiff City, NY 14609

The above-referenced company has given your concern's name as a credit reference. Please provide us with your experience with them so that we may determine their credit worthiness. Please fax this information back to us as soon as possible. Thank you in advance for the information that you provide and be assured that it will be kept confidential.

Sincerely,

I. B. Strict
Credit Department

If business is not incorporated, please provide owners' name & address:

SAVINGS ACCOUNT   LOW __   MEDIUM __   HIGH __ $__ FIGURE ___
OPEN ___   CLOSED ___

CHECKING ACCOUNT   LOW __   MEDIUM X_   HIGH __ $ 6_ FIGURE
SATISFACTORY X__   UNSATISFACTORY ___

CREDIT EXPERIENCE

Loans are granted: Frequently ___   Occasionally ___   Seldom _X

Type: Working Capital _X_ Mortgage __ Installment ___

Maximum Credit Extended $ Med 7 Figures_ Secured _X_ Unsecured ___

Present Outstandings: Secured $Med 7 Figures_ Unsecured $_____

Relationship: SATISFACTORY X__   UNSATISFACTORY____

Have "NSF" checks been issued: Yes ___   No X

Prepared By: I. M. Loose,_____   Title: Ex. Vice President

Locktight Seals Company
235 St. Patrick Drive
Rochester, NY 14623
PHONE (716) 555-2810
FAX   (716) 555-2932

CREDIT INQUIRY

*Pump Components U.S.A., Inc.   REF: Perfect Image Supplies Inc.
*1136 Fallinarut Way   640 Downhill Road
*Skyhigh, ME 33659   Stiff City, NY 14609

The above-referenced company has given your concern's name as a credit reference.
Please provide us with your experience with them so that we may determine their credit
worthiness. Please fax this information back to us as soon as possible. Thank you in
advance for the information that you provide and be assured that it will be kept
confidential.

Sincerely,

  I.B. Strict
Credit Department

Sold From _1984_____   MANNER OF PAYMENT
                                      _X_ Discounts
Terms of Sales _2% 10, Net 30__   ___ Prompt & Satisfactory
                                      ___ Prompt to __ Days Slow
Largest Amount Now Owing $300,000   ___ Pays on Account
                                      ___ Asks for More Time
Amount Past Due $0_____   ___ Slow but Collectible
                                      ___ Accepts COD's Promptly
Recent Trend Toward _X_Promptness   ___ Settles by Trade Acceptance
                    __ Slowness   ___ Notes Paid at Maturity
Makes Unjust Claims (State) _____ ___ Account Secured
_____
_____
Credit Refused (State Cause) _____
_____
_____
Remarks: _____   _10_ Average Days Paid
_____
_____
Information Given By: _Ken I. Think, Credit Manager_ Date _5/26/96_

WE REQUEST THE RETURN OF THIS FORM TO FACILITATE OUR SYSTEM OF
FILING REPORT.

Locktight Seals Company
235 St. Patrick Drive
Rochester, NY 14623
PHONE (716) 555-2810
FAX   (716) 555-2932

CREDIT INQUIRY

*Rubber Components Inc.   REF: Perfect Image Supplies Inc.
*2235 Fallonface Way   640 Downhill Road
*Deadend, MI 55699   Stiff City, NY 14609

The above-referenced company has given your concern's name as a credit reference.
Please provide us with your experience with them so that we may determine their credit
worthiness. Please fax this information back to us as soon as possible. Thank you in
advance for the information that you provide and be assured that it will be kept
confidential.

Sincerely,

  I.B. Strict
Credit Department

Sold From _1988_____   MANNER OF PAYMENT
                                     _X_ Discounts
Terms of Sales __1% 10, Net 30__   ___ Prompt & Satisfactory
                                     ___ Prompt to __ Days Slow
Largest Amount Now Owing $100,000   ___ Pays on Account
                                     ___ Asks for More Time
Amount Past Due $0_____   ___ Slow but Collectible
                                     ___ Accepts COD's Promptly
Recent Trend Toward _X_Promptness   ___ Settles by Trade Acceptance
                    __ Slowness   ___ Notes Paid at Maturity
Makes Unjust Claims (State) _____ ___ Account Secured
_____
_____

Credit Refused (State Cause) _____
_____
_____

Remarks: _____   _12_ Average Days Paid
_____

Information Given By: _Ken I. Act, Credit Manager__ Date _5/26/96_

WE REQUEST THE RETURN OF THIS FORM TO FACILITATE OUR SYSTEM OF
FILING REPORT.

Locktight Seals Company
235 St. Patrick Drive
Rochester, NY 14623
PHONE (716) 555-2810
FAX   (716) 555-2932

CREDIT INQUIRY

*Steel Parts Now Inc.
*8935 Nowork Way
*Lazyland, CA 99658

REF: Perfect Image Supplies Inc.
640 Downhill Road
Stiff City, IL 14609

The above-referenced company has given your concern's name as a credit reference. Please provide us with your experience with them so that we may determine their credit worthiness. Please fax this information back to us as soon as possible. Thank you in advance for the information that you provide and be assured that it will be kept confidential.

Sincerely,

 I.B. Strict
Credit Department

Sold From 1990

Terms of Sales   1.5% 10, Net 30

Largest Amount Now Owing $250,000

Amount Past Due $0

Recent Trend Toward X Promptness
                     __ Slowness
Makes Unjust Claims (State) _____
_____
_____

Credit Refused (State Cause) _____
_____
_____

Remarks: _____
_____
_____

MANNER OF PAYMENT
 X Discounts
___ Prompt & Satisfactory
___ Prompt to __ Days Slow
___ Pays on Account
___ Asks for More Time
___ Slow but Collectible
___ Accepts COD's Promptly
___ Settles by Trade Acceptance
___ Notes Paid at Maturity
___ Account Secured

 11 Average Days Paid

Information Given By: Ken I. Decide, Credit Manager Date 5/26/96

WE REQUEST THE RETURN OF THIS FORM TO FACILITATE OUR SYSTEM OF FILING REPORT.

Perfect Image Supplies Inc.
640 Downhill Road
Stiff City, NY 14609

SIC 5084

ACCOUNT # 123456

$141,286,300.00
$8,841,900.00

	12/31/95				12/31/94				12/31/93			
	$	% Change	% Assets	Ind % Assets	$	% Change	% Assets	Ind % Assets	$	% Change	% Assets	Ind % Assets
Cash	$79,300.00	16.62	0.24	8.40	$68,000.00	1.95	0.18	7.20	$66,700.00	100.00	0.18	7.50
Accounts Receivable	$13,000,400.00	-21.88	38.89	33.80	$16,640,900.00	14.89	43.85	34.20	$14,484,200.00	100.00	38.74	33.50
Inventory	$12,702,500.00	-7.96	38.00	35.30	$13,800,900.00	6.01	36.36	36.50	$13,018,600.00	100.00	34.82	35.40
Due from Shareholder	$0.00	0.00	0.00	---	$0.00	0.00	0.00	---	$0.00	0.00	0.00	---
Due From Affiliate	$0.00	0.00	0.00	---	$0.00	0.00	0.00	---	$0.00	0.00	0.00	---
Other Current	$318,900.00	21.12	0.95	1.40	$263,300.00	-78.07	0.69	1.30	$1,200,700.00	100.00	3.21	1.70
Total Current	$26,101,100.00	-15.18	78.09	78.90	$30,773,100.00	6.96	81.08	79.20	$28,770,200.00	100.00	76.94	78.10
Fixed Assets	$3,240,200.00	25.87	9.69	14.60	$2,574,200.00	8.03	6.78	14.40	$2,382,900.00	100.00	6.37	14.90
Notes Receivable	$3,539,600.00	-8.58	10.59	---	$3,871,900.00	-26.13	10.20	---	$5,241,800.00	100.00	14.02	---
Deposits	$0.00	0.00	0.00	---	$0.00	0.00	0.00	---	$0.00	0.00	0.00	---
Cash Value of Life Insur.	$0.00	0.00	0.00	5.40	$0.00	0.00	0.00	5.30	$0.00	0.00	0.00	6.40
Intangible Assets	$543,600.00	-26.01	1.63	1.10	$734,700.00	-26.38	1.94	1.10	$998,000.00	100.00	2.67	0.60
Total Assets	$33,424,500.00	-11.93	100.00	100.00	$37,953,900.00	1.50	100.00	100.00	$37,392,900.00	100.00	100.00	100.00
Account Payable	$9,737,600.00	-46.15	29.13	20.50	$18,082,500.00	19.00	47.64	24.80	$15,194,800.00	100.00	40.64	23.10
Bank Loans + N.P.	$8,500,000.00	1,973.17	25.43	11.60	$410,000.00	100.00	1.08	13.50	$0.00	0.00	0.00	14.00
Cur. Mat.-L.T.D.	$0.00	-100.00	0.00	3.20	$3,200,000.00	0.00	8.43	3.60	$3,200,000.00	100.00	8.56	4.40
Income Tax Payables	$0.00	-100.00	0.00	2.30	$164,200.00	100.00	0.43	0.50	$0.00	0.00	0.00	0.30
Accrued Expenses	$3,981,500.00	95.89	11.91	8.90	$2,032,500.00	144.82	5.36	7.10	$830,200.00	100.00	2.22	7.30
Total Current	$22,219,100.00	-6.99	66.48	46.50	$23,889,200.00	24.26	0.00	49.50	$19,225,000.00	100.00	51.41	49.10
Long Term Debt	$0.00	-100.00	0.00	10.50	$1,200,000.00	-73.33	3.16	10.20	$4,500,000.00	100.00	12.03	10.40
Deferred Taxes	$0.00	0.00	0.00	0.10	$0.00	0.00	0.00	0.20	$0.00	0.00	0.00	0.30
All Other L.T. Debt	$2,363,500.00	-45.53	7.07	2.40	$4,339,300.00	-19.18	11.43	2.40	$5,369,200.00	100.00	14.36	1.80
Net Worth	$8,841,900.00	3.71	26.45	40.50	$8,525,400.00	2.73	22.46	37.70	$8,298,700.00	100.00	22.19	38.40
Total Liab & Equity	$33,424,500.00	-11.93	100.00	100.00	$37,953,900.00	1.50	37.06	100.00	$37,392,900.00	100.00	100.00	100.00
Net Sales	$141,286,300.00	6.52	100.00	100.00	$132,633,300.00	4.22	100.00	100.00	$127,259,800.00	100.00	100.00	100.00
Cost of Goods Sold	$88,590,600.00	7.96	62.70	68.20	$82,058,900.00	1.13	61.87	68.70	$81,144,400.00	100.00	63.76	68.50
Gross Profit	$52,695,700.00	4.19	37.30	31.80	$50,574,400.00	9.67	38.13	31.30	$46,115,400.00	100.00	36.24	31.50
Depreciation	$316,500.00	39.61	0.22	---	$226,700.00	-19.78	0.17	---	$282,600.00	100.00	0.22	---
Lease Payments	$0.00	0.00	0.00	---	$0.00	0.00	0.00	---	$0.00	0.00	0.00	---
Other Operating Exps.	$50,681,900.00	5.06	35.87	29.30	$48,241,300.00	4.99	36.37	28.90	$45,948,700.00	100.00	36.11	29.20
Tot. Operating Exps.	$50,998,400.00	5.22	36.10	2.60	$48,468,000.00	4.84	36.54	2.40	$46,231,300.00	100.00	36.33	2.30
Operating Profit	$1,697,300.00	-19.42	1.20	0.40	$2,106,400.00	-1,917.43	1.59	0.60	($115,900.00)	100.00	-0.09	0.90
Interest Inc./(Exp.)	($466,300.00)	-52.33	-0.33	---	($978,100.00)	-31.31	-0.74	---	($1,424,000.00)	100.00	-1.12	---
G/(L) on sale of Fxd Assets	$0.00	0.00	0.00	---	$0.00	0.00	0.00	---	$0.00	0.00	0.00	---
Profit Before Taxes	$1,231,000.00	9.10	0.87	2.20	$1,128,300.00	-173.27	0.85	1.80	($1,539,900.00)	100.00	-1.21	1.40
Taxes	$263,300.00	-52.50	0.19	---	$554,300.00	100.00	0.42	---	$0.00	0.00	0.00	---
Net Profit	$967,700.00	68.59	0.68	---	$574,000.00	-137.28	0.43	---	($1,539,900.00)	100.00	-1.21	---
Other Data:												
Working Capital	$3,882,000.00	-43.61	11.61	32.40	$6,883,900.00	-27.88	81.08	29.70	$9,545,200.00	100.00	25.53	29.00
Tangible Equity	$8,298,300.00	6.52	24.83	39.40	$7,790,700.00	6.71	20.53	36.60	$7,300,700.00	100.00	19.52	37.80
Recommended Credit Limit:	$896,216.40	30.72	---	---	$685,581.60	11.79	---	---	$613,258.80	---	---	---

Perfect Image Supplies Inc.
640 Downhill Road
Stiff City, NY 14609

RATIOS

Ratio	Unit	12/31/95	% Change	UQ	Med	LQ	12/31/94	% Change	UQ	Med	LQ	12/31/93	% Change	UQ	Med	LQ
SOLVENCY																
Current Ratio	($)	1.17	-8.81	2.50	1.70	1.30	1.29	-13.92	2.30	1.60	1.20	1.50	100.00	2.20	1.60	1.20
Quick Ratio	($)	0.59	-117.04	1.40	0.90	0.60	0.70	-7.59	1.20	0.80	0.60	0.76	100.00	1.20	0.80	0.60
Net Profit B4 Tax + Depr./Cur LTD	(X)	0.00	-100.00	3.40	1.40	0.50	0.42	-207.77	4.00	1.50	0.60	-0.39	100.00	3.20	1.30	0.40
Sales to Fixed Assets	(X)	43.60	195.74	64.50	32.70	12.90	14.74	-72.39	74.20	33.30	12.80	53.41	100.00	64.80	32.10	12.60
Sales to Total Assets	(X)	4.23	20.96	3.80	2.70	1.90	3.49	2.68	3.70	2.80	3.30	3.40	100.00	3.70	2.80	2.00
Total Liab. to NW	(X)	2.78	-19.46	0.80	1.60	3.10	3.45	-1.54	0.90	1.70	3.30	3.51	100.00	0.90	1.70	3.60
Fixed Assets to NW	(%)	0.37	21.37	0.10	0.30	0.70	0.30	5.16	0.10	0.30	0.80	0.29	100.00	0.10	0.30	0.80
Tot. Liab. to Tot. Assets	(X)	73.55	-5.15	N/A	N/A	N/A	77.54	-0.35	N/A	N/A	N/A	77.81	100.00	N/A	N/A	N/A
Oper. Prof. to Int. Exp.		3.64	69.02	N/A	N/A	N/A	2.15	-2,745.97	N/A	N/A	N/A	-0.08	100.00	N/A	N/A	N/A
Oper Prof+Lease Py to Int Exp+LP	(X)	3.64	69.02	N/A	N/A	N/A	2.15	-2,745.97	N/A	N/A	N/A	-0.08	100.00	N/A	N/A	N/A
EFFICIENCY																
Sales to Receivables	(X)	10.87	36.35	11.80	8.40	6.80	7.97	-9.29	11.40	8.80	6.80	8.79	100.00	12.00	8.60	6.80
Days Sales Outstanding	(D)	34	-26.09	31	43	54	46	9.52	32	41	54	42	100.00	30	42	54
Cost of Sales to Inv.	(X)	6.97	17.30	10.20	5.70	3.30	5.95	-4.61	9.70	5.60	3.40	6.23	100.00	11.20	5.60	3.20
Days' Sales in Inventory	(D)	52	-14.75	36	64	111	61	3.39	38	65	107	59	100.00	33	65	114
Sales to Net Working Cap.	(X)	36.40	88.90	5.30	8.10	19.50	19.27	44.51	5.60	10.50	24.80	13.33	100.00	6.00	10.30	22.80
Cost of Sales/Payables	(X)	9.10	100.48	23.20	10.30	6.70	4.54	-15.02	15.50	9.30	5.90	5.34	100.00	16.30	9.20	6.10
A/P Turnover	(D)	40	-50.00	16	35	54	80	17.65	24	39	62	68	100.00	22	40	60
PROFITABILITY																
Depreciation to Sales	(%)	0.22	31.06	0.50	1.00	1.80	0.17	-23.03	0.50	0.90	1.70	0.22	100.00	0.60	0.90	1.80
Prof bef Tax to Tot Assets	(%)	3.68	23.89	11.20	4.70	0.60	2.97	-172.19	8.70	3.20	0.80	-4.12	100.00	9.20	3.70	0.30
Profit before Taxes to TNW	(%)	13.92	5.20	29.80	13.30	2.50	13.23	-171.32	24.20	9.70	2.10	-18.56	100.00	25.00	10.30	1.60

		(X)=TIMES			(D) = DAYS		(%) = PRECENT			($) = DOLLARS						

OTHER RATIOS NOT AVAILABLE WITH INDUSTRY STANDARDS

Ratio	Unit	12/31/95	% Change	UQ	Med	LQ	12/31/94	% Change	UQ	Med	LQ	12/31/93	% Change	UQ	Med	LQ
SOLVENCY																
Inv. to Net Work. Capital	(X)	3.27	63.22	N/A	N/A	N/A	2.00	46.99	N/A	N/A	N/A	1.36	100.00	N/A	N/A	N/A
Current Liab. to NW	(X)	2.51	-10.32	N/A	N/A	N/A	2.80	20.96	N/A	N/A	N/A	2.32	100.00	N/A	N/A	N/A
LT Debt to Tot. Debt & Capital	(%)	7.07	-51.54	N/A	N/A	N/A	14.59	-44.71	N/A	N/A	N/A	26.39	100.00	N/A	N/A	N/A
Fixed Assets to LT Debt	(X)	0.00	-100.00	N/A	N/A	N/A	2.15	305.66	N/A	N/A	N/A	0.53	100.00	N/A	N/A	N/A
EFFICIENCY																
Net Sales to NW	(X)	15.98	2.70	N/A	N/A	N/A	15.56	1.50	N/A	N/A	N/A	15.33	100.00	N/A	N/A	N/A
Net Sales to Inventory	(X)	11.12	15.71	N/A	N/A	N/A	9.61	-1.74	N/A	N/A	N/A	9.78	100.00	N/A	N/A	N/A
Cost of Sales/Working Capital	(X)	22.82	91.44	N/A	N/A	N/A	11.92	40.24	N/A	N/A	N/A	8.50	100.00	N/A	N/A	N/A
Short Term Loan Turnover	(X)	35.00	1,650.00	N/A	N/A	N/A	2.00	100.00	N/A	N/A	N/A	0.00	0.00	N/A	N/A	N/A
LT Liabilities Payback *	($)	$1,284.20	-153.52	N/A	N/A	N/A	($2,399.30)	-46.17	N/A	N/A	N/A	($4,457.30)	100.00	N/A	N/A	N/A
PROFITABILITY																
Gross Profit on Net Sales	(%)	37.30	-2.18	--	31.80	N/A	38.13	5.22	--	31.30	--	36.24	100.00	--	31.50	--
Net Oper Inc on Net Sales	(%)	1.20	-24.53	--	2.60	N/A	1.59	-135.54	--	2.40	--	-0.09	100.00	--	2.30	--
Net Profit on Net Sales	(%)	0.68	58.14	N/A	N/A	N/A	0.43	-1,866.67	N/A	N/A	N/A	-1.21	100.00	N/A	N/A	N/A
Net Prof on Total Assets	(%)	2.90	92.05	N/A	N/A	N/A	1.51	-136.65	N/A	N/A	N/A	-4.12	100.00	N/A	N/A	N/A
Tot Assets to Equity	(%)	3.78	-15.09	N/A	N/A	N/A	4.45	-1.20	N/A	N/A	N/A	4.51	100.00	N/A	N/A	N/A
Net Prft on Stkhldrs Eqty	(%)	10.94	62.56	N/A	N/A	N/A	6.73	-136.26	N/A	N/A	N/A	-18.56	100.00	N/A	N/A	N/A

* IN THOUSANDS

OVERVIEW

Let us look at the financial condition and the credit status of this customer. The customer's liquidity has dropped over the last three years and is below the lowest quartile ($0.59 to a $1.00 compared to $0.60 to $1.00). Its DSO, however, has been improving over the last three years and is far better than industry average (34 days compared to 43 days). The debt to net worth has been improving over the last three years but still is only a little better than the lowest quartile ($2.78 to $1.00 compared to $3.10 to $1.00). Inventory turnover has been improving in the same time period and is better than industry average (52 days compared to 64 days).

A/P turnover has improved over the last three years but is worse than industry average (40 days compared to 35 days). Gross profits declined slightly over the last three years but still were better than industry average (37.3% compared to 31.8%). Operating profits also declined over the last three years and were below the industry average (1.2% compared to 2.6%).

The three trade credit references reflect a trend toward promptness, discounts with all three firms are taken, and the high credit is $300,000. The credit report reflects promptness with only minor 15-day delinquency and a high credit balance of $300,000. The bank, once again, holds a first lien on all assets, and the business owns it premises. One man owns 100% of the business. It is family run and in business for 41 years. The bank has a medium seven-figure working capital line of credit with the company with a medium seven-figure balance outstanding ($4 million to $6 million) and it is satisfactory.

To save some time and repetition, I will highlight the main market points that could affect everyone's credit decision. The first point to focus on is that this is a very competitive market and any market movement can have a real impact on the players. Locktight stands to make better-than-average profit on Perfect Images' order if Locktight signs up. If Perfect Images signs on, Locktight will gain new sales totaling between $3.5 to $5 million annually or 3.5 to 5% more sales. Currently Perfect Images controls 75% of its regional market. Its largest customer, a Fortune 50 firm, represents 30% of its total sales. Thus Perfect Images faces a great market and financial risk if this customer is lost, and the contract is up for renewal in two months. Perfect Images wants to place an initial order for $1,000,000 at terms of 2% 30 days, net 60 days, which is different from the industry standard terms of 1% 10 days, net 30 days.

WHAT OTHER CREDIT MANAGERS THOUGHT

As before, let us meet our group of three to discuss their insights into each question thrown at them in the case.

Student One

Paula J. is a credit manager from a multinational electronics firm that deals with many distributors worldwide. The biggest positive in dealing with Perfect Images is the fact that it pays its debts very well and is financially sound. The biggest drawback is its sole owner, who is difficult to get along with. This fact is reflected in the company's recent loss of its two top salespersons, including the one who sold directly to its largest customer. This situation can have a drastic effect on the future orders that Perfect Images can obtain, which in turn reduces its value to Locktight.

One area that needs additional investigation is the whereabouts of the two salespeople who have left Perfect Images. Did they go to work for a competitor? Is it a competitor that buys products from someone other than Locktight?

Student Two

The second student is Cheryl S., the credit manager for a manufacturer of plumbing supplies that sells mainly to distributors. Cheryl emphasized similar points to those of Paula but also was concerned that Perfect Images was a Subchapter "S" corporation. This can be a major drain on cash if the owner needs money to meet tax needs. It is also a family-owned and operated firm, and Arnold Stopgap has never worked outside of the business. Since he appears to have driven off his two top salespeople, the possibility exists that if you are not a Stopgap, you may not last in the firm.

Student Three

Gary M., a credit manager for a manufacturer of pipe fittings that sells to firms very much like Perfect Images, wanted to know why there were problems in dealing with Arnold Stopgap. The best place to obtain information on the attitude problem was from the industrial trade credit group that he is a member of. Since others in his group have been selling to Arnold for years, he felt there might be a way around this problem. The ultimate question that he had for Arnold would be that if he lost the Fortune 50 customer, how did he intend to replace those sales?

WHAT ABOUT COLLATERAL?

Student One

Paula J. felt that due to the attitude factor, the loss of the two top salespersons, and the pending expiration of Perfect Images' contract with its largest customer, collateral may be needed. She would justify this requirement to top management and support the idea, as long as it does not jeopardize getting this new business. She would use all of the reasons stated earlier to clarify why collateral is needed.

Student Two

Cheryl S. thought that collateral was less of a factor in this case than the fact that Locktight may be faced with a major customer that might want to return its entire inventory two months after it signed up. The amount of the initial sale is larger than any shown on the credit report or references received, and Perfect Images is asking not only for extended terms but for a higher cash discount than what is commonly given in the industry. These and the other factors mentioned must be discussed with top management. Cheryl felt that if collateral is needed, she would meet with Arnold personally and discuss all of her concerns before covering any need for collateral.

Student Three

Gary M., on the other hand, felt that in this case, the risk of extending this much credit required that Arnold's bank be involved. Considering that it had a first lien on all assets and are merely trading off our product for that of a competitor, the bank would be less receptive to helping to finance this change. Arnold's attitude will also come to bear when the determination is made as to who needs whom more. Since he owns 75% of the regional market, Locktight needs him more than he needs Locktight. Yet if Perfect Images loses its largest customer in two months, it will not be as big a player in the area.

Convincing top management, Arnold, and Arnold's bank that collateral is needed will be another matter. While the reasons for the need for collateral are clear, as long as Perfect Images is still in business and hope is there that it will continue, no one will be receptive to collateral being required to shore up sales.

RECOMMENDATIONS TO MANAGEMENT

Student One

Paula J. summarizes her findings this way. In order to improve Locktight's position with Perfect Images, she would first require that Perfect Images return all of its inventory to Locktight's competitor except that which is needed to fill current orders. This would increase Perfect Images' need of Locktight. She would then require that Perfect Images sign a UCC-1, taking a second lien against all assets behind the bank. With assets totaling over $33 million and the bank being owed about $6 million, equity does exist even at fire-sale prices. She also would require that Arnold sign a personal guarantee to cover the amount of the credit extension.

In exchange for this, she would have top management sign a policy change that states all new accounts that place a stocking order get credit terms of 2% 30 days, net 60 days. She would address Arnold's objection to providing collateral that he did not have to do for the competitor by pointing out that he just lost his two top salespersons and also may lose his top customer in two months. Locktight's competitor was never in this position, never extended him $1 million in credit at any one time, and never gave him special terms on the first order. She would present this entire program to Arnold in person at his office with the director of sales and marketing in tow.

Student Three

Cheryl S. decided that considering the past payment performance and current financial strengthen, Perfect Images could still weather the loss of its biggest customer. She had no concerns over getting paid for the first order, as she was sure that it would take the cash discount. This would drop Perfect Images from owing Locktight over $1 million to about $350,000. If Perfect Images did lose its top customer, it in all probability would not be returning $1 million in product. Even if it returned enough to cover its current balance, Locktight would still be ahead of the game as it would have successfully sold $1 million in product that it would not have if it did not sign on Perfect Images.

After getting through with the first major order and seeing if Perfect Images loses its major customer, orders would then be handled on a case-by-case basis. As for the terms, she would recommend to top management that it start offering these terms to all new customers for initial stocking orders. This solves any possible problem with the Robinson-Patman Act.

Student Three

Gary M. was less optimistic about the ability of Perfect Images to hang on if it lost its biggest customer. He felt that Locktight needed outside security to cover any shortfalls that could occur if this were to take place. He would opt for a standby letter of credit for $500,000 to cover the first order to expire in three months followed by a $200,000 letter of credit for a year. This would give Locktight at least a 50% coverage on the first order and about 30 to 50% coverage on the limit needed thereafter. After the first year, if all is well, if no payment problems occur, and if the largest customer remains intact, then Perfect Images can drop its standby letter of credit for Locktight.

He would sell this to top management based on the possible loss of the largest customer and the turnover experienced at Perfect Images due to the president's attitude problem. Gary would explain to top management that, if Arnold Stopgap became upset, he could just as easily not pay or try to return large quantities of product. The fact that the company president is a "loose cannon" does not make a long-term relationship a possibility without hedging bets. Gary had talked to the credit manager at his competitor, and she relayed that her company was dropping Perfect Images as a customer (supposition only!). Gary planned to meet with Arnold Stopgap and advise him that it is in his best interest to cooperate, as he may not have a product source if he continues to have an attitude toward working with his vendors. Gary would emphasize the profitability of this order for both companies and the fact that if Arnold does not have materials to sell to his customers, he will not be in business long.

RECOMMENDATIONS IF OVERRIDEN BY MANAGEMENT

Student One

Paula J. was not surprised that top management might override her. When a piece of business this size waltzes in the door, sales and marketing and top management usually dance together. She felt that the best that she could do was to put on her company cap and dance as well. She did plan to be on the phone to Mr. Stopgap on the 26th day from invoice date to remind him of the discount terms and to encourage him to take them. And if he decided not to, she would have the salesperson standing at his door on the 60th day to pick up the check for the $1 million. Once they got past the date for Perfect Images to renew its largest customer and assuming it was successful, she would relax some but she would definitely stay on top of this account.

Student Two

Cheryl S., like Paula, was not surprised at an override. She felt that if she could get top management to agree to the initial terms change as the normal terms offered for all first-stocking orders, there would be no need to have her decision overridden.

Student Three

Gary M. felt that top management was not clear on how much it stood to lose in this case if it overrode his decision. He did, however, decide to be a team player and would watch this company like a hawk. He planned on making a visit up to meet with Arnold Stopgap around the time that the discount due date was up and see if he could leave with a check. He felt that if Arnold knew that he was being monitored closely, he might cooperate. He also planned to require Arnold to fax him a copy of the signed renewed contract with Perfect Images' largest customer. This might help him and top management to sleep at night. If the contract fell through, he would discuss with top management some of the fallout that might occur and prepare for some returns that might hit the docks soon.

WHAT REALLY HAPPENED

In this case, the two top salespeople formerly from Perfect Images had contacted the Locktight director of sales and marketing to see if they could become Locktight distributors. After having a blowout with Arnold Stopgap and knowing that he had mistreated the former customer after they left, they decided to try to take this piece of business away from Perfect Images. Their former largest customer had contacted them first to offer them a job and then decided to offer them a proposition instead.

Locktight had offered to guarantee some credit for them and provide them with some start up capital in exchange for them giving the Fortune 50 customer better service and a steady stream of the product they were buying from Arnold. This company would certainly be good for the order. During the next two months until the contract expired, the two salespeople were setting up their operations. They would be ready to open their doors and service their new, largest customer precisely when it needed to be serviced. Locktight was given the first option to become the new company's supplier and would be given a corporate guarantee by the Fortune 50 company to cover the order. The new company requested regular terms and would come to Locktight's office to work out all details on this order and all future business.

Accepting this arrangement (and a higher margin of 40%), Locktight agreed to set them up as a distributor. As for Arnold, after losing his top customer, his business started to deteriorate and he soon filed Chapter 11 bankruptcy that was later converted to a Chapter 7 liquidation, putting Perfect Images out of business. The new firm started by his two former salespeople has grown to about a $20 million distributor and continues to be a Locktight customer.

CONCLUSION

The moral to this story is that you should always be nice to your greatest asset, your employees.

12

CASE STUDY 8: BASIC NEEDS, INC.

Considering Increased Credit Limits for Existing Customers

INTRODUCTION

This case will provide readers with new insights into the ways to look at old customers. It also will consider what makes an established customer lose its sparkle so that companies do not want to extend additional credit. The chapter discusses ways to overcome the lackluster appearance of some old customers by helping them improve their financial lot in life through the use of financial trend analysis. The student group reviews using a value-added approach to firming up a potentially shaky deal. Readers will scrutinize alternatives to traditional credit terms for soundness, uniqueness, simplicity, and strength of logic. Finally, they will gain a new respect for the steadfastness of established customers and how they support the company's bottom line.

By reviewing this real day in the life of a credit department, readers will learn to make effective use of data, facts, and alternative methods in reaching a decision. An appreciation for how other people in marketing or finance think will hone negotiating skills. Readers can use new insight into the creation of a sound business credit decision to prevent gaps or weaknesses in their decision-making processes.

Case study 8 looks at selling to a marginal customer in a highly competitive industry. Occasionally an order may even be obtained from such a customer at a more profitable margin. Now comes the tough part: how do you grant credit without gambling everything and giving away the house, the car, and your first born? Every credit professional must face these challenges when selling to companies that really represent your profit and are not customers who cover overhead.

While it is easy to sell to customers who never give you any headaches, never pay you slowly, have a solid financial statement, and never want to buy 20 times more than their established credit limit, it is marginal customers who are the reason companies employ credit professionals.

THE FACTS

You have been approached by the marketing manager to increase the credit limit of Basic Needs Inc. from $30,000 to $100,000 to accommodate a large new order for a major manufacturer. This would be new incremental business for your firm as Basic Needs has never sold to this firm before. The total dollar amount of the yearlong order will be $600,000, and competition in your industry has been tough.

Basic Needs has been your customer since April 1988. It pays you on average of 57 days from invoice date. You have allowed it to go as high as $39,000, and its current balance is $20,000. Basic Needs has not officially asked yet but the marketing manager has stated that since this is new business for it and the customer is very demanding, Basic Needs may ask for extended terms to deal with payment time delays by its customer. The gross margin to your company for this $80,000+ order will be 35% with standard terms. Keep in mind that things have been slow due to a recession. Your terms are 1% 10 net 30, and your normal margin on this order is 25%. An updated credit check was done recently and updated financials are available for your review.

INSTRUCTIONS

1. Analyze all data available on the case, summarizing your findings using the following:

    A. Trend analysis, common-size analysis, ratio analysis, and comparison to industry standings

    B. Summarize the information available in the credit report, references, and information available above

2. Will you increase the limit and sell Basic Needs the product on open account, or will you increase the credit limit and sell the product on a secured basis?

3. Will you leave the limit the same but sell the product on open account, or will you leave the limit the same but sell it the product on a secured basis?

4. Will you refuse to ship Basic Needs the order?

5. If the customer asked for extended terms of net 90 or net 120, how would this effect your decision?

6. What facts would you use to defend your decision to management and to the customer?

7. If overridden by management, what steps would you take to prevent a possible loss?

CREDIT REPORT

FILE #: 141236591	DATE PRINTED MAY 30, 1996	SUMMARY RATING ------
BASIC NEEDS (INC.)		STARTED 1981
35 LOCK STREET	WHOLESALES &	PAYMENTS SEE BELOW
AND BRANCHES	MANUFACTURES	SALES Over $2,000,000
OR DIVISION(S)	RUBBER GASKETS	EMPLOYS 8 (6 Here)
STIFF, NY 14923	SIC NO.	HISTORY CLEAR
TEL: (212) 555-1234	5085 3559	

CHIEF EXECUTIVE: ARNOLD FLOPPER, PRES.

PAYMENTS (Amounts may be rounded to nearest figure in prescribed ranges)
REPORTED

	PAYING RECORD	HIGH CREDIT	NOW OWES	PAST DUE	SELLING TERMS	LAST SALE WITHIN
5/96	Ppt	100	-0-	-0-	N30	6-12 Mos
	Ppt-Slow 30	50000	-0-	-0-	N30	6-12 Mos
	Slow 35	5000	5000	5000	N30	1 Mo
4/96	Ppt	250	50	-0-	N15	1 Mo
	Ppt	250	250	-0-	N15	1 Mo
	Ppt-Slow 30	30000	25000	5000	N30	1 Mo
	Ppt-Slow 30	250	-0-	-0-		2-3 Mos
	Slow 5	750	250	100		1 Mo
	Slow 30	5000	-0-	-0-	N30	4-5 Mos
	Slow 30	500	-0-	-0-	N30	1 Mo
	Slow 30	500	-0-	-0-	N30	1 Mo
3/96	Slow 30	7500	-0-	-0-		2-3 Mos
2/96	Ppt-Slow 30	500	-0-	-0-	N30	6-12 Mos

* Payment experiences reflect how bills are met in relation to the terms granted. In some instances payment beyond terms can be the result of disputes over merchandise, skipped invoices, etc.

* Each experience shown represents a separate account reported by a supplier. Updated trade experiences replace those previously reported.

PUBLIC FILINGS
The following data is for information purposes only and is not the official record. Certified copies can only be obtained from the official source.

---

* * * UCC FILING * * *

BASIC NEEDS (INC)   May 30, 1996   PAGE 002

COLLATERAL: Unspecified and proceeds
FILING #:   146238   DATE FILED: 08/11/1990
TYPE: Original   FILED WITH: UCC Commercial
SEC. PARTY: Barnes Leasing Corp.   Recording Division,
               Slippery Rock, IL   NY
DEBTOR: Basic Needs (Inc.)

COLLATERAL: Negotiable instruments - Specified accounts receivable - Chattel
paper - Contract rights - General intangibles and proceeds
FILING #:   15686423   DATE FILED: 07/21/92
TYPE: Original   FILED WITH: Secretary of State
SEC. PARTY: Chase Manhattan Bank NA,   NY
               NY
DEBTOR: Basic Needs (Inc.)

The public record items reported above under "Public Filings" and "UCC Filings" may
have been paid, terminated, vacated or released prior to the date this report was printed.

HISTORY
12/31/95
          Arnold Flopper, Pres   Mary Flopper, Sec-Treas
          Director(s): The Officer(s)

          Business Type: Corporation   Date Incorporated: 11/07/1985
                      Profit   State of Incorp: New York

          Auth Shares - Common: 200
          Par Value -   Common: No par value

          Authorized to do business in New York State 11/07/1985.
          Business started 1981 by Arnold Flopper as a sole proprietorship. 100% of
          capital is owned by Arnold Flopper.

          Arnold Flopper born 1938. 1960–1969 Federal Bureau of Investigation, New
          York, NY Special Agent. 1969–1981Jack's Rubber & Packing Co., Inc.,
          Queen, NY, Treasurer. 1981–present here.

          Mary Flopper born 1940. 1981–present here. Prior to this was a housewife.

OPERATION
12/31/95   Wholesales (distributes) (80%) and Manufactures (20%) rubber gaskets,
rings and non-metallic stamped washers.

Terms are Net 30 days. Has 3,000 accounts. Sells to Manufacturers. Territory:

BASIC NEEDS (INC)   May 30, 1996   PAGE 003

Connecticut, New York, and New Jersey.

Nonseasonal.

Employees: 8 including officers. 6 employed here.

Facilities: Rents 15,000 sq. ft. in a two-story brick building.

Location: Central business section on a side street.

FULL DISPLAY COMPLETE

New Deal Products Inc.
235 St. Patrick Drive
Rochester, TX 77653
FAX#: (716) 555-2932

BANK CREDIT INQUIRY

Chase Manhattan Bank NA
1589 Super Rich Way   Ref: Basic Needs Inc.
New York, TX 10011   35 Lock Street
(212) 555-2810   Stiff, NY 14923

The above-referenced company has given your concern's name as a credit reference.
Please provide us with your experience with them so that we may determine their credit
worthiness. Please fax this information back to us as soon as possible. Thank you in
advance for the information that you provide and be assured that it will be kept
confidential.

Sincerely,

I. M. Tracer
Credit Department

If business is not incorporated, please provide owners' name & address:

SAVINGS ACCOUNT   LOW __   MEDIUM __   HIGH __ $__ FIGURE
                  OPEN ___   CLOSED ___

CHECKING ACCOUNT   LOW _X_   MEDIUM __   HIGH __ $_4_ FIGURE
                   SATISFACTORY _X_   UNSATISFACTORY ___

CREDIT EXPERIENCE

Loans are granted: Frequently _X_ Occasionally ___ Seldom ___

Type: Working Capital _X_ Mortgage __ Installment __

Maximum Credit Extended $Low 5 Figures Secured _X_ Unsecured ___

Present Outstandings: Secured $Low 5 Figures Unsecured $_____

Relationship: SATISFACTORY _X_   UNSATISFACTORY ____

Have "NSF" checks been issued: Yes ___ No _X_

Prepared By: B. A. Badger_____ Title: Vice President

New Deal Products Inc.
235 St. Patrick Drive
Rochester, TX 77653
PHONE (713) 555-2810
FAX   (713) 555-2932

CREDIT INQUIRY

*Sheet Material Company Inc.   REF: Basic Needs Inc.
*1235 Skyhigh Lane   35 Lock Street
*Runuptown, TX 77653   Stiff, NY 14923

The above-referenced company has given your concern's name as a credit reference.
Please provide us with your experience with them so that we may determine their credit
worthiness. Please fax this information back to us as soon as possible. Thank you in
advance for the information that you provide and be assured that it will be kept
confidential.

Sincerely,

 I. M. Tracer
Credit Department

Sold From 1985   MANNER OF PAYMENT
                                         ___ Discounts
Terms of Sales Net 30   ___ Prompt & Satisfactory
                                          X Prompt to 60 Days Slow
Largest Amount Now Owing $20,000   ___ Pays on Account
                                         ___ Asks for More Time
Amount Past Due $18,000   ___ Slow but Collectible
                                         ___ Accepts COD's Promptly
Recent Trend Toward __Promptness   ___ Settles by Trade Acceptance
                     X Slowness   ___ Notes Paid at Maturity
Makes Unjust Claims (State) _____   ___ Account Secured
_____
_____
Credit Refused (State Cause) _____
_____
_____
Remarks: _____   55 Average Days Paid
_____
_____
Information Given By: Jack A. Deadbeat, Credit Mgr. Date 05/26/96

WE REQUEST THE RETURN OF THIS FORM TO FACILITATE OUR SYSTEM OF
FILING REPORT.

New Deal Products Inc.
235 St. Patrick Drive
Rochester, TX 77653
PHONE (713) 555-2810
FAX   (713) 555-2932

CREDIT INQUIRY

*Gasket Maker Company Inc.   REF: Basic Needs Inc.
*1345 Giveup Street   35 Lock Street
*Runmedown, TX 77643   Stiff, NY 14923

The above-referenced company has given your concern's name as a credit reference. Please provide us with your experience with them so that we may determine their credit worthiness. Please fax this information back to us as soon as possible. Thank you in advance for the information that you provide and be assured that it will be kept confidential.

Sincerely,

I. M. Tracer
Credit Department

Sold From 1978

Terms of Sales 1% 10 Net 30

Largest Amount Now Owing $30,000

Amount Past Due $10,000

Recent Trend Toward X Promptness
                     __ Slowness
Makes Unjust Claims (State) _____
_____
_____

Credit Refused (State Cause) _____
_____
_____

Remarks: _____
_____

MANNER OF PAYMENT
__ Discounts
__ Prompt & Satisfactory
 X Prompt to 20 Days Slow
__ Pays on Account
__ Asks for More Time
__ Slow but Collectible
__ Accepts COD's Promptly
__ Settles by Trade Acceptance
__ Notes Paid at Maturity
__ Account Secured

45 Average Days Paid

Information Given By: Maye Theforce-Bewithyou, Credit Mgr. Date 05/26/96

WE REQUEST THE RETURN OF THIS FORM TO FACILITATE OUR SYSTEM OF FILING REPORT.

New Deal Products Inc.
235 St. Patrick Drive
Rochester, TX 77653
PHONE (713) 555-2810
FAX   (713) 555-2932

CREDIT INQUIRY

*Rubber U.S.A. Inc.   REF: Basic Needs Inc.
*1569 Lowdown Varmit Highway   35 Lock Street
*Rolloverme, TX 77543   Stiff, NY 14923

The above-referenced company has given your concern's name as a credit reference.
Please provide us with your experience with them so that we may determine their credit
worthiness. Please fax this information back to us as soon as possible. Thank you in
advance for the information that you provide and be assured that it will be kept
confidential.

Sincerely,

I. M. Tracer
Credit Department

Sold From 1990   MANNER OF PAYMENT
                                         __ Discounts
Terms of Sales _____ Net 30 _____   __ Prompt & Satisfactory
                                         _X_ Prompt to _30_ Days Slow
Largest Amount Now Owing $40,000   __ Pays on Account
                                         __ Asks for More Time
Amount Past Due $25,000   __ Slow but Collectible
                                         __ Accepts COD's Promptly
Recent Trend Toward _X_Promptness   __ Settles by Trade Acceptance
                    __ Slowness   __ Notes Paid at Maturity
Makes Unjust Claims (State) _____   __ Account Secured
_____
_____
Credit Refused (State Cause) _____
_____
_____
Remarks: _____   53 Average Days Paid

Information Given By: _Rank Smelling, Credit Manager_ Date _05/26/96_

WE REQUEST THE RETURN OF THIS FORM TO FACILITATE OUR SYSTEM OF
FILING REPORT.

Basic Needs Inc.
35 Lock Street
Stiff, NY 14923

SIC 5085

$2,029,702.00
$76,927.00

ACCOUNT # 123456

	12/31/95 $	12/31/95 % Change	12/31/95 % Assets	12/31/95 Ind % Assets	12/31/94 $	12/31/94 % Change	12/31/94 % Assets	12/31/94 Ind % Assets	12/31/93 $	12/31/93 % Change	12/31/93 % Assets	12/31/93 Ind % Assets
Cash	$1,601.00	-95.15	0.34	6.10	$32,979.00	181.41	6.26	5.80	$11,719.27	100.00	1.99	0.00
Accounts Receivable	$208,476.00	28.57	44.10	34.40	$162,147.00	-33.11	30.80	33.40	$242,405.37	100.00	41.25	0.00
Inventory	$223,874.00	-24.75	47.36	37.60	$297,504.00	13.19	56.52	38.60	$262,825.30	100.00	44.73	0.00
Due from Shareholder	$0.00	0.00	0.00	--	$0.00	0.00	0.00	--	$0.00	0.00	0.00	--
Due From Affiliate	$0.00	0.00	0.00	--	$0.00	0.00	0.00	--	$0.00	0.00	0.00	--
Other Current	$6.00	-97.66	0.00	1.30	$256.00	17.23	0.05	1.30	$218.37	100.00	0.04	0.00
Total Current	$433,957.00	-11.96	91.81	79.40	$492,886.00	-4.70	93.63	79.10	$517,168.31	100.00	88.01	0.00
Fixed Assets	$33,781.00	36.31	7.15	14.10	$24,783.00	-29.11	4.71	13.50	$34,962.10	100.00	5.95	0.00
Notes Receivable	$0.00	0.00	0.00	--	$0.00	0.00	0.00	0.00	$0.00	0.00	0.00	--
Deposits	$4,949.00	-41.66	1.05	5.30	$8,483.00	1,596.06	1.61	6.30	$500.16	100.00	0.09	--
Cash Value of Life Insur.	$0.00	0.00	0.00	--	$0.00	0.00	0.00	--	$0.00	0.00	0.00	--
Intangible Assets	$0.00	-100.00	0.00	1.20	$250.00	-99.29	0.05	1.10	$34,969.74	100.00	5.95	100.00
Total Assets	$472,687.00	-10.20	100.00	100.00	$526,402.00	-10.41	100.00	100.00	$587,600.31	100.00	100.00	100.00
Account Payable	$162,283.00	-26.12	34.33	25.30	$219,653.00	5.61	41.73	24.20	$207,989.12	100.00	35.40	0.00
Bank Loans + N.P.	$1,961.00	100.00	0.41	12.60	$0.00	-100.00	0.00	11.60	$79,000.00	100.00	13.44	0.00
Cur. Mat.-L.T.D.	$174,675.00	-3.77	36.95	4.20	$181,515.00	293.10	34.48	4.10	$46,174.95	100.00	7.86	0.00
Income Tax Payables	$4,327.00	100.00	0.92	0.30	$0.00	-100.00	0.00	0.40	$19,100.00	100.00	3.25	0.00
Accrued Expenses	$43,519.00	-31.79	9.21	7.00	$63,800.00	66.05	12.12	5.60	$38,421.82	100.00	6.54	0.00
Total Current	$386,765.00	-16.82	81.82	49.40	$464,968.00	19.01	88.33	45.90	$390,685.89	100.00	66.49	0.00
Long Term Debt	$8,995.00	-34.12	1.90	11.90	$13,654.00	-76.16	2.59	11.60	$57,278.63	100.00	9.75	0.00
Deferred Taxes	$0.00	0.00	0.00	0.30	$0.00	0.00	0.00	0.20	$0.00	0.00	0.00	0.00
All Other L.T. Debt	$0.00	0.00	0.00	1.80	$0.00	0.00	0.00	2.30	$0.00	0.00	0.00	0.00
Net Worth	$76,927.00	61.00	16.27	36.60	$47,780.00	-65.78	9.08	40.00	$139,635.79	100.00	23.76	100.00
Total Liab & Equity	$472,687.00	-10.20	100.00	100.00	$526,402.00	-10.41	100.00	100.00	$587,600.31	100.00	100.00	100.00
Net Sales	$2,029,702.00	-15.05	100.00	100.00	$2,389,253.00	-12.81	100.00	100.00	$2,740,421.11	100.00	100.00	100.00
Cost of Goods Sold	$1,200,261.00	-14.36	59.13	67.90	$1,401,599.00	-13.20	58.66	68.10	$1,614,820.48	100.00	58.93	100.00
Gross Profit	$829,441.00	-16.02	40.87	32.10	$987,654.00	-12.26	41.34	31.90	$1,125,600.63	100.00	41.07	0.00
Depreciation	$9,127.00	-11.19	0.45	--	$10,277.00	-48.42	0.43	--	$19,923.28	100.00	0.73	--
Lease Payments	$0.00	0.00	0.00	--	$0.00	0.00	0.00	--	$0.00	0.00	0.00	--
Other Operating Exps.	$783,861.00	-20.25	38.62	29.40	$982,887.00	-2.87	41.14	29.60	$1,011,916.88	100.00	36.93	100.00
Tot. Operating Exps.	$792,988.00	-20.16	39.07	--	$993,164.00	-3.75	41.57	--	$1,031,840.16	100.00	37.65	100.00
Operating Profit	$36,453.00	-761.58	1.80	2.70	($5,510.00)	-105.88	-0.23	2.30	$93,760.47	100.00	3.42	100.00
Interest Inc./(Exp.)	$0.00	0.00	0.00	0.80	$0.00	0.00	0.00	0.60	$0.00	0.00	0.00	0.00
G/(L) on sale of Fxd Assets	$0.00	0.00	0.00	--	$0.00	0.00	0.00	--	$0.00	0.00	0.00	0.00
Profit Before Taxes	$36,453.00	-761.58	1.80	2.00	($5,510.00)	-105.88	-0.23	1.70	$93,760.47	100.00	3.42	100.00
Taxes	$7,396.00	278.12	0.36	--	$1,956.00	-89.76	0.08	--	$19,100.00	100.00	0.70	100.00
Net Profit	$29,057.00	-489.19	1.43	--	($7,466.00)	-110.00	-0.31	--	$74,660.47	100.00	2.72	--
Other Data:												
Working Capital	$47,192.00	69.04	9.98	30.00	$27,918.00	-77.93	5.30	33.20	$126,482.42	100.00	21.53	0.00
Tangible Equity	$76,927.00	61.85	16.27	35.40	$47,530.00	-54.59	9.03	38.90	$104,666.05	100.00	17.81	0.00
Recommended Credit Limit:	$8,000.41	68.32	--	--	$4,753.00	-60.85	--	--	$12,141.26	--	--	--

Basic Needs Inc.
35 Lock Street
Stiff, NY 14923

RATIOS		12/31/95 Value	% Change	UQ	Med	LQ	12/31/94 Value	% Change	UQ	Med	LQ	12/31/93 Value	% Change	UQ	Med	LQ
SOLVENCY																
Current Ratio	($)	1.12	5.85	2.40	1.70	1.30	1.06	-19.92	2.70	1.80	1.30	1.32	100.00	2.50	1.70	1.20
Quick Ratio	($)	0.54	-112.48	1.20	0.80	0.60	0.42	-35.48	1.40	0.90	0.60	0.65	100.00	1.20	0.80	0.60
Net Profit B4 Tax + Depr/Cur LTD	(X)	0.26	893.60	2.90	1.20	0.50	0.03	-98.93	2.80	1.30	0.20	2.46	100.00	5.00	1.80	0.70
Sales to Fixed Assets	(X)	60.08	182.88	62.70	31.80	14.50	21.24	-72.90	70.70	32.70	13.90	78.38	100.00	70.10	32.70	19.60
Sales to Total Assets	(X)	4.29	-5.40	3.90	3.00	2.30	4.54	-2.68	3.70	3.10	2.20	4.66	100.00	3.80	3.00	2.20
Total Liab. to NW	(X)	5.14	-48.64	0.90	1.80	4.30	10.02	212.25	0.80	1.40	3.70	3.21	100.00	0.90	1.70	3.60
Fixed Assets to NW	(X)	0.44	-15.34	0.10	0.30	0.60	0.52	107.16	0.10	0.30	0.80	0.25	100.00	0.10	0.30	0.60
Tot. Liab. to Tot. Assets	(%)	83.73	-7.92	N/A	N/A	N/A	90.92	19.27	N/A	N/A	N/A	76.24	100.00	N/A	N/A	N/A
Oper. Prof. to Int. Exp.	(X)	0.00	0.00	N/A	N/A	N/A	0.00	0.00	N/A	N/A	N/A	0.00	0.00	N/A	N/A	N/A
Oper Prof+Lease Py to Int Exp+LP	(X)	0.00	0.00	N/A	N/A	N/A	0.00	0.00	N/A	N/A	N/A	0.00	0.00	N/A	N/A	N/A
EFFICIENCY																
Sales to Receivables	(X)	9.74	-33.93	10.90	9.10	7.70	14.74	30.34	11.60	9.10	7.90	11.31	100.00	11.00	9.20	7.10
Days Sales Outstanding	(D)	37	48.00	33	40	47	25	-21.88	31	40	46	32	100.00	33	40	51
Cost of Sales to Inv.	(X)	5.36	13.80	9.10	5.10	3.60	4.71	-23.32	8.50	5.00	3.50	6.14	100.00	9.90	5.10	3.30
Days' Sales in Inventory	(D)	68	-11.69	40	72	101	77	30.51	43	73	104	59	100.00	37	72	111
Sales to Net Working Cap.	(X)	43.01	-49.74	5.90	9.30	21.40	85.58	294.99	5.40	9.00	18.40	21.67	100.00	5.10	9.30	23.60
Cost of Sales/Payables	(X)	7.40	15.91	15.40	8.80	6.60	6.38	-17.81	15.30	9.20	6.00	7.76	100.00	14.80	9.20	6.20
A/P Turnover	(D)	49	-14.04	24	41	58	57	21.28	24	40	61	47	100.00	25	40	59
PROFITABILITY																
Depreciation to Sales	(%)	0.45	4.54	0.60	1.00	1.60	0.43	-40.84	0.50	0.80	1.60	0.73	100.00	0.60	0.90	1.40
Prof bef Tax to Tot Assets	(%)	7.71	-836.76	10.70	4.30	0.40	-1.05	-106.56	10.30	4.50	0.00	15.96	100.00	10.40	4.70	0.40
Profit before Taxes to TNW	(%)	47.39	-510.91	32.40	14.70	2.60	-11.53	-117.17	29.40	10.70	0.00	67.15	100.00	29.20	13.00	1.70
		(X)=TIMES		(D) = DAYS												

OTHER RATIOS NOT AVAILABLE WITH INDUSTRY STANDARDS

		12/31/95 Value	% Change	UQ	Med	LQ	12/31/94 Value	% Change	UQ	Med	LQ	12/31/93 Value	% Change	UQ	Med	LQ
SOLVENCY																
Inv. to Net Work. Capital	(X)	4.74	-55.48	N/A	N/A	N/A	10.66	412.82	N/A	N/A	N/A	2.08	100.00	N/A	N/A	N/A
Current Liab. to NW	(X)	5.03	-48.34	N/A	N/A	N/A	9.73	247.81	N/A	N/A	N/A	2.80	100.00	N/A	N/A	N/A
LT Debt to Tot. Debt & Capital	(%)	1.90	-26.64	N/A	N/A	N/A	2.59	-73.44	N/A	N/A	N/A	9.75	100.00	N/A	N/A	N/A
Fixed Assets to LT Debt	(X)	3.76	106.59	N/A	N/A	N/A	1.82	198.36	N/A	N/A	N/A	0.61	100.00	N/A	N/A	N/A
EFFICIENCY																
Net Sales to NW	(X)	26.38	-47.25	N/A	N/A	N/A	50.01	154.76	N/A	N/A	N/A	19.63	100.00	N/A	N/A	N/A
Net Sales to Inventory	(X)	9.07	12.95	N/A	N/A	N/A	8.03	-23.01	N/A	N/A	N/A	10.43	100.00	N/A	N/A	N/A
Cost of Sales/Working Capital	(X)	25.43	-49.34	N/A	N/A	N/A	50.20	293.11	N/A	N/A	N/A	12.77	100.00	N/A	N/A	N/A
Short Term Loan Turnover	(X)	1.00	100.00	N/A	N/A	N/A	0.00	-100.00	N/A	N/A	N/A	18.00	100.00	N/A	N/A	N/A
LT Liabilities Payback *	($)	($136.49)	-23.62	--	32.10	--	($178.70)	-469.16	--	31.90	--	$48.41	100.00	--	0.00	--
PROFITABILITY																
Gross Profit on Net Sales	(%)	40.87	-1.14	--	2.70	--	41.34	0.66	--	2.30	--	41.07	100.00	--	0.00	--
Net Oper Inc on Net Sales	(%)	1.80	-882.61	N/A	N/A	N/A	-0.23	-106.73	N/A	N/A	N/A	3.42	100.00	N/A	N/A	N/A
Net Profit on Net Sales	(%)	1.43	-561.29	N/A	N/A	N/A	-0.31	-111.40	N/A	N/A	N/A	2.72	100.00	N/A	N/A	N/A
Net Prof on Total Assets	(%)	6.15	-533.10	N/A	N/A	N/A	-1.42	-111.17	N/A	N/A	N/A	12.71	100.00	N/A	N/A	N/A
Tot Assets to Equity	(X)	6.14	-44.23	N/A	N/A	N/A	11.02	161.81	N/A	N/A	N/A	4.21	100.00	N/A	N/A	N/A
Net Prft on Stkhldrs Eqty	(%)	37.77	-341.65	N/A	N/A	N/A	-15.63	-129.23	N/A	N/A	N/A	53.47	100.00	N/A	N/A	N/A
				(D) = DAYS					(%) = PRECENT					($) = DOLLARS		

* IN THOUSANDS

OVERVIEW

Let us look at the financial condition and the credit status of this customer. The liquidity, as expected, is below the bottom of the barrel as compared to the industry standard ($0.54 to $1.00 compared to $0.60 to $1.00 for the lowest quartile). This has actually improved from the previous year but worsened from two years ago. While worsening compared to the previous year, the DSO is better that industry average (37 days to 40 days).

A/P turnover has greatly improved compared to the previous year but is poor compared with the industry average (49 days to 41 days). This average, by the way, is better than how Basic Needs has been paying you, the supplier, and it needs to increase its credit limit. The debt ratio also has greatly improved compared to last year but is far worse than the industry's lowest quartile ($5.14 to $1.00 compared to $4.30 to $1.00). Inventory turnover also has improved from the previous year and is even better than industry average (68 days compared to 72 days).

Gross profits have worsened slightly from the previous year but are better than the industry average (40.87% compared to 32.1%). The operating income improved greatly from the previous year but is worse than industry average (1.8% compared to 2.7%). Net worth, while dropping substantially from two years ago, has almost doubled last year's total. Unfortunately, sales are also down from the previous two years. It would appear on the surface that every sale is important to Basic Needs.

The high credit on Basic Needs' credit report was $50,000, and the company appears to pay on average about 30 days slow. Once again, the bank has a first lien on everything. The business is owned by a husband and wife and it has been in existence for 15 years. The husband had 11 years of prior experience in this field before starting this firm. They rent the company's facility and have a total of eight employees. The high credit on the three trade references was $40,000, and the three were paid on average between 45 to 55 days slow. Two of the references state that Basic Needs' payment trend is leaning toward promptness while one states that the trend is toward slowness.

The bank has extended a low five-figure ($10,000 to $20,000) working capital line of credit, which appears to be fully utilized and is satisfactory.

WHAT OTHER CREDIT MANAGERS THOUGHT

Now let us meet the first of our three marginal experts to see how they will deal with this case.

Student One

Tracey T., a corporate credit manager for a major office supplies manu-facturer, has the distinct pleasure of dealing with a large number of cus-tomers just like this. Realizing that the initial part of the year-long order is $80,000 leaving increments of about $47,000 plus any other orders that Basic Needs might get from its other customers, leaves Tracey with the dilemma of being paid while not losing business.

Since the bank's total outstanding is about $20,000 and Basic Needs' assets equal $472,000 (as an ongoing concern), there is some room for security. To whom does the company owe the current balance of the long-term debt, and does this party have a second lien on all the assets behind the bank? If the security is available, Tracey decided to increase the line to $110,000 while taking a second on all assets. This would give Basic Needs some room to breathe to cover the first order while still having some room to cover other orders that might come along. Tracey felt that selling the idea of security to top management would be easy as the com-pany has been hit recently with a rash of bankruptcies where it had not been paid more than $0.05 on every $1.00 (supposition).

After reviewing Tracey's assessment of the financial statements, top management could see that Basic Needs was a potential bankruptcy can-didate. Considering the customer's slow payment performance and the fact that giving the security would not cost it anything but would give it access to the product that it needed, she felt top management would most likely readily agree to this requirement.

Student Two

Robert A. is a credit manager from a manufacturer of bathroom fixtures. Having looked at the falling sales numbers, the less-than-perfect way that Basic Needs has been paying its bills, and its low net worth, Robert was not interested in increasing the credit limit under any circumstances. He did, however, offer to sell to the end user directly and to pay Basic Needs a sales commission equal to its profit less his costs in carrying its receivables.

By doing it this way, the sale is not lost and Basic Needs has its prof-its without the hassle of dealing with its argumentative, demanding cus-tomer. Robert planned on selling his idea to top management by showing the likelihood that the Basic Needs would end up going on credit hold due to its inability to pay on time. Basic Needs would then tell the end user that it was Robert's company's fault for the holdups in delivering the goods. This could damage Robert's firm's reputation with the end user and make it look elsewhere for a new supplier. To sell the strategy to Arnold Flopper, Basic Needs' owner, Robert would emphasize that he would get his money without any of the headache or worry over being paid and have improved cash flow.

Student Three

Doreen W., a divisional credit manager of a major national chemical company, does not feel that it is necessary to raise the limit now. She feels that, considering Basic Needs' faltering sales, low net worth, and general delinquency with everyone except the bank, some security must be held to approve this pending sale. Since the bank outstanding is so low and it has first on everything, her firm needs to take a first on the goods that are being shipped.

A dual-step security is needed to cover this large credit extension. A purchase money security interest in her inventory would be step one; then a second lien on all assets behind the bank would finish the deal. This would provide her company with the maximum amount of coverage needed to guarantee payment of the balance even in the face of a bankruptcy and would give it substantial leverage over having Basic Needs pay on time.

Selling top management may require more than just giving them a synopsis of the financial statements and credit checks to get them to buy in to her decision. Doreen decided to show them some bankruptcy statistics on recoveries made by unsecured creditors on claims submitted to the court. This would help them understand why it is important not only to have a first on inventory and proceeds but also to have a follow-up lien behind the bank to cover the company in case its inventory was gone. By having a second, once the bank was paid in full it would be able to sell off the remaining assets to clear the final debt owed by Basic Needs.

She knew that Arnold Flopper was in no position to argue about what her company did or did not need as collateral and would simply acquiesce to her firm's demand to cover a credit extension of this magnitude.

EXTENDED TERMS

As a side note, all three students agreed that no matter what, the sale did need to go through. The next consideration for our three students is the matter of extended terms.

Student One

Tracey T. too felt that extended credit was the first thing Arnold Flopper of Basic Needs would ask for. She said, "I could see him now telling me that he is a poor small company that has to deal with a large customer who demands everything and pays when it feels like it." This is true with a lot of large customers; Tracey can be very empathetic but will not let that interfere with her decision. Unless Basic Needs can prove that a competitor is getting extended terms from its supplier and is bidding against it for this contract, any change of terms would be a direct violation of the Robinson-Patman Act. Since she is not willing to violate a federal statute and also upset other distributors that her company sells to, the answer would definitely be no and would make no difference to her earlier decision.

Student Two

Robert A. likewise sympathized with Basic Needs on being stretched out for payment by large customers. For him, offering extended terms was not in the cards. For starters, it would be a violation of the Robinson-Patman Act. However, of even greater concern to him was the fact that with the company's poor financial condition, it was a prime candidate for bankruptcy. With longer terms, the company would have more time to sell off the inventory, use the money to cover other needs, and (not necessarily in this case) close the firm, or intentionally bankrupt it in a fraudulent "bustout" operation.

Student Three

Doreen W.'s attitude was that this is business and if a company chooses to sell to major corporations that bully small vendors into doing things that make it unprofitable, then it has to pay the penalty for these actions. Only those more profitable or more liquid firms should attempt to deal with these "800-pound gorillas."

To expect the vendor to cover the shortfall of these small, poorly managed firms is unreasonable as the profit margin on these sales goes down proportionately the longer the payments are strung out, legally (via legally offered terms) or illegally (through delinquency). This is, of course, in addition to it being a violation of the Robinson-Patman Act.

RECOMMENDATIONS IF OVERRIDEN BY TOP MANAGEMENT

Student One

Tracey T. knew full well that if Basic Needs' customer strings it out for too long, it would not pay this debt and may be forced to file once pushed by Tracey's collection efforts. The only tool available to Tracey to deal with Basic Needs is to start collection efforts very early on and put it on hold at 35 days from invoice date if payment is not received. It would remain on hold until the account is paid current. If and when payment is received (and the check cleared), then the next order would be shipped. She would work with the local salesperson to try to keep the end user from being misled about the reason for goods not being delivered.

By being very visible on the site, the local salesperson can prevent this misconception from occurring, as it would make little sense to be there physically to take abuse from the end user when it has a problem getting goods to Basic Needs. With these two steps taken, the best controls possible will be in place to keep both the end user and Arnold Flopper under control.

Student Two

Robert A. felt that being put into this position by top management meant that his company needed a tax write-off and had found a likely candidate in Basic Needs. He would hold orders at 35 days but planned to have the local salesperson, the regional sales manager, and himself alternately "sitting on Basic Needs' doorstep" until a check was in hand and had cleared the bank. Since the president of his firm had chosen to override him, Robert would agree to call the end user personally to explain any delays caused by Flopper's lack of funds. This would cover both the money issue and the reputation issue.

Student Three

Doreen W. felt that top management's decision to override her was shortsighted and she would require a signoff on the approval to ship. Her steps to safeguard the outstanding balance started with pushing

Arnold Flopper to pay by way of wire transfer, at her firm's expense, on the 35th day. She warned Arnold that she had access to her trade credit group's notification system and would notify all the members that sold to him that she had put him on credit hold again. At 45 days, all future shipments would go out on a COD certified basis once the account was up to date. Notification of a terms change would likewise be filtered down to all other members once payment was received. As to the reputation problem, she would e-mail the local salesperson the minute the account went on credit hold so it could begin being visible at the end user's location. Arnold would be warned that no game-playing would be tolerated on this order. If he could not meet his obligations in a timely manner, he should allow her firm to sell the end user direct and pay Basic Needs a commission.

WHAT REALLY HAPPENED

Sometimes even the most obvious credit decisions escape the eagle eye of top management. In this case, I presented them with my recommendations of selling direct to the end user and paying Basic Needs its income less our expenses for carrying the receivable. On this very rare occasion, the president decided to pay Russian roulette and loaded the gun with six bullets rather than just one. Taking it upon himself to approve this credit, not only did he approve the order but he also granted Basic Needs extended terms of 120 days.

After assuring him that I would be a team player and would keep an eye on this to keep our chance of a loss low, he assured me that there would be no loss. Later that day I met with the CFO. He agreed with my final recommendation to increase our reserve for bad debt by the amount of the approved credit limit. After getting the initial $80,000 shipment and three subsequent $47,000 shipments thereafter, we received a notice of bankruptcy filing (Chapter 7).

Because it had been 30 days since the last shipment, we had no chance at filing a reclamation claim, and our A/R balance of over $220,000 was virtually gone. To our chagrin, we discovered that we were the largest unsecured creditor and our balance was greater than the bank's. Since most of the assets were gone and a great deal of the receivables were nonperforming, after the liquidation only enough was left to pay the bank off, the administrative debt, and a token payment of $0.005 on the $1.00 to the unsecured creditors.

We attempted to salvage the business with the end user, but it was so soured by Basic Needs' poor performance that it would have nothing to do with us. Our firm's auditors reviewed this particular bad debt writeoff with the CFO and me, then presented their findings to the president. While disappointed that the end result was a loss, he advised them that he would have done the same thing all over again if he were presented with the same circumstances.

About three months later the president resigned and the CFO was promoted to president. He later informed me that he was promoted not only for his hard work but also for his foresight in setting up a reserve for this $220,000 disaster. He thanked me formally for wearing my company hat during that time and also for doing my best to keep this disaster under control. Then he showed me a notice that formally announced my promotion to director of credit and confirmed that I would remain reporting to him in the future.

CONCLUSION

Regardless of how much you try, losses do occur. Given the choice to have no loss or a major loss that resulted in a promotion for me, I would take the promotion every time!

13

CASE STUDY 9: DRUGS "R" US PRODUCTS, INC.

Addressing a Customer's "Shady" Past

INTRODUCTION

This case provides guidance on how to deal with customers whose past credit history has been less than favorable. It covers how to deal with former bankrupt companies and compares various methods to protect the company. Readers will learn how to negotiate with difficult, egotistical individuals with a jaded past. The goal is to minimize the potential for loss while still confirming the sale. Readers will play "devil's advocate" to hone their ability to bring home a done deal.

By reviewing this real day in the life of a credit department, readers will learn to make effective use of data, facts, and alternative methods in reaching a decision. An appreciation for how other people in marketing or finance think will hone negotiating skills. Readers can use new insight into the creation of a sound business credit decision to prevent gaps or weaknesses in their decision-making processes.

Case study 9 looks at dealing with not only a company run by an argumentative president but also one that used bankruptcy in the past as a tool for controlling the firm's creditors. This aspect makes it difficult to determine if your firm can make a profit on the sales to the company and also whether you may lose money as a result of being pulled into your customer's bankruptcy filing. In this particular case, we will be using the five "C's" of credit to justify our decision and the best way to minimize the risks involved in dealing with this type of individual.

Typically, most commercial credit managers do not have the luxury of getting to know all the people who manage the companies to which they extend credit. Generally the exception to the rule either allows or forces them to get to know those individuals at the top. In this case, because of my connections with a credit trade group, I was informed of the president's past track record so I did get to know him.

THE FACTS

I. B. Strict, the corporate credit manager for Hipower Drug Manufacturing Company, the world's leader in pharmaceutical manufacturing, is reviewing a new account with his credit analyst, Jane Dough. The customer, Drugs "R" Us Products, Inc. (a Subchapter S corporation), has been in business since 1955. It has fair financials for a company of its size. It is a top distributor in the region, controlling nearly 75% of the market, and has had great success in areas that Hipower could not penetrate. Hipower's product would replace its largest current supplier of "Hyperion" (an "instantaneous" cure for the common cold) and Hipower's number-two competitor in the industry. If Hipower agrees to sign them on, it would become one of Drugs "R" Us's top five suppliers.

Anticipated additional sales for Hipower as reflected in its sales manager's report would be between $13.5 million and $15 million per year, which would be a 0.5 to 1% overall increase. Large sales increases in this very competitive and narrow market is critical to the growth and survival of all industry players. The paying habits are average, taking some larger discounts when offered and paying at about 8 days over terms when only net is offered.

The initial order placed by Drugs "R" Us is for $1.5 million to be shipped complete in the next 30 days. Hipower's margin on the order is 55%, which is above average for the industry. It is asking for terms of 3% 60 net 90 for the first purchase. Hipower's standard terms of sale are 2% 30 net 31 days. A check with some members of its national industry credit trade group reveals that the president and CEO, Arnold Stopgap, had at a previous firm of which he was president filed bankruptcy demanding that suppliers accept a $0.10 on the $1.00 in a reorganization plan or face liquidation and no payment at all.

Arnold has a reputation as a tough negotiator and would pay more for product at another source just to spite a supplier that put him on credit hold. As a result, he just lost two top product lines to a local competitor, which will cause serious problems in contract negotiations with customers. He has a large contract with a Fortune 50 company, which will be up for renewal in two months, and there have been rumors that the Fortune 50 company may be looking for a new supplier. This customer represents some 40% of Hipower Drugs' total sales. A credit report and financial analysis are available for review.

QUESTIONS

1. Analyze capital: Discuss the firm's creditworthiness based on the credit report and the financial analysis report provided. Provide a summary of how they compare to industry standards provided.

2. Analyze market conditions: Discuss the facts available on the condition of the market, your profitability, and other factors that could affect your credit decision.

3. Analyze character and management capacity: How does their background and management style affect your credit decision? What factors do you consider important? Is more investigation needed and if so what?

4. Analyze collateral: Is this a factor to be considered? Will you need it, and if so, how do you justify it to the customer, its bank, and your company's officials?

5. Summarize your findings: Use your findings to formulate and justify a course of action. Be complete, creative, and specific with your response.

CREDIT REPORT

FILE #123456789	DATE PRINTED MAY 23, 1996	SUMMARY
		RATING 3A2
DRUGS "R" US PRODUCTS INC.		STARTED 1955
400 RUNDOWN LANE	DIST DRUGS	SALES $46,724,750
BLOWDOWNTOWN, TN 30606		WORTH $1,713,700
TEL: 412 555-9000	SIC NO.	HISTORY CLEAR
	51 22	CONDITION GOOD

CHIEF EXECUTIVE: ARNOLD STOPGAP, PRES.

PAYMENTS (Amounts may be rounded to nearest figure in prescribed ranges)
REPORTED

	PAYING RECORD	HIGH CREDIT	NOW OWES	PAST DUE	SELLING TERMS	LAST SALE WITHIN
4/96	Ppt	25000	250	-0-		1 Mo
	Slow 15	25000	15000	10000		1 Mo
3/96	Disc	10000	5000	-0-		
	Ppt	250	-0-			6-12 Mos
	Ppt	50	50	-0-	N30	1 Mo
	Ppt-Slow 10	85000	55000	40000	N30	1 Mo
	Ppt-Slow 10	5000	5000	1000	N30	1 Mo
	Slow 15	2500	100			6-12 Mos
	Slow 15	1000	1000			4-5 Mos
	Slow 15	250	-0-			4-5 Mos
	Slow 15	5000	-0-	-0-	N30	4-5 Mos
	Ppt	2500	2500	-0-	N30	
	Ppt	250	-0-	-0-		2-3 Mos
2/96	Ppt	250000	-0-	-0-	N15	2-3 Mos
	Ppt	75000			N30	
	Ppt	500	500	-0-	N15	1 Mo
	Ppt	250	250	-0-		2-3 Mos
	Ppt-Slow 10	2500	750	250	N30	1 Mo
	Ppt-Slow 15	500	-0-	-0-	N30	4-5 Mos
1/96	Disc	10000	-0-	-0-	1 Prox N30	
	Ppt	60000	10000	-0-		1 Mo
	Ppt-Slow 10	250	250	250	N30	2-3 Mos
12/95	Disc	300000	10000	-0-	1 10 N30	1 Mo
	Ppt-Slow 15	500	500	500		1 Mo
	Slow 15	15000	2500	500		1 Mo
	Slow 15	100	-0-	-0-		6-12 Mos
	Slow 10-15	2500	2500	2500		
11/95	Ppt	50000	2000	-0-		1 Mo
	Ppt	5000	-0-	-0-	N30	6-12 Mos
	Ppt	5000				

DRUGS "R" US PRODUCTS INC.   May 23, 1996   PAGE 002

Ppt-Slow 10	100	-0-	-0-		1 Mo
10/95 Ppt	10000	5000	-0-		1 Mo

       * Payment experiences reflect how bills are met in relation to the terms granted. In some instances payment beyond terms can be the result of disputes over merchandise, skipped invoices, etc.

       * Each experience shown represents a separate account reported by a supplier. Updated trade experiences replace those previously reported.

FINANCE
* Financial information is attached for your review. Good condition is indicated based on debt to net worth. Sales for 1996 were forecasted to be $50,000,000.

PUBLIC FILINGS
UCC FILINGS
4/15/95
    Financing statement #984345 filed 9/11/94 with Secretary, State of N.Y. Debtor Drugs "R" Us Products Inc., Blowdowntown, TN, Secured Party: All Secured Bank, NA, Stiff, TN.

Collateral: Accounts receivable, inventory, all other fixed assets.

HISTORY
4/15/96
        ARNOLD L. STOPGAP, PRES.
        JACK L. GAP, V. PRES.
        BARRY R. STOP, TREAS.
        DIRECTOR(S): The officer(s)

        INCORPORATED Tennessee January 20, 1955

        Authorized capital consists of 500,000 shares Common Stock, $100 par value.

        Business started 1955 by Arnold G. Stopgap. 100% of capital is owned by Arnold L. Stopgap.

        Arnold L. Stopgap born 1935, married 1960. started here in 1990. Former employer Hiedge Drugs, Inc. there 1965–1990. Company filed Chapter 11 on 1/86 emerged from bankruptcy on 10/89. He is the son of founder and is now president.

        Jack L. Gap born 1960, single. Graduate Jackson University, Wheatland, NY 1982. 1982–Present: Vice President here and continues.

DRUGS "R" US PRODUCTS INC.   May 23, 1996   PAGE 003

Barry R. Stop born 1961. Active here since 1985.

OPERATION
4/15/96
    Distributes drugs (100%)

    Terms 1/10 Net 30 days. Has 1,000 accounts. Sells to Hospitals and Retailers, Territory: U.S. and international. Non-seasonal.

    EMPLOYEES: 300 including officers. 275 employed here.

    FACILITIES: Owns 100,000 sq. ft. in 1-story concrete block building in good condition. Premises neat.

    LOCATION: Suburban business section on side street.

FULL DISPLAY COMPLETE

Hipower Drug Manufacturing Co.
400-16 Still Moon Crescent
Rochester, NY 14624
FAX#: (716) 555-5860

BANK CREDIT INQUIRY

All Secured Bank, NA
235 St. Patrick Drive   Ref: Drugs "R" US Products Inc.
Stiff, TN 30609   400 Rundown Lane
(412) 555-2810   Blowdowntown, TN 30606

The above-referenced company has given your concern's name as a credit reference. Please provide us with your experience with them so that we may determine their credit worthiness. Please fax this information back to us as soon as possible. Thank you in advance for the information that you provide and be assured that it will be kept confidential.

Sincerely,

I. B. Strict
Credit Department

If business is not incorporated, please provide owners' name & address:

SAVINGS ACCOUNT   LOW ___   MEDIUM ___   HIGH ___ $__ FIGURE ___
                  OPEN ___   CLOSED ___

CHECKING ACCOUNT   LOW ___   MEDIUM _X_   HIGH ___ $_7_ FIGURE

          SATISFACTORY _X_   UNSATISFACTORY ___

CREDIT EXPERIENCE

Loans are granted: Frequently ___ Occasionally _X_ Seldom ___

Type: Working Capital _X_ Mortgage ___ Installment ___

Maximum Credit Extended $ High 7 Figures Secured _X_ Unsecured ___

Present Outstandings: Secured $High 7 Figures Unsecured $_____

Relationship: SATISFACTORY _X_   UNSATISFACTORY ____

Have "NSF" checks been issued: Yes ___ No _X_
Prepared By: I. M. Loose,_____ Title: Ex. Vice President

Hipower Drug Manufacturing Co.
400-16 Still Moon Crescent
Rochester, NY 14624
PHONE (716) 555-5860
FAX (716) 555-5860

CREDIT INQUIRY

*Drug Components U.S.A., Inc.   REF: Special Materials Inc.
*1136 Fallinarut Way   1234 Creek Drive
*Skyhigh, ME 33659   Taos, NM 82345

The above-referenced company has given your concern's name as a credit reference.
Please provide us with your experience with them so that we may determine their credit
worthiness. Please fax this information back to us as soon as possible. Thank you in
advance for the information that you provide and be assured that it will be kept
confidential.

Sincerely,

I.B. Strict
Credit Department

Sold From 1984   MANNER OF PAYMENT
                                             ___ Discounts
Terms of Sales   Net 30   X Prompt & Satisfactory
                                             ___ Prompt to __ Days Slow
Largest Amount Now Owing $300,000   ___ Pays on Account
                                             ___ Asks for More Time
Amount Past Due $0   ___ Slow but Collectible
                                             ___ Accepts COD's Promptly
Recent Trend Toward X Promptness   ___ Settles by Trade Acceptance
                     __ Slowness   ___ Notes Paid at Maturity
Makes Unjust Claims (State) _____   ___ Account Secured
_____
_____
Credit Refused (State Cause) _____
_____
_____
Remarks: _____   30 Average Days Paid
_____
_____

Information Given By: Ken I. Think, Credit Manager   Date 5/26/96

WE REQUEST THE RETURN OF THIS FORM TO FACILITATE OUR SYSTEM OF
FILING REPORT.

Hipower Drug Manufacturing Co.
400-16 Still Moon Crescent
Rochester, NY 14624
PHONE (716) 555-5860
FAX   (716) 555-5860

CREDIT INQUIRY

*Drug Components U.S.A., Inc.   REF: Drugs "R" Us Products Inc.
*1136 Fallinarut Way   400 Rundown Lane
*Skyhigh, ME 33659   Blowdowntown, TN 30606

The above-referenced company has given your concern's name as a credit reference.
Please provide us with your experience with them so that we may determine their credit
worthiness. Please fax this information back to us as soon as possible. Thank you in
advance for the information that you provide and be assured that it will be kept
confidential.

Sincerely,

I.B. Strict
Credit Department

Sold From _1984_____   MANNER OF PAYMENT
                                        ___ Discounts
Terms of Sales __Net 30_____   _X_ Prompt & Satisfactory
                                        ___ Prompt to __ Days Slow
Largest Amount Now Owing $300,000   ___ Pays on Account
                                        ___ Asks for More Time
Amount Past Due $0_____   ___ Slow but Collectible
                                        ___ Accepts COD's Promptly
Recent Trend Toward _X_ Promptness   ___ Settles by Trade Acceptance
                     __ Slowness   ___ Notes Paid at Maturity
Makes Unjust Claims (State) _____   ___ Account Secured
_____
_____

Credit Refused (State Cause) _____
_____
_____

Remarks: _____   _30_ Average Days Paid
_____

Information Given By: _Ken I. Think, Credit Manager_ Date _5/26/96_

WE REQUEST THE RETURN OF THIS FORM TO FACILITATE OUR SYSTEM OF
FILING REPORT.

Hipower Drug Manufacturing Co.
400-16 Still Moon Crescent
Rochester, NY 14624
PHONE (716) 555-5860
FAX   (716) 555-5860

CREDIT INQUIRY

*Drugs Withoutend Inc.
*2169 Jumpinarut Way
*Deadhead, MD 24589

REF: Drugs "R" Us Products Inc.
400 Rundown Lane
Blowdowntown, TN 30606

The above-referenced company has given your concern's name as a credit reference. Please provide us with your experience with them so that we may determine their credit worthiness. Please fax this information back to us as soon as possible. Thank you in advance for the information that you provide and be assured that it will be kept confidential.

Sincerely,

I.B. Strict
Credit Department

Sold From 1990

Terms of Sales 2% 30 Net 31

Largest Amount Now Owing $200,000

Amount Past Due $0

Recent Trend Toward X Promptness
                     ___ Slowness
Makes Unjust Claims (State) _____
_____
_____
Credit Refused (State Cause) _____
_____
_____
Remarks: _____
_____
_____

MANNER OF PAYMENT
___ Discounts
 X Prompt & Satisfactory
___ Prompt to ___ Days Slow
___ Pays on Account
___ Asks for More Time
___ Slow but Collectible
___ Accepts COD's Promptly
___ Settles by Trade Acceptance
___ Notes Paid at Maturity
___ Account Secured

42 Average Days Paid

Information Given By: I. Bea Easy, Credit Manager Date 5/23/96

WE REQUEST THE RETURN OF THIS FORM TO FACILITATE OUR SYSTEM OF FILING REPORT.

Drug "R" Us Products Inc.
400 Rundown Lane
Blowndowntown, TN 30606

SIC 5122   ACCOUNT # 123456

$46,724,750.00
$2,007,600.00

Account	12/31/95 $	95 % Change	95 % Assets	95 Ind % Assets	12/31/94 $	94 % Change	94 % Assets	94 Ind % Assets	12/31/93 $	93 % Change	93 % Assets	93 Ind % Assets
Cash	$348,190.00	-14.79	4.12	5.40	$408,640.00	100.00	5.09	7.60	$0.00	0.00	0.00	0.00
Accounts Receivable	$3,979,240.00	25.00	47.14	37.30	$3,183,440.00	100.00	39.62	35.40	$0.00	0.00	0.00	0.00
Inventory	$3,320,540.00	-11.35	39.34	34.10	$3,745,570.00	100.00	46.62	33.70	$0.00	0.00	0.00	0.00
Due from Shareholder	$0.00	0.00	0.00	---	$0.00	0.00	0.00	---	$0.00	0.00	0.00	0.00
Due From Affiliate	$0.00	0.00	0.00	---	$0.00	0.00	0.00	---	$0.00	0.00	0.00	---
Other Current	$79,640.00	172.55	0.94	3.80	$29,220.00	100.00	0.36	2.30	$0.00	0.00	0.00	0.00
Total Current	$7,727,610.00	4.90	91.55	80.60	$7,366,870.00	100.00	91.69	79.00	$0.00	0.00	0.00	0.00
Fixed Assets	$407,320.00	7.95	4.83	9.30	$377,330.00	100.00	4.70	10.90	$0.00	0.00	0.00	0.00
Notes Receivable	$0.00	0.00	0.00	---	$0.00	0.00	0.00	---	$0.00	0.00	0.00	---
Deposits	$12,200.00	-14.69	0.14	---	$14,300.00	100.00	0.18	---	$0.00	0.00	0.00	---
Cash Value of Life Insur.	$0.00	0.00	0.00	5.70	$0.00	0.00	0.00	6.20	$0.00	0.00	0.00	0.00
Intangible Assets	$293,900.00	6.50	3.48	4.40	$275,970.00	100.00	3.43	3.90	$0.00	0.00	0.00	100.00
Total Assets	$8,441,030.00	5.06	100.00	100.00	$8,034,470.00	100.00	100.00	100.00	$0.00	0.00	0.00	0.00
Account Payable	$4,918,440.00	21.50	58.27	31.10	$4,048,130.00	100.00	50.38	27.10	$0.00	0.00	0.00	0.00
Bank Loans + N.P.	$745,000.00	-45.42	8.83	15.10	$1,365,000.00	100.00	16.99	16.00	$0.00	0.00	0.00	0.00
Cur. Mat.-L.T.D.	$0.00	0.00	0.00	1.20	$0.00	0.00	0.00	2.20	$0.00	0.00	0.00	0.00
Income Tax Payables	($46,050.00)	30.01	-0.55	0.50	($35,420.00)	100.00	-0.44	0.80	$0.00	0.00	0.00	0.00
Accrued Expenses	$70,250.00	-24.95	0.83	8.70	$93,600.00	100.00	1.16	8.20	$0.00	0.00	0.00	0.00
Total Current	$5,687,640.00	3.95	67.38	56.60	$5,471,310.00	100.00	68.09	54.30	$0.00	0.00	0.00	0.00
Long Term Debt	$694,730.00	0.02	8.23	7.80	$694,610.00	100.00	8.65	7.30	$0.00	0.00	0.00	0.00
Deferred Taxes	$51,060.00	-22.68	0.60	0.40	$66,040.00	100.00	0.82	0.40	$0.00	0.00	0.00	0.00
All Other L.T. Debt	$0.00	0.00	0.00	3.40	$0.00	0.00	0.00	4.30	$0.00	0.00	0.00	0.00
Net Worth	$2,007,600.00	11.38	23.78	31.80	$1,802,510.00	100.00	22.43	33.70	$0.00	0.00	0.00	100.00
Total Liab & Equity	$8,441,030.00	5.06	100.00	100.00	$8,034,470.00	100.00	100.00	100.00	$0.00	0.00	0.00	0.00
Net Sales	$46,724,750.00	15.73	100.00	100.00	$40,374,240.00	17.84	100.00	100.00	$34,260,970.00	100.00	100.00	100.00
Cost of Goods Sold	$45,657,500.00	15.73	97.72	79.10	$39,451,720.00	17.92	97.72	69.10	$33,457,560.00	100.00	97.66	70.70
Gross Profit	$1,067,250.00	15.69	2.28	20.90	$922,520.00	14.83	2.28	30.90	$803,410.00	100.00	2.34	29.30
Depreciation	$62,790.00	8.02	0.13	---	$58,130.00	2.50	0.14	---	$56,710.00	100.00	0.17	---
Lease Payments	$0.00	0.00	0.00	---	$0.00	0.00	0.00	---	$0.00	0.00	0.00	---
Other Operating Exps.	$625,550.00	24.42	1.34	17.10	$502,790.00	16.06	1.25	26.90	$433,220.00	100.00	1.26	25.00
Tot. Operating Exps.	$688,340.00	22.72	1.47	3.80	$560,920.00	14.49	1.39	4.00	$489,930.00	100.00	1.43	4.40
Operating Profit	$378,910.00	4.79	0.81	1.00	$361,600.00	15.35	0.90	1.10	$313,480.00	100.00	0.91	0.50
Interest Inc./(Exp.)	($101,270.00)	-9.46	-0.22	---	($111,850.00)	-25.08	-0.28	---	($149,300.00)	100.00	-0.44	---
G/(L) on sale of Fxd Assets	$0.00	0.00	0.00	---	$0.00	0.00	0.00	---	$0.00	0.00	0.00	3.80
Profit Before Taxes	$277,640.00	11.17	0.59	2.90	$249,750.00	52.12	0.62	2.90	$164,180.00	100.00	0.48	---
Taxes	$113,830.00	11.16	0.24	---	$102,400.00	49.40	0.25	---	$68,540.00	100.00	0.20	---
Net Profit	$163,810.00	11.17	0.35	---	$147,350.00	54.07	0.36	---	$95,640.00	100.00	0.28	---
Other Data:												
Working Capital	$2,039,970.00	7.62	24.17	24.00	$1,895,560.00	100.00	23.59	24.70	$0.00	0.00	0.00	0.00
Tangible Equity	$1,713,700.00	12.26	20.30	27.40	$1,526,540.00	100.00	19.00	29.80	$0.00	0.00	0.00	0.00
Recommended Credit Limit:	$205,644.00	16.13	---	---	$0.00				$0.00			

Drug "R" Us Products Inc.
400 Rundown Lane
Blowndowntown, TN 30606

RATIOS

RATIOS	Unit	12/31/95 Value	95 % Change	95 UQ	95 Med	95 LQ	12/31/94 Value	94 % Change	94 UQ	94 Med	94 LQ	12/31/93 Value	93 % Change	93 UQ	93 Med	93 LQ
SOLVENCY																
Current Ratio	($)	1.36	0.91	2.00	1.40	1.20	1.35	100.00	1.90	1.50	1.20	0.00	0.00	2.20	1.60	1.20
Quick Ratio	($)	0.76	-134.82	1.10	0.70	0.50	0.66	100.00	1.10	0.80	0.60	0.00	0.00	1.10	0.80	0.60
Net Profit B4 Tax + Depr./Cur LTD	(X)	0.00	0.00	9.70	2.80	1.20	0.00	0.00	9.80	3.20	1.30	0.00	0.00	6.20	2.50	1.10
Sales to Fixed Assets	(X)	114.71	438.74	167.50	59.70	19.60	21.29	100.00	161.30	44.70	17.70	0.00	0.00	105.50	42.30	19.60
Sales to Total Assets	(X)	5.54	10.16	5.10	3.40	2.10	5.03	100.00	4.30	2.90	2.20	0.00	0.00	4.40	3.20	2.40
Total Liab. to NW	(X)	3.20	-7.31	1.20	2.80	6.30	3.46	100.00	1.10	2.30	5.30	0.00	0.00	1.00	2.60	4.30
Fixed Assets to NW	(X)	0.20	-3.08	0.10	0.20	0.70	0.21	100.00	0.10	0.30	0.70	0.00	0.00	0.10	0.30	0.70
Tot. Liab. to Tot. Assets	(%)	76.22	-1.74	N/A	N/A	N/A	77.57	100.00	N/A	N/A	N/A	0.00	0.00	N/A	N/A	N/A
Oper. Prof. to Int. Exp.	(X)	3.74	15.73	N/A	N/A	N/A	3.23	53.97	N/A	N/A	N/A	2.10	100.00	N/A	N/A	N/A
Oper Prof+Lease Py to Int Exp+LP	(X)	3.74	15.73	N/A	N/A	N/A	3.23	53.97	N/A	N/A	N/A	2.10	100.00	N/A	N/A	N/A
EFFICIENCY																
Sales to Receivables	(X)	11.74	-7.42	15.30	9.60	6.10	12.68	100.00	13.30	9.00	6.60	0.00	0.00	14.40	8.90	6.30
Days Sales Outstanding	(D)	31	6.90	24	38	60	29	100.00	27	41	55	0	0.00	25	41	58
Cost of Sales to Inv.	(X)	13.75	30.54	14.40	9.80	5.20	10.53	100.00	12.10	6.30	3.90	0.00	0.00	11.60	6.80	4.50
Days' Sales in Inventory	(D)	27	-22.86	25	37	70	35	100.00	30	58	94	0	0.00	31	54	81
Sales to Net Working Cap.	(X)	22.90	7.54	9.30	13.80	33.90	21.30	100.00	7.30	12.50	37.00	0.00	0.00	7.20	12.30	25.00
Cost of Sales/Payables	(X)	9.28	-4.75	13.10	9.50	6.70	9.75	100.00	14.70	9.20	5.70	0.00	0.00	14.30	9.10	5.80
A/P Turnover	(D)	39	5.41	28	38	54	37	100.00	25	40	64	0	0.00	26	40	63
PROFITABILITY																
Depreciation to Sales	(%)	0.13	-6.66	0.20	0.30	0.90	0.14	-13.02	0.20	0.60	1.40	0.17	100.00	0.30	0.60	1.30
Prof bef Tax to Tot Assets	(%)	3.29	5.81	13.70	4.80	1.60	3.11	100.00	15.80	7.00	1.70	0.00	0.00	16.20	6.40	1.50
Profit before Taxes to TNW	(%)	13.83	-0.19	43.00	26.20	12.20	13.86	100.00	56.80	25.30	11.10	0.00	0.00	58.80	25.40	6.30

OTHER RATIOS NOT AVAILABLE WITH INDUSTRY STANDARDS

RATIOS	Unit	12/31/95 Value	95 % Change	95 UQ	95 Med	95 LQ	12/31/94 Value	94 % Change	94 UQ	94 Med	94 LQ	12/31/93 Value	93 % Change	93 UQ	93 Med	93 LQ
SOLVENCY																
Inv. to Net Work. Capital	(X)	1.63	-17.63	N/A	N/A	N/A	1.98	100.00	N/A	N/A	N/A	0.00	0.00	N/A	N/A	N/A
Current Liab. to NW	(X)	2.83	-6.66	N/A	N/A	N/A	3.04	100.00	N/A	N/A	N/A	0.00	0.00	N/A	N/A	N/A
LT Debt to Tot. Debt & Capital	(%)	8.84	-6.65	N/A	N/A	N/A	9.47	100.00	N/A	N/A	N/A	0.00	0.00	N/A	N/A	N/A
Fixed Assets to LT Debt	(X)	0.59	9.26	N/A	N/A	N/A	0.54	100.00	N/A	N/A	N/A	0.00	0.00	N/A	N/A	N/A
EFFICIENCY																
Net Sales to NW	(X)	23.27	3.88	N/A	N/A	N/A	22.40	100.00	N/A	N/A	N/A	0.00	0.00	N/A	N/A	N/A
Net Sales to Inventory	(X)	14.07	30.52	N/A	N/A	N/A	10.78	100.00	N/A	N/A	N/A	0.00	0.00	N/A	N/A	N/A
Cost of Sales/Working Capital	(X)	22.38	7.54	N/A	N/A	N/A	20.81	100.00	N/A	N/A	N/A	0.00	0.00	N/A	N/A	N/A
Short Term Loan Turnover	(X)	6.00	-53.85	N/A	N/A	N/A	13.00	100.00	N/A	N/A	N/A	0.00	0.00	N/A	N/A	N/A
LT Liabilities Payback *	($)	$226.60	10.28	---	---	---	$205.48	34.87	---	---	---	$152.35	100.00	---	---	---
PROFITABILITY																
Gross Profit on Net Sales	(%)	2.28	0.00	---	20.90	---	2.28	-2.56	---	30.90	---	2.34	100.00	---	29.30	---
Net Oper Inc on Net Sales	(%)	0.81	-10.00	---	3.80	---	0.90	-1.10	---	4.00	---	0.91	100.00	---	4.40	---
Net Profit on Net Sales	(%)	0.35	-2.78	N/A	N/A	N/A	0.36	28.57	N/A	N/A	N/A	0.28	100.00	N/A	N/A	N/A
Net Prof on Total Assets	(%)	1.94	6.01	N/A	N/A	N/A	1.83	100.00	N/A	N/A	N/A	0.28	100.00	N/A	N/A	N/A
Tot Assets to Equity	(X)	4.20	-5.67	N/A	N/A	N/A	4.46	100.00	N/A	N/A	N/A	0.00	0.00	N/A	N/A	N/A
Net Prft on Stkhldrs Eqty	(%)	8.16	-0.12	N/A	N/A	N/A	8.17	100.00	N/A	N/A	N/A	0.00	0.00	N/A	N/A	N/A

(X) = TIMES   (D) = DAYS   (%) = PRECENT   ($) = DOLLARS

* IN THOUSANDS

OVERVIEW

Let us look at the financial condition and the credit status of this customer. Here we have only two years' worth of balance sheet information and three years' worth of income statement information to analyze. Starting with liquidity, the most recent quick ratio is better than the previous year and is slightly better than average ($0.76 to $1.00 compared to $0.70 to a $1.00). Even though DSO worsened by two days, it is far better than industry average (31 days compared to 38 days).

A/P turnover likewise worsened by two days but is only slightly worse than industry average (39 days compared to 38 days). Inventory turnover improved significantly over the previous year and is almost as good as the industry upper quartile (27 days compared to 25 days). Debt to net worth improved greatly over the previous year but is worse than industry average ($3.20 to $1.00 compared to $2.80 to $1.00).

This firm's gross margin remained the same from the previous year but it is tremendously below the industry average (2.28% compared to 20.9%). Its operating profit is down from the previous year and is also far under industry average (0.81% compared to 3.8%). Sales have increased substantially each year, and net worth has also increased from the previous year.

The high credit on the credit report was $300,000 with payments being made anywhere from discounted up to 15 days slow. The bank has a first lien on everything. The firm has been operating for 40 years and is 100% owned by the president. The previous firm that employed the president filed bankruptcy nine years earlier. The firm has 275 employees and owns its facilities.

The high credit on the three trade references obtained was $500,000 and the average days paid ranged from 30 days to 42 days from invoice date. All reflected payment trends were toward promptness; however, in two of the references where a 2% 30 days discount was offered, no mention of discounting took place. The bank has extended the firm a high seven-figure ($8 million to $9 million) working capital line of credit, which appears to be fully utilized and is satisfactory.

WHAT OTHER CREDIT PROFESSIONALS THOUGHT

Now let us meet the first of our three students and see how he dealt with this case. Our group will tie questions 2 and 3 together in replying to the important aspects of this case.

Student One

Bob D. is the corporate credit manager for a major vacuum cleaner manufacturer. This case was a very intriguing and complicated puzzle for him.
In assessing the positives, Bob felt that the potential for admittance into a
market that Hipower has not been able to penetrate was a major plus, as
were the higher margins on the product and the size of this order. The
financials for Drugs "R" Us, not great, were at least adequate to make the
request for credit plausible. Its paying habits on the whole were good to
average.

The negatives, he felt, included dealing with Arnold Stopgap, a self-
described tough negotiator. Another major factor is the fact that Drugs
"R" Us has a customer that represents 40% of its total sales, and that contract is up for renewal in the next two months. There have been rumors
that this customer is planning on dumping it at that time.

Since gains in this very tight market are made only through reducing
the market share of a competitor, this might be an excellent opportunity to
increase market share. Currently, Drugs "R" Us controls 75% of the
regional market that it services, which is excellent. If Hipower decides to
set up Drugs "R" Us as its distributor, Hipower will become one of its top
five suppliers, which should give Hipower some control over Drugs "R"
Us's more errant ways of doing business.

Additional information on what prompted the bankruptcy in the previous drug firm that Arnold Stopgap ran would provide insights into the
possibility of him taking this type of action again. Since this is a Subchapter "S" corporation, all income or losses flow down to the owner.
When funds are needed to meet tax requirements, they are taken directly
out of the firm's coffers, which is another reason for knowing more about
the previous bankruptcy. All these elements directly affect not only
whether credit will be extended but, if it is extended, whether it is on a
secured or unsecured basis.

Student Two

Susan D., a credit manager who works for a large consumer and industrial
agricultural supplies manufacturer, agreed with what Bob had said. She
later added that with his less-than-stellar background and poor attitude,
Arnold Stopgap may be the force that brings down the 40-year-old, well-
established firm created by his father. This is compounded by the rumor

that the largest customer, who represents 40% of its business, is about to drop them.

Susan also was concerned by Arnold's request for extended dating on the initial order. His requesting terms of 3% 60 days, net 90 days could mean that he already is experiencing financial difficulties. Since the initial order is for only $1.5 million and considering that the total annual purchases are going to be between $13.5 million and $15 million, each monthly shipment thereafter will range between $1 million and $1.225 million. This is not a great deal less than the initial shipment; thus the initial shipment should not require any special terms compared to the regular monthly purchases. Susan wants to know why the extended terms are needed.

Student Three

Mitch P., a controller for a national paper corporation, was disturbed by the large size of the working capital line of credit and how the company could have such a high balance now when at the end of the year the bank and long-term debt totaled only $1.4 million. Unless this money was used to pay down the A/P outstanding, where did the money go?

While it is critical for Hipower to break into this market, it is also critical to know if the firm that controls it will be around at all, especially if its top customer may leave it in the dust in two months.

THE COLLATERAL ISSUE

Student One

Bob D. stated that the need for security in this case is obvious. The potential loss of its largest customer, the past track record of a bankruptcy, the only fair financials, the request for extended terms, and the missing money question makes this a no-brainer. Since drugs typically are not readily salable once they are returned, a purchase money security interest would not be of much value in this case. On the other hand, a standby letter of credit would be ideal since such letters generally are not affected by a bankruptcy filing of the firm that offered the letters as collateral. Considering the margin on this product is 55%, a standby letter of credit for at least half of the credit line would not only protect the company's costs but also a small amount of their profit. All of these reasons would help to sell top management, but Bob doubted that anything would sell Arnold on the idea of providing security against this potential line of credit.

If indeed the bank line has been totally used up, then the bank would not be interested in providing a standby letter of credit and would be totally against a purchase money security interest if Arnold requested one.

Student Two

Susan D. added that she believed that it might already be too late to worry about collateral in this case. The factors that affect the possibility that collateral will not even be available include the working capital line of credit being used up and the fact that drugs are something that you do not wish to take back. This only leaves a second lien behind the bank. With the company's debt structure, it is likely that nothing would be left to pay Hipower.

If security can be obtained, then it would indeed be a standby letter of credit for at least $1 million coupled with a personal guarantee signed by Arnold Stopgap. This would not allow him to bankrupt the company without being responsible for the debt. It would then force him to pay it, be sued and attached, or file personal bankruptcy. As far as convincing top management to agree to this decision, the emphasis would be on the possibility of a substantial loss occurring in about two months if Drugs "R" Us were approved.

While there is a definite need to obtain access to this market, it is likewise smart to keep the owner in check if he refuses to cooperate. The potential loss of the largest customer and the quick use of the working capital line of credit coupled with Arnold's poor attitude and previous bankruptcy track record should be all that is needed to convince top management that collateral is required.

Arnold's attitude and the bank being tapped out on the working capital line of credit do not leave much room for discussion or convincing him. In Arnold's case, though, it should be a take-it-or-leave-it offer with no exceptions made.

Student Three

Mitch P. felt that security was required. Before demanding it, though, he would be willing to sit down with Arnold Stopgap to discuss all the problems in the case. Mitch P. felt that before a final requirement of security is made and how much is needed is determined, he must have answers to some hard questions.

The details of the former bankruptcy, the draw down of the working capital line of credit, the status of the relationship between Drugs "R" Us and the Fortune 50 customer, and whether the contract will be renewed among other things need to be clarified. Without solid answers to what is happening on these aspects of the case, a sound business credit decision cannot be rendered. With answers, though, negotiations could begin and a resolution could be reached fairly quickly.

Student One

Bob D. recommended that a meeting be set up with Arnold Stopgap to discuss questions. Arnold's level of cooperation, answers to the questions, and ability to provide security will either make or break this sale. Even though Hipower needs this sale and access to this market, it needs even more to avoid getting connected to a firm that is on its way out.

Student Two

Susan D.'s biggest concern revolved around whether there was any truth to the rumor that Drugs "R" Us was being dumped by its largest customer. She recommended a meeting with both the end user and Arnold prior to credit being considered. If the end user agrees to renewing its contract because Hipower signs up Arnold's firm, then the decision to move forward on the sale is greatly improved. Although answers to other questions still need to be provided, with some security and some cooperation on Arnold's part, the sale can go through.

Student Three

Mitch P. was not so optimistic about the answers that he anticipated receiving. He felt that all the news may be bad, such as the bank line being tapped out and the end user definitely dropping Arnold's firm. He also believed that Arnold's earlier bankruptcy was a means to force the creditors to accept far less than what was due them due to Arnold's mismanaging of that firm. Knowing this, Mitch would recommend that top management consider approaching the Fortune 50 company with an offer either to sell direct to it or, if it chose to buy from a distributor, to sign up that firm as the new distributor. Once getting either the Fortune 50 firm or a new distributor on board, a "foot in the door" will have been established and Hipower will have safely entered this very desirable market.

WHAT REALLY HAPPENED

To no one's surprise, Arnold did lose his largest customer and file bankruptcy, but that is really only part of the story. I had flown out to meet Arnold at his office with the regional sales manager to discuss my concerns over the new alliance Hipower was considering.

What Arnold did not know was that we also planned a meeting with the buyer at the Fortune 50 firm the next day. After getting literally no cooperation from Arnold, listening to many innuendoes that we were trying to beat up on a small defenseless distributor just like all the major drug manufacturers do, and that his past was none of our business, we left knowing that he was in trouble. I decided that his firm may be in the process of being dropped by a large number of manufacturers. This meant that the end was rapidly approaching and would explain why our closest competitor was relieved about losing Arnold as a customer.

The meeting with Arnold's customer was enlightening. Speaking with their director of purchasing, I discovered that not only was his company planning to drop Arnold as a vendor but a great many other customers also were planning to drop Arnold at the expiration of their contracts. Knowing that he was going down the tubes quickly, we asked the director how we could be of service to his firm. He requested that we consider doing business with some ex-employees of Arnold's. These same ex-employees were being bankrolled by a number of firms that needed focal point vendors for all their pharmaceutical needs. We were told to ask the ex-employees the specifics.

That day I traveled to meet the new vendor being created by the end users. Soon I found myself in the presence of Arnold's son, Jack Stopgap. Floored by this revelation that Arnold had fired his own son and that the end users were excited about dealing with Jack, I had millions of questions.

As it turned out, Arnold had used the company's working capital line of credit to pay off some extremely large personal gambling debts. He was now in trouble and needed to get his customers to pay very quickly so he could cover his payables and meet his weekly payroll. When Jack confronted Arnold with this information, Jack was fired and escorted off the premises by security. This same thing had occurred with his former business that filed bankruptcy. Jack had always been a favorite of the end users, as he had set up the contracts directly and had worked well with their buyers and marketing staff. When the end users discovered that they would now have to deal directly with Arnold instead of Jack, they were upset and made an effort to contact Jack directly. They offered to bankroll a new company for him to keep their supplies flowing and to keep alive the great relationship that they had with him. Jack told me they were providing interest-free loans and corporate guarantees to his suppliers so he could obtain the credit lines needed to hit the road running. Jack was excited about the possibility of selling our product to his customers and was able to get us a corporate guarantee from the Fortune 50 customer for the first three years that we did business with him. After that time we would need to reevaluate the relationship and approve his firm on its own merits.

Once all the paperwork was received, signed, and the firm was set up and running, we immediately began shipping products into this formerly impenetrable area of the market. Arnold has retired, is being treated for a gambling addiction, and has reestablished his relationship with his son.

14

CASE STUDY 10: FREEZY REFRIGERATION REPAIR CO.

Addressing the Problems with the Sale of a Service

INTRODUCTION

This chapter provides techniques for dealing with customers who need your service at the time but, once the work is done, leave you "hanging" for your payment. Readers will study how to deal with applications that say nothing and compare countermethods for protecting themselves. The art of negotiating with a difficult collection yet keeping collection expenses tight will be discussed in this case. The goal is to minimize the potential for loss while still confirming the sale. Readers will play devil's advocate to hone their ability to bring home a satisfied customer.

By reviewing this real day in the life of a credit consulting firm, readers will learn to make effective use of data, facts, and alternative methods in reaching a decision. An appreciation for how other people in marketing or finance think will hone negotiating skills. Readers can use new insight into the creation of a sound business credit decision to prevent gaps or weaknesses in their decision-making processes.

Case study 10 is completely different from the previous nine. Here you will become a consulting firm and try to solve the working problems of a small service company. This situation is unlike the ones you are likely to encounter as the credit manager for a large firm. Here your time is limited and you lack the controls and the resources that you have at the larger firm. In addition, the firm that hired you has only a limited amount of money to spend for your services and may not pay you unless real results are obtained.

In this chapter I do not present financials or credit reports or the three students.

THE FACTS

Cash Flow Inc. is your business, created to help small and midsize businesses compete against large firms. Your first client, Freezy Refrigeration Repair Co., Inc., has some unique problems to be solved to make its significant delinquency drop. As background information, commercial freezer units can be anything from a small portable case to a large walk in unit. This company does not do repairs on consumer refrigerators.

ISSUES TO BE RESOLVED

Problem One

When Freezy receives a call on a repair from a new customer, it immediately dispatches a service truck and the clock starts ticking on the bill. Phone arrangements are made to request a check at the completion of work. Small restaurants, convenience stores, and grocery stores are serviced. When the service person arrives, the owner typically assures him that he will have the check ready when the work is completed. Many times, when the work is completed, no one is available to pay and the service person is told that a check will be sent. Credit is thereby given whether Freezy wants to or not.

Problem Two

When a credit application is received, the references are always food suppliers. They must be paid on time or the customer will be out of business.

These are poor references as they do not compare to the level of value that someone who offers a service provides. Service people are important only until the problem is fixed, then they are no longer significant.

Problem Three

Freezy Refrigeration Co. does not have much expertise in collections. It is a company started by a husband and wife. The husband is the expert in repairs and has a group of technicians to help with service calls. The wife is the office manager and has all the responsibilities for accounts receivable and payables and keeping her staff of three clerks covering day-to-day activities. They cannot afford to hire a high-powered credit manager to watch over their accounts receivables. They also cannot afford a D&B contract. Their one major advantage is that there is a significant amount of business out there and they readily can select their clientele.

QUESTIONS

1. What can be done to protect them against problem 1? Be creative!
2. List other types of companies that are similar to Freezy and could be asked for as a specific reference on a credit application.
3. What credit factors should Freezy consider in extending credit to customers?
4. What special and normal collection techniques could be used to improve Freezy's delinquency?
5. When should Freezy write off an account? What factors should it consider when it chooses a collection agency?

OVERVIEW

As part of this case, readers can re-create forms and documents that would be of use to Freezy in solving its credit problems. Those readers who think that "credit is credit" no matter to whom or what is being sold are sadly mistaken. A manufacturer or a distributor grants the credit and sells goods from an industrial or consumer product line is radically different than when a service firm extends credit. Besides the obvious fact that there is no physical product to be had, some service firms, such as this one, must deal with the fact that before they perform the service they are the most critical firm to that customer, but once their service has been completed, they are valueless.

Other service firms offer a continuous service that is constantly critical to their customers, which eliminates the problems that this small firm experiences on a daily basis. While reference checking, credit report review, and to some extent even financial analysis are the same in all types of credit, the approval conditions may be very much different to a service firm, as can be the credit terms that are extended. Even the analysis of the financial statements of a service firm compared to that of a manufacturer, distributor, or retailer varies greatly in some very important aspects, such as inventory turnover and DSO, to name only two. Now take some time to answer the questions, and then I will provide my efforts to solve this company's credit issues.

SOLUTION

Here I take you through my recommendations for dealing with new customer approval and collection difficulties. In question 1, we deal with the problem of how not to be stiffed after doing the work. There is a way to deal with being stuck for the payment after the work is done, no matter when the company receives the call.

Off Hours

Let us take the wee hours of the morning situation first, as it is the most difficult. Since most of the customers are small, usually family-owned firms such as restaurants, mom-and-pop grocery stores, or franchise food stores, the owner typically is the one who discovers the problem. If you have never done business with them before, you should require a credit card number to hold the guarantee of service before you dispatch a repair truck. If you are given a credit card number, you should inform the caller that a hold will be placed against the card for the basic service fee. If the caller pays at the end of the service work, the charge will be canceled. Clear the card while the customer is on the line; if the charge is approved, dispatch the truck.

If a check is received after the work is done, the credit card hold will be released (assuming that the check clears). If the check bounces, the charge is reinstated. When the work is completed, the owner must be shown the work and that the refrigeration unit is working perfectly. The owner then signs a form confirming that the unit was working perfectly when the work was completed and that payment was made either via a check or a credit card (assuming that the check does not clear). A credit application will be left. See Exhibit 10.1 for an example of a credit application form.

If future service is needed and an account is established for that particular firm, there is no need for either a credit card or a check at completion of the service work. The confirmed work order is kept in the customer's credit folder. Once either the check is cleared or the credit card pays the service firm, it is retained for use as a means to solicit future business. The work order also can be referred to if the customer ever defaults on a future invoice for other service work; then you can charged the credit card given at that time (as authorized on your credit application).

A photocopy of the customer's check should be kept in the credit file for use if a customer's credit card is canceled or closed and an asset is needed to attach under a judgment for the amount owed.

Normal Business Hours

Now let us look at the situation that deals with a call coming in during normal business hours. When the owner calls in the request for service, a credit application is taken over the phone. If the owner refuses to complete it over the phone, then a credit card number is required before a truck can be dispatched. The same procedure is followed as described in the wee-hours scenario. Once the credit application is completed, a quick call to the references is made. If the references come back satisfactory, a truck is dispatched. If the information that comes back is poor or no information can be obtained, the owner is contacted again and a credit card number is requested before a truck will be dispatched.

As before, the owner signs the confirmation of completion of the service work, which is returned to the customer's credit folder along with the signed copy of the credit application taken over the phone. The service technician has this application signed when he arrives at the customer's location or the work is not done. When payment is received, a copy of the check is retained in the customer's file for future use.

Exhibit 10.1.   Credit application form

FREEZY REFRIGERATION REPAIR COMPANY, INC.
CREDIT APPLICATION FORM

Firm's Legal Name: _____ Phone #: _____

Physical Address: _____ Fax #: _____

City: _____ State: _____ Zip: _____

# of Years in Business: _____ Liquor License #: _____

Expiration date of license: _____ State issued: _____

If Incorporated and have sales under $5,000,000 or are a Proprietorship or a Partnership,
List Name, Home Address, Social Security #, & Date of Birth of Owners:

_____
_____
_____
_____
_____
_____
_____
_____
_____
_____

Date & Location of Incorporation: _____
Federal Tax ID #: _____ Own or Rent Building: _____

Name & Address of Mortgage Holder or Landlord: _____
_____
_____
_____

Bank Name: _____

Bank Address: _____
_____

Phone #: _____ Fax #: _____
Bank Account #: _____ Loan #: _____
Person To Contact & Title: _____
_____

Exhibit 10.1.   Continued

<u>FREEZY REFRIGERATION REPAIR COMPANY, INC.</u>
<u>CREDIT APPLICATION FORM (Cont.)</u>

Advertising Reference: _____

Address: _____

Person To Contact & Title: _____

Phone #: _____ Fax #: _____

Printer Reference: _____

Address: _____

Person To Contact & Title: _____

Phone #: _____ Fax #: _____

Refrigeration Repair Reference: _____

Address: _____

Person To Contact & Title: _____

Phone #: _____ Fax #: _____

By signing, I attest to the truthfulness of the above information and agreement with all terms. For value received, I hereby authorize Freezy Refrigeration Repair Co., Inc. in the event of non-payment to charge my credit card for any services rendered now or in the future for my firm with interest. In the event of a default all expenses of collection including court costs, collection and attorney's fees will be added to the total due Freezy Refrigeration Repair Co., Inc. I agree to pay interest (at the state legal limit interest rate where the vendor is located) per month on all invoices over 15 days past due. I hereby authorize Freezy Refrigeration Repair Co., Inc. to check my consumer and business credit for consideration in the extension of credit for services rendered by them.

By: _____ Date: _____

By: _____ Date: _____

REFERENCES

Service firms are critical when the call comes in but once the work is completed, they lose their worth. Many firms fall into this same category; one such firm is an advertising firm such as a newspaper, "penny saver" type publication, radio, and occasionally a local television station. While the advertisement is being prepared and is being run, the newspaper or television station is crucial; once the ad has run its course, the firm is of little or no use to the advertiser. Another such firm is a printer.

References should be obtained from companies that are in the same payment situation as the company supplying the service.

CREDIT FACTORS

One factor that should be checked in particular with the customer's bank is whether it has run any nonsufficient funds (NSF) checks through the bank. A firm that is "writing bad paper" is in trouble. Since most of these firms are "cash-type" firms, they should maintain a respectable average balance in their checking account. A number that is low for a firm of this size might mean serious trouble.

As stated earlier, information supplied by other service firms that are in the same boat as you are in is of vital importance to your credit decision. A last piece of advice is to join a local trade credit group to exchange credit information on these types of customers. Check exchange information before approving a new customer. If it did not pay another service firm that sold to it, then likely it will not pay you.

COLLECTIONS

Fifteen days after completion of the work, call the owner to determine whether he or she is satisfied with the work. If all factors are positive, then a confirmation of receipt of Freezy's invoice should be made. End the call by reminding that payment will be expected according to Freezy's terms (net 30 days from invoice date). If there is a problem, solve it immediately and then confirm the invoice's receipt and the due date. Call again at 45 days due; refuse to do more work at 60 days due. If more service is requested, advise the customer that payment in full of the past due amount must be made before work is started. Have the company provide a

MasterCard or Visa credit card number before a service person leaves and have an authorization form signed before work commences to cover all new work. If the account has reached a serious state (60 or more days past due), send a letter advising that an artisan's lien is being considered for the work that was done. If no payment is received, send a final letter and forward the account to a collection agency with instructions to proceed with the lien and a lawsuit.

BAD DEBT AND COLLECTION AGENCIES

When an account goes 90 days past due, it should be written off and placed with a collection agency. You should be willing to extend credit to an agency in an amount equal to the balance that you are placing with them. The use of agencies that are National Association of Credit Management (NACM) affiliates or those backed by well-known companies, such as Dun & Bradstreet, would be acceptable. If the company has a large amount or anticipates a high volume of accounts to be written off, it should negotiate for a better rate. It also should demand a monthly status report on all accounts placed with the agency.

15

CASE STUDY 11: TERRA TECHNOLOGY, INC.

The Risk of a Custom Order Sale

INTRODUCTION

Risk factors include dealing with the possibility of a canceled order, lack of funds to meet progress payments, and having the funds available to pay your creditors for materials. In this case study, the business must consider developing a terms and collection strategy. It also looks at dealing with a service firm that contracts for others from the point of view of managing risk/rewards factors. Readers will learn how to consummate the deal with all the "I's" dotted and the "T's" crossed, which will help to bring home a done deal.

By reviewing this real day in the life of a credit department, readers will learn to make effective use of data, facts, and alternative methods in reaching a decision. An appreciation for how other people in marketing or finance think will hone negotiating skills. Readers can use new insight into the creation of a sound business credit decision to prevent gaps or weaknesses in their decision-making processes.

Case study 11 deals with a large construction job of a very customized product that has high overhead costs and is paid for over a much longer period of time than the typical 30 days. The risks involve creating a product that cannot be sold elsewhere; exposure for the initial costs involved in designing, buying of materials, storage of materials, labor, and storage costs of work in process; and transportation of the finished goods. Although progress payments are made in these types of construction jobs, they rarely begin to cover the amount of initial cash outlay that can occur in projects of this size. Your firm must be financially sound and able to deal with these issues and with the biggest issue of all, a default.

THE FACTS

I.B. Strict, the division credit manager for Locktight Tanks Company (a manufacturer), is reviewing a new account with his credit analyst, Jane Dough. The customer, Terra Technology, Inc., has been in business for about 14 years. It had refused to provide financials at first but finally agreed to release them. Terra is a market leader in the engineering and design of water treatment plants and has had great success in areas that Locktight could not penetrate. Anticipated additional sales for Locktight as reflected in its sales manager's report on Terra Technology would be between $10 million to $15 million per year.

Its paying habits are excellent, taking discounts when offered and paying at terms when only net is offered. The initial order placed by Terra Technology is for $3.5 million to be shipped in the next 150 days. Locktight's margin on the order is 25%, which is average for the industry. The standard terms of sale for customized construction jobs are 10% down payment due at order placement, 10% due at start of fabrication, 10% due at 120 days from date of order, 10% due at shipment, and 60% due at start up but not to exceed 90 days from the date of shipment. A credit check and financial analysis are available for review.

INSTRUCTIONS

1. Analyze all data available on the case, summarizing your findings using the following:
   A. Trend analysis, common-size analysis, ratio analysis, and comparison to industry standards

    B. Summarize the information available in the credit report, references, and information available above

2. What is your credit decision?

3. If approved, will open account terms be offered? Is security needed? If so, what type? Or should the order be declined?

4. What facts would you use to defend your decision to management and to the customer?

5. If overridden by management, what steps would you take to prevent a possible loss?

CREDIT REPORT

FILE #123456789   DATE PRINTED   SUMMARY
                            MAY 23, 1996   RATING 4A1
TERRA TECHNOLOGY INC.   STARTED 1982
323 DONEIN ROAD   ENGINEERING &   SALES $179,492,000
BLOWMEDOWN, WI 70606   GENERAL CONTRACTOR   WORTH $24,676,000
   TEL: 505 555-9000   SIC NO.   HISTORY CLEAR
                                 73 53   CONDITION STRONG

CHIEF EXECUTIVE: ARNOLD STOPGAP, PRES.

PAYMENTS (Amounts may be rounded to nearest figure in prescribed ranges)
REPORTED

	PAYING RECORD	HIGH CREDIT	NOW OWES	PAST DUE	SELLING TERMS	LAST SALE WITHIN
4/96	Ppt	250000	250	-0-		1 Mo
3/96	Disc	100000	5000	-0-		
2/96	Ppt	2500000	-0-	-0-	N15	2-3 Mos
	Ppt	750000			N30	
1/96	Disc	100000	-0-	-0-	1 Prox N30	
	Ppt	600000	10000	-0-		1 Mo
12/95	Disc	3000000	10000	-0-	1 10 N30	1 Mo
8/95	Ppt	500000	2000	-0-		1 Mo
	Ppt	50000	-0-	-0-	N30	6-12 Mos
	Ppt	50000				
5/95	Ppt	100000	5000	-0-		1 Mo

   * Payment experiences reflect how bills are met in relation to the terms granted.
   In some instances payment beyond terms can be the result of disputes over
   merchandise, skipped invoices, etc.
   * Each experience shown represents a separate account reported by a supplier.
   Updated trade experiences replace those previously reported.

FINANCE
* Financial information is attached for your review. Strong condition is indicated based
on debt to net worth. Sales for 1995 were forecasted to be $40,000,000.

PUBLIC FILINGS
UCC FILINGS
4/15/95
   Financing statement #984345 filed 9/11/93 with Secretary, State of WI. Debtor Terra
   Technology Inc., Blowmedown WI, Secured Party: All Secured Bank, NA,
   Watertown, WI.

Collateral: Accounts receivable, inventory, all other fixed assets.

TERRA TECHNOLOGY INC.   May 23, 1996   PAGE 002

HISTORY
4/15/96
    ARNOLD L. STOPGAP, PRES.
    JACK L. STOPGAP, V. PRES.
    BARRY R. STOPGAP, TREAS.
    DIRECTOR(S): The officer(s)

    INCORPORATED Wisconsin January 20, 1982

    Authorized capital consists of 500,000 shares Common Stock, $100 par value.

    Business started 1982 by Arnold L. Stopgap 100% of capital is owned by him.

    Arnold L. Stopgap born 1920, married. 1960 retired US Army. In 1961, he was a
    vice president at Modest Co. and in 1982 started this company and became its
    president.

    Jack L. Stopgap born 1950, single. Graduate Jackson University, Wheatland, WI
    1972. 1972–1982 employed by Modest Company. 1982–Present: Vice President
    here and continues.

    Barry R. Stopgap born 1951. Brother of Jack. Active here since 1982.

OPERATION
4/15/96
    Engineering and General Contract (100%)

    Terms progress payments. Has 200 accounts. Sells to industrial and government
    accounts. Territory: Worldwide. Nonseasonal.

    EMPLOYEES: 300 including officers. 230 employed here.

    FACILITIES: Owns 10,000 sq. ft. in 1-story concrete block building in good
    condition. Premises neat.

    LOCATION: Suburban business section on side street.

        FULL DISPLAY COMPLETE

Locktight Tanks Company
400-16 Still Moon Cres.
Rochester, NY 14624
FAX#: (716) 555-5860

BANK CREDIT INQUIRY

All Secured Bank, NA
235 St. Patrick Drive   Ref: Terra Technology Inc.
Watertown, WI 94355   1234 Creek Drive
(515) 555-2810   Taos, WI 82345

The above-referenced company has given your concern's name as a credit reference.
Please provide us with your experience with them so that we may determine their credit
worthiness. Please fax this information back to us as soon as possible. Thank you in
advance for the information that you provide and be assured that it will be kept
confidential.

Sincerely,

I. B. Strict
Credit Department

If business is not incorporated, please provide owners' name & address:

SAVINGS ACCOUNT   LOW __   MEDIUM __   HIGH __ $__ FIGURE ___
                  OPEN ___   CLOSED ___

CHECKING ACCOUNT   LOW __   MEDIUM _X_   HIGH __ $ 9_ FIGURE
                   SATISFACTORY _X_   UNSATISFACTORY ___

CREDIT EXPERIENCE

Loans are granted: Frequently ___   Occasionally ___   Seldom _X_

Type: Working Capital _X_ Mortgage __ Installment ___

Maximum Credit Extended $ High 10 Figures Secured _X_ Unsecured ___

Present Outstandings: Secured $High 9 Figures Unsecured $ _____

Relationship: SATISFACTORY _X_   UNSATISFACTORY ___

Have "NSF" checks been issued: Yes ___ No _X_

Prepared By: _I. M. Loose_____   Title: Ex. Vice President

Locktight Tanks Company
400-16 Still Moon Crescent
Rochester, NY 14624
PHONE (716) 555-5860
FAX   (716) 555-5860

CREDIT INQUIRY

*Pump Components U.S.A., Inc.   REF: Special Materials Inc.
*1136 Fallinarut Way   1234 Creek Drive
*Skyhigh, WI 33659   Taos, WI 82345

The above-referenced company has given your concern's name as a credit reference. Please provide us with your experience with them so that we may determine their credit worthiness. Please fax this information back to us as soon as possible. Thank you in advance for the information that you provide and be assured that it will be kept confidential.

Sincerely,

I.B. Strict
Credit Department

Sold From __1984__   MANNER OF PAYMENT
                                      ___ Discounts
Terms of Sales __Net 30__   _X_ Prompt & Satisfactory
                                      ___ Prompt to __ Days Slow
Largest Amount Now Owing $3,000,000   ___ Pays on Account
                                      ___ Asks for More Time
Amount Past Due $0_____   ___ Slow but Collectible
                                      ___ Accepts COD's Promptly
Recent Trend Toward _X_ Promptness   ___ Settles by Trade Acceptance
                  ___ Slowness   ___ Notes Paid at Maturity
Makes Unjust Claims (State) _____   ___ Account Secured
_____
_____

Credit Refused (State Cause) _____
_____
_____

Remarks: _____   _30_ Average Days Paid
_____

Information Given By: _Ken I. Think, Credit Manager_ Date _5/26/96_

WE REQUEST THE RETURN OF THIS FORM TO FACILITATE OUR SYSTEM OF FILING REPORT.

Locktight Tanks Company
400-16 Still Moon Crescent
Rochester, NY 14624
PHONE (716) 555-5860
FAX   (716) 555-5860

CREDIT INQUIRY

*Rubber Components Inc.   REF: Special Materials Inc.
*2235 Fallonface Way   1234 Creek Drive
*Deadend, WI 55699   Taos, WI 82345

The above-referenced company has given your concern's name as a credit reference.
Please provide us with your experience with them so that we may determine their credit
worthiness. Please fax this information back to us as soon as possible. Thank you in
advance for the information that you provide and be assured that it will be kept
confidential.

Sincerely,

I.B. Strict
Credit Department

Sold From _1988_____   MANNER OF PAYMENT
                                             ___ Discounts
Terms of Sales __Net 30_____   X Prompt & Satisfactory
                                             ___ Prompt to __ Days Slow
Largest Amount Now Owing $5,000,000   ___ Pays on Account
                                             ___ Asks for More Time
Amount Past Due $0_____   ___ Slow but Collectible
                                             ___ Accepts COD's Promptly
Recent Trend Toward X _Promptness   ___ Settles by Trade Acceptance
                    ___ Slowness   ___ Notes Paid at Maturity
Makes Unjust Claims (State) _____   ___ Account Secured
_____
_____

Credit Refused (State Cause) _____
_____
_____

Remarks: _____   30 Average Days Paid
_____
_____

Information Given By: _Ken I. Act, Credit Manager_ Date 5/26/96

WE REQUEST THE RETURN OF THIS FORM TO FACILITATE OUR SYSTEM OF
FILING REPORT.

Locktight Tanks Company
400-16 Still Moon Crescent
Rochester, NY 14624
PHONE (716) 555-5860
FAX   (716) 555-5860

CREDIT INQUIRY

*Steel Parts Now Inc.   REF: Special Materials Inc.
*8935 Nowork Way   1234 Creek Drive
*Lazyland, WI 99658   Taos, WI 82345

The above-referenced company has given your concern's name as a credit reference.
Please provide us with your experience with them so that we may determine their credit
worthiness. Please fax this information back to us as soon as possible. Thank you in
advance for the information that you provide and be assured that it will be kept
confidential.

Sincerely,

I.B. Strict
Credit Department

Sold From 1990   MANNER OF PAYMENT
                                         ___ Discounts
Terms of Sales Net 30   X Prompt & Satisfactory
                                         ___ Prompt to ___ Days Slow
Largest Amount Now Owing $6,000,000   ___ Pays on Account
                                         ___ Asks for More Time
Amount Past Due $0   ___ Slow but Collectible
                                         ___ Accepts COD's Promptly
Recent Trend Toward X Promptness   ___ Settles by Trade Acceptance
                     ___ Slowness   ___ Notes Paid at Maturity
Makes Unjust Claims (State) _____   ___ Account Secured
_____
_____

Credit Refused (State Cause) _____
_____
_____

Remarks: _____   30 Average Days Paid
_____

Information Given By: Ken I. Decide, Credit Manager Date 5/26/96

WE REQUEST THE RETURN OF THIS FORM TO FACILITATE OUR SYSTEM OF
FILING REPORT.

Terra Technology Inc.
323 Donein Road
Blowmedown, WI 70606

SIC 8711 ACCOUNT # 123456

$179,492,000.00
$24,676,000.00

	12/31/95				12/31/94				12/31/93			
	$	% Change	% Assets	Ind % Assets	$	% Change	% Assets	Ind % Assets	$	% Change	% Assets	Ind % Assets
Cash	$4,572,000.00	63.11	4.81	6.70	$2,803,000.00	100.00	2.82	8.40	$0.00	0.00	0.00	0.00
Accounts Receivable	$55,396,000.00	-0.48	58.28	48.30	$55,662,000.00	100.00	55.99	50.00	$0.00	0.00	0.00	0.00
Inventory	$0.00	0.00	0.00	3.20	$0.00	0.00	0.00	4.00	$0.00	0.00	0.00	0.00
Due from Shareholder	$0.00	0.00	0.00	---	$0.00	0.00	0.00	---	$0.00	0.00	0.00	---
Due From Affiliate	$0.00	0.00	0.00	---	$0.00	0.00	0.00	---	$0.00	0.00	0.00	---
Other Current	$5,121,000.00	-33.69	5.39	11.10	$7,723,000.00	100.00	7.77	6.30	$0.00	0.00	0.00	0.00
Total Current	$65,089,000.00	-1.66	68.48	69.30	$96,188,000.00	100.00	66.58	68.70	$0.00	0.00	0.00	0.00
Fixed Assets	$15,442,000.00	-16.94	16.25	17.10	$18,592,000.00	100.00	18.70	20.10	$0.00	0.00	0.00	0.00
Notes Receivable	$0.00	0.00	0.00	---	$0.00	0.00	0.00	---	$0.00	0.00	0.00	---
Deposits	$2,579,000.00	23.93	2.71	---	$2,081,000.00	100.00	2.09	---	$0.00	0.00	0.00	---
Cash Value of Life Insur.	$0.00	0.00	0.00	9.10	$0.00	0.00	0.00	9.00	$0.00	0.00	0.00	0.00
Intangible Assets	$11,936,000.00	-4.88	12.56	4.50	$12,549,000.00	100.00	12.62	2.20	$0.00	0.00	0.00	100.00
Total Assets	$95,046,000.00	-4.39	100.00	100.00	$99,410,000.00	100.00	100.00	100.00	$0.00	0.00	0.00	100.00
Account Payable	$14,466,000.00	-23.02	15.22	12.60	$18,791,000.00	100.00	18.90	11.40	$0.00	0.00	0.00	0.00
Bank Loans + N.P.	$0.00	0.00	0.00	8.20	$0.00	0.00	0.00	12.40	$0.00	0.00	0.00	0.00
Cur. Mat.-L.T.D.	$1,196,000.00	-73.13	1.26	2.70	$4,451,000.00	100.00	4.48	3.70	$0.00	0.00	0.00	0.00
Income Tax Payables	$0.00	-100.00	0.00	1.50	$599,000.00	100.00	0.60	1.20	$0.00	0.00	0.00	0.00
Accrued Expenses	$17,763,000.00	6.31	18.69	20.20	$16,709,000.00	100.00	16.81	14.90	$0.00	0.00	0.00	0.00
Total Current	$33,425,000.00	-17.57	35.17	45.20	$40,550,000.00	100.00	0.00	43.60	$0.00	0.00	0.00	0.00
Long Term Debt	$18,700,000.00	48.97	19.67	9.10	$12,553,000.00	100.00	12.63	9.20	$0.00	0.00	0.00	0.00
Deferred Taxes	$107,000.00	100.00	0.11	3.70	$0.00	0.00	0.00	3.70	$0.00	0.00	0.00	0.00
All Other L.T. Debt	$18,138,000.00	-16.87	19.08	4.90	$21,820,000.00	100.00	21.95	3.20	$0.00	0.00	0.00	0.00
Net Worth	$24,676,000.00	0.77	25.96	37.10	$24,487,000.00	100.00	24.63	40.30	$0.00	0.00	0.00	100.00
Total Liab & Equity	$95,046,000.00	-4.39	100.00	100.00	$99,410,000.00	100.00	59.21	100.00	$0.00	0.00	0.00	100.00
Net Sales	$179,492,000.00	1.87	100.00	100.00	$176,199,000.00	-6.01	100.00	100.00	$187,487,000.00	100.00	100.00	100.00
Cost of Goods Sold	$65,853,000.00	2.63	36.69	100.00	$64,165,000.00	-18.37	36.42	100.00	$78,606,000.00	100.00	41.93	100.00
Gross Profit	$113,639,000.00	1.43	63.31	0.00	$112,034,000.00	2.91	63.58	0.00	$108,861,000.00	100.00	58.07	0.00
Depreciation	$0.00	0.00	0.00	---	$0.00	0.00	0.00	---	$0.00	0.00	0.00	---
Lease Payments	$0.00	0.00	0.00	---	$0.00	0.00	0.00	---	$0.00	0.00	0.00	---
Other Operating Exps.	$107,482,000.00	-1.46	59.88	95.60	$109,073,000.00	-4.17	61.90	94.90	$113,825,000.00	100.00	60.72	94.60
Tot. Operating Exps.	$107,482,000.00	-1.46	59.88	4.40	$109,073,000.00	-4.17	61.90	5.10	$113,825,000.00	100.00	60.72	5.40
Operating Profit	$6,157,000.00	107.94	3.43	0.70	$2,961,000.00	-159.65	1.68	0.80	($4,964,000.00)	100.00	-2.65	0.90
Interest Inc./(Exp.)	($2,717,000.00)	-18.51	-1.51	---	($3,334,000.00)	-25.88	-1.89	---	($4,498,000.00)	100.00	-2.40	---
G/(L) on sale of Fxd Assets	$0.00	0.00	0.00	3.60	$0.00	0.00	0.00	4.20	$0.00	0.00	0.00	4.50
Profit Before Taxes	$3,440,000.00	-1,022.25	1.92	---	($373,000.00)	-96.06	-0.21	---	($9,462,000.00)	100.00	-5.05	---
Taxes	$3,776,000.00	762.10	2.10	---	$438,000.00	-190.68	0.25	---	($483,000.00)	100.00	-0.26	---
Net Profit	($336,000.00)	-58.57	-0.19	---	($811,000.00)	-90.97	-0.46	---	($8,979,000.00)	100.00	-4.79	---
Other Data:												
Working Capital	$31,664,000.00	23.50	33.31	24.10	$25,638,000.00	100.00	66.58	25.10	$0.00	0.00	0.00	0.00
Tangible Equity	$12,740,000.00	6.72	13.40	32.60	$11,938,000.00	100.00	12.01	38.10	$0.00	0.00	0.00	0.00
Recommended Credit Limit:	$1,146,600.00	2.18	---	---	$1,122,172.00	100.00	---	---	$0.00	---	---	---

Terra Technology Inc.
323 Donein Road
Blowmeadow, WI 70606

RATIOS

Ratio	Unit	12/31/95 Value	% Change	UQ	Med	LQ	12/31/94 Value	% Change	UQ	Med	LQ	12/31/93 Value	% Change	UQ	Med	LQ
SOLVENCY																
Current Ratio	($)	1.95	19.30	2.10	1.60	1.30	1.63	100.00	2.50	1.70	1.20	0.00	0.00	2.50	1.60	1.20
Quick Ratio	($)	1.79	24.44	1.70	1.30	0.90	1.44	100.00	2.20	1.40	1.00	0.00	0.00	2.20	1.40	1.00
Net Profit B4 Tax + Depr./Cur LTD	(X)	2.88	-3,532.23	14.10	4.00	1.70	-0.08	100.00	7.70	2.70	1.40	0.00	0.00	6.80	2.70	1.20
Sales to Fixed Assets	(X)	11.62	117.39	31.10	19.10	9.90	5.35	100.00	35.70	18.90	10.30	0.00	0.00	33.80	18.90	10.90
Sales to Total Assets	(X)	1.89	6.55	3.30	2.40	1.90	1.77	100.00	3.50	2.60	1.90	0.00	0.00	3.50	2.60	2.00
Total Liab. to NW	(X)	2.85	-6.80	1.10	1.70	3.30	3.06	100.00	0.80	1.50	3.30	0.00	0.00	0.80	1.50	3.40
Fixed Assets to NW	(X)	0.63	-17.58	0.20	0.40	1.00	0.76	100.00	0.20	0.40	0.90	0.00	0.00	0.20	0.40	0.90
Tot. Liab. to Tot. Assets	(%)	74.04	-1.76	N/A	N/A	N/A	75.37		N/A	N/A	N/A	0.00	0.00	N/A	N/A	N/A
Oper. Prof. to Int. Exp.	(X)	2.27	155.16	N/A	N/A	N/A	0.89	-180.47	N/A	N/A	N/A	-1.10	100.00	N/A	N/A	N/A
Oper Prof+Lease Py to Int Exp+LP	(X)	2.27	155.16	N/A	N/A	N/A	0.89	-180.47	N/A	N/A	N/A	-1.10	100.00	N/A	N/A	N/A
EFFICIENCY																
Sales to Receivables	(X)	3.24	2.36	6.80	5.10	4.00	3.17	100.00	7.40	5.10	3.60	0.00	0.00	7.70	5.00	3.60
Days Sales Outstanding	(D)	113	-1.74	54	72	91	115	100.00	49	72	101	0	0.00	47	73	101
Cost of Sales to Inv.	(X)	0.00	0.00	0	0	0	0.00	0.00	0	0	0	0	0.00	0	0	0
Days' Sales in Inventory	(D)	0	0.00	0	0	0	0	0.00	0	0	0	0	0.00	0	0	0
Sales to Net Working Cap.	(X)	5.67	-17.52	6.30	8.60	18.00	6.87	100.00	5.20	9.80	30.30	0.00	0.00	5.70	10.00	28.70
Cost of Sales/Payables	(X)	4.55	33.31	0.00	0.00	0.00	3.41	100.00	0.00	0.00	0.00	0.00	0.00	0.00	0.00	0.00
A/P Turnover	(D)	80	-25.23	0	0	0	107	100.00	0	0	0	0	0.00	0	0	0
PROFITABILITY																
Depreciation to Sales	(%)	0.00	0.00	1.00	1.60	2.60	0.00	0.00	1.10	1.80	2.90	0.00	0.00	1.20	1.80	2.80
Prof bef Tax to Tot Assets	(%)	3.62	-1,064.60	13.50	8.70	4.70	-0.38	100.00	19.10	8.50	1.80	0.00	0.00	19.50	8.30	1.70
Profit before Taxes to TNW	(%)	13.94	-1,015.19	42.40	24.90	14.30	-1.52	100.00	49.90	23.20	5.90	0.00	0.00	50.60	22.90	6.00

OTHER RATIOS NOT AVAILABLE WITH INDUSTRY STANDARDS

Ratio	Unit	12/31/95 Value	% Change	UQ	Med	LQ	12/31/94 Value	% Change	UQ	Med	LQ	12/31/93 Value	% Change	UQ	Med	LQ
SOLVENCY																
Inv. to Net Work. Capital	(X)	0.00	0.00	N/A	N/A	N/A	0.00	0.00	N/A	N/A	N/A	0.00	0.00	N/A	N/A	N/A
Current Liab. to NW	(X)	1.35	-18.20	N/A	N/A	N/A	1.66	100.00	N/A	N/A	N/A	0.00	0.00	N/A	N/A	N/A
LT Debt to Tot. Debt & Capital	(%)	38.87	12.41	N/A	N/A	N/A	34.58	100.00	N/A	N/A	N/A	0.00	0.00	N/A	N/A	N/A
Fixed Assets to LT Debt	(X)	0.83	-43.92	N/A	N/A	N/A	1.48	100.00	N/A	N/A	N/A	0.00	0.00	N/A	N/A	N/A
EFFICIENCY																
Net Sales to NW	(X)	7.27	0.97	N/A	N/A	N/A	7.20	100.00	N/A	N/A	N/A	0.00	0.00	N/A	N/A	N/A
Net Sales to Inventory	(X)	0.00	0.00	N/A	N/A	N/A	0.00	0.00	N/A	N/A	N/A	0.00	0.00	N/A	N/A	N/A
Cost of Sales/Working Capital	(X)	2.08	-16.80	N/A	N/A	N/A	2.50	100.00	N/A	N/A	N/A	0.00	0.00	N/A	N/A	N/A
Short Term Loan Turnover	(X)	0.00	0.00	N/A	N/A	N/A	0.00	0.00	N/A	N/A	N/A	0.00	0.00	N/A	N/A	N/A
LT Liabilities Payback.*	($)	($1,532.00)	-70.89	N/A	N/A	N/A	($5,262.00)	-41.40	N/A	N/A	N/A	($8,979.00)	100.00	N/A	N/A	N/A
PROFITABILITY																
Gross Profit on Net Sales	(%)	63.31	-0.42	--	0.00	--	63.58	9.49	--	0.00	--	58.07	100.00	--	0.00	--
Net Oper Inc on Net Sales	(%)	3.43	104.17	--	4.40	--	1.68	-163.40	--	5.10	--	-2.65	100.00	--	5.40	--
Net Profit on Net Sales	(%)	-0.19	-58.70	N/A	N/A	N/A	-0.46	-90.40	N/A	N/A	N/A	-4.79	100.00	N/A	N/A	N/A
Net Prof on Total Assets	(%)	-0.35	-57.32	N/A	N/A	N/A	-0.82	100.00	N/A	N/A	N/A	0.00	0.00	N/A	N/A	N/A
Tot Assets to Equity	(%)	3.85	-5.12	N/A	N/A	N/A	4.06	100.00	N/A	N/A	N/A	0.00	0.00	N/A	N/A	N/A
Net Prft on Stkhldrs Eqty	(%)	-1.36	-58.91	N/A	N/A	N/A	-3.31	100.00	N/A	N/A	N/A	0.00	0.00	N/A	N/A	N/A

(X)=TIMES   (D) = DAYS   (%) = PERCENT   ($) = DOLLARS

* IN THOUSANDS

OVERVIEW

Let us look at the financial condition and the credit status of this customer. Since this is a service firm, some of the usual numbers, including inventory turnover, are not available. Also, only two years of balance sheet numbers and three years of income statement numbers are available for analysis. Looking at the liquidity of this firm, the numbers not only improve greatly compared to the previous year's numbers but also are above the highest quartile number for the industry ($1.79 to $1.00 compared to $1.70 to $1.00).

On the down side, while the DSO is better than the previous year, it is far worse than the lowest quartile of its industry (113 days compared to 91 days). This situation can be explained in one of two possible ways; Terra could have been forced to offer extended terms on a very large construction job, or much worse, it could have some nonperforming receivables in its total accounts receivables portfolio.

Unfortunately, even though its A/P turnover has dropped considerably from the previous year, industry numbers were not available to do a comparison against. Debt to net worth has certainly decreased from the previous year to this year and is far worse and much higher than the industry average ($2.85 to $1.00 compared to $1.70 to $1.00). Gross profit has decreased only slightly from the previous year, but once again no information is available for the industry to compare against. Operating profit, while completely doubling the previous year's figures, is still below the industry average (3.4% compared to 4.4%).

One unusual item that does appear on the income statement is a tremendously large increase in taxes from the previous year to this year ($3,776,000 compared to $438,000). Both sales and net worth are up from the previous year, but the net worth is low compared to industry average (26% of all assets compared to 37.1% of all assets for the industry average).

There is a high credit amount of $3 million on the credit report, and all accounts were either paid on a prompt or discount basis. The bank has a first lien on everything. The firm is 14 years old and the owner's previous experience is in the same type of work. The firm has 230 employees and owns its facilities. The high credit on the three trade references has been up to $6 million, and all were paid promptly. All three showed a trend toward promptness, and none currently has a balance.

The bank currently reflects a low eight-figure limit ($10 million to $20 million) and a working capital line of credit with a balance of a high seven-figure balance ($7 million to $9 million), which is satisfactory.

WHAT OTHER CREDIT PROFESSIONALS THOUGHT

Student One

Monte J., a credit manager from a national firm that manufactures customized heat transfer equipment for large industrial plants, is the first reviewer. (Since questions 2, 3, 4, and 5 tie together, each student will make a decision based on the concerns stated in these three questions.) Having dealt with this type of large customized project in the past, Monte felt very comfortable with all of the credit facts he saw but was slightly disconcerted about some of the numbers in the financial analysis.

The fact that the DSO was so high, although improving, and the net worth was off considerably compared to industry average also was bewildering. The major increase in the taxes was also a puzzle that did not set well with him. From everything here this should be an open-and-shut easy credit approval, but he was not convinced that everything was right with this deal. Although uncomfortable, Monte decided to approve the deal with a few changes. He was going to require that the customer pay 30% at time of order, 20% at time of fabrication, 20% at 120 days, 10% at time of shipment, and the balance in 90 days. This would cover overhead before the finished product left the plant.

Due to the nature of the numbers, Monte also felt it necessary that his company should retain ownership of the goods until the remaining payment was made. A UCC-1 would be taken on the product and would be released on clearance of the final payment. Monte felt that it was justified to require more on this first job because it is only an average-income piece of business and Terra it was at first reluctant to provide financials and acquiesced only after some solid pushing. By reviewing these details with top management, Monte felt he could convince them that this was the smartest move for their company and would use this icebreaker as the gauge for future business.

He would meet with the customer personally to review his concerns and ask some questions concerning the strange financial items.

Student Two

Judy H. is a credit manager with a global manufacturer of customized vacuum and heat transfer systems for major petrochemical plants. Judy was not as apprehensive as Monte was on this case and felt that Terra had a lot going for it. The positives included access to a fair amount of cash from its working capital line of credit, a high credit with another firm that was almost twice the size of this initial order, and the fact that it has always paid either by taking a cash discount or within terms.

The fact that it had solid experience in this field also was a major plus because dealing with seasoned pros is far easier than dealing with rank amateurs. The only downside that she was concerned about was the tax issue, which was a puzzle, and Terra's reluctance to provide a financial statement when it wished to do a regular series of projects with her firm. She would discuss this with management before giving her approval. If there were no oddities in the answers, she would approve this deal but would require more of a down payment for this first order. If all went well after that she would return to her firm's standard terms of sales. She would require a 30% down payment and then progress payments of 10% until the end and the balance would be due in 90 days. Her firm would retain ownership of the product until the finished goods left the dock.

She felt that the margin was only average and this was the first time the two firms would be working together would help her convince both management and the customer that her recommendations were not an unreasonable way to start the relationship.

Student Three

Tom V. is a credit manager for a national customized plant supply house. His firm also creates custom components for petrochemical manufacturers. Tom was a little less enraptured by this whole deal. He was upset over the time that he had spent prying financials out of Terra and by the fact that, after comparing them to the industry, they turned out to be less than stellar. He was also not all that sold on the terms of this deal, due to the level of profit (just average), the terms (10%, 10%, 10%, 10%, and 60% 90 days after the delivery of the goods), and finally the fact that his company had never done business with this firm before.

Since this customer had been in business for 14 years and contracts constantly with the same type of end users that Locktight delivers finished product to on a regular basis, why hadn't it approached Tom's firm before? What happened to its regular supplier, and why did its three top suppliers have a zero balance when they were contacted?

With all of this in mind, Tom did not feel comfortable with this deal at all. He would consider it with some positive answers to his questions and with a major change of terms. He would require terms of 30% with the order, 20% at the start of fabrication, 20% at 120 days from order date, 20% at date of shipment, and the balance in 30 days from shipment date. He definitely would retain ownership of the goods until the final payment was made.

As far as convincing top management, Tom felt that his company had seen enough of these firms that come out of nowhere and want to grace you with their presence that they would not be overwhelmed by an average-profit deal. As to the customer, if Terra really wanted to do business with Locktight, then it would need to be more open and willing to discuss the issues that make this a less than interesting deal. As a show of good faith, Terra should agree to his terms on this deal and if all went well the relationship could be built on this foundation.

ACTIONS IF OVERRIDEN BY TOP MANAGEMENT

Now students must face the prospect of getting overridden by top management and dealing with the fallout that results.

Student One

Monte J. was not happy about being overridden and not used to this kind of treatment. But as a team player, he would do his level best to make sure that all "I's" were dotted and all "T's" were crossed. When the first 10% was due, he would notify the customer that payment should be sent via ACH transfer or wire transfer or the project would stop immediately. Having seen the past payment record, he doubted that there would be a problem, but he was not quite 100% sold on that idea. His biggest concern arose when the completed project left the dock and became part of the end user's plant. Since 60% was not due for 90 days, there was a long time for things to go wrong, and his company would have more than twice as much outstanding than it was due to make on the sale.

He planned to stay in close contact with both the sales staff and the engineering staff to make sure that no excuses could be used to delay payment on this project.

Student Two

Judy H. was less worried about this deal but was not happy about not getting more money down. She knew in this particular case if she was overridden that it was not smart to rock the boat. She did, however, plan on staying on Terra's heels about getting paid and staying in touch with the group working on this project to try to nip any problems in the bud before Terra had an excuse for not paying. Her fears will coalesce around the time after the goods are delivered to the end user's plant as her company will have to wait a long time for the biggest part of its money to be paid. It might be a good idea for the salesperson or her to be in Terra's area on the 90th day to finish the deal.

Student Three

Tom V., although unhappy, was not surprised. This kind of tactic happened all the time when marketing and sales saw a chance at new business and was willing to beg top management to not let credit interfere. Because he had a great relationship with the purchasing and engineering staff, Tom would be kept up to the minute on anything that may cause problems in getting paid for this project. He would be on the phone the day after the due date, but before the ink dried on the contract, he would make sure that Terra knew how to make an ACH transfer to his company's account. He also planned to be in Terra's area the day after the last invoice was due.

WHAT REALLY HAPPENED

As always, I immediately pulled a credit report on the customer. When this order was dropped into my lap, I was surprised to see a deal where the customer's paying habits were perfect. After having a rare fight with the director of sales and marketing over requiring financial information on this customer, he finally agreed to back my efforts to get the information.

I hit a solid wall of resistance to getting the information, and both he and I became suspicious that the customer had a skeleton in its closet. After two calls each from both the director and me, which had no effect in freeing up the information, we asked our firm's president to contact them personally. While even he had to argue to get the company to finally relent (he threatened to walk away from the deal if it would not release the information), the financials appeared in his office the next day. After seeing the very large tax figure in the income statement for this past year, I made an appointment to sit with the president to discuss my feelings on the whole deal. He instantly got suspicious that something was wrong with this firm and phoned Terra's president to ask just what was going on. When he twice got a recording that the phone had been disconnected, he called in the director of sales and marketing who arrived looking very pale. Together they decided to contact the local salesperson to go over there to find out what was going on.

The salesperson was already on her way there, as she could not reach the firm by phone either. When she arrived not five minutes later, she announced that the door to the office had been padlocked. A notice pinned to the front door stated that the IRS had closed the firm down in connection with a criminal tax fraud investigation and that all inquiries should be referred to a special agent. Stunned and thankful that we had not started any work on this project, we discussed the possibility of contacting the end user to see if it was aware of what had happened. It was indeed aware of the situation and was scrambling to locate another firm to take over the entire project. While typically our firm did not get involved in this type of work, our president convinced its president that we would like to discuss the details of this project and that we could meet at their convenience.

The next day there was an article in the paper in the town where Terra Technology was located, and our local sales rep faxed a copy of it to me. The IRS had followed a long audit trail to determine the tax evasion that had taken place at Terra. Apparently all of the top officers were in jail for tax evasion and racketeering and would be arraigned in the next 30 days. After showing this to both the president and the director of sales and marketing, they were very relieved to not have gotten mixed up with this firm. The meeting arranged with the petrochemical firm netted our company a $100 million construction contract that had a 40% margin.

The president wanted me to ride roughshod over this entire contract so as to prevent any problems in dealing with subcontractors and suppliers. He also wanted me to make sure that the customer had no reason to pay us late on any of the progress payments. This job, which took about two years to complete, was one of the most satisfying pieces of business I had ever been involved in. As an aside, the officers of Terra Technology are currently serving 10 years in a federal penitentiary for tax evasion and racketeering.

16

CASE STUDY 12: COMPANIA SWIFT, INC.

Sale of Goods to Foreign Customers

INTRODUCTION

This chapter looks at ways to minimize risk while maximizing the sale. It assesses techniques used in the extension of credit to foreign customers for viability and effectiveness in making the sale from a sound business credit perspective. Here the ultimate goal is achieving a balance-of-risk reduction and maximizing the sale.

By reviewing this real day in the life of a credit department, readers will learn to make effective use of data, facts, and alternative methods in reaching a decision. An appreciation for how other people in marketing or finance think will hone negotiating skills. Readers can use new insight into the creation of a sound business credit decision to prevent gaps or weaknesses in their decision-making processes.

Case study 12 involves extending credit to a foreign company in Mexico, which presents additional risks that the domestic credit manager never faces. One is country risk, which covers the dangers in dealing with the laws, government, political risk, and customs of a foreign country. The next form of foreign risk is economic risk, which deals with the current level of development of the country, its levels of inflation, its foreign trade status, and other economic factors that affects a country's ability to participate in international trade.

The final risk involves monetary risk, which deals with how the currency of a country compares to that of the home country. If the exchange rate is favorable, there is less of a risk and vice versa. If a letter of credit is payable only through the customer's bank and if there is a shortage of the currency on hand in the customer's country, the bank may delay payment due to government pressures. In some cases the banks are owned by the government and are simply following its dictates.

Additional differences that exist in international transactions are the terms extended and the instruments used for payment. Terms can be longer due to the distances that goods are shipped and the need to get them through customs. These time delays can be compounded by the foreign country setting restrictions on the length of time for the terms of sale of goods into the country. Letters of credit and drafts are payment tools commonly used in foreign transactions. Both can be payable on sight or over a time period. Letters of credit are irrevocable (otherwise they are useless) and may or may not be confirmed by another bank in the seller's country, a third country, or in a branch of the buyer's home issuing bank. Letters of credit issued in international transactions are used to pay for the credit transaction; a domestic standby letter of credit is used as security for a credit extension.

Credit reports and financial information for foreign firms tend to be sketchier and the information is less timely, due to the greater degree of difficulty in getting accurate information in a foreign country compared to the United States. It may not be easy to get credit ratings and financial information on a firm in a particular foreign country. Accounting and auditing standards in some foreign countries are not as thorough as that of the United States and are sometimes ineffective due to exchange rates that are greatly affected by inflation and hyperinflation.

THE FACTS

I. B. Strict, the division credit manager for Locktight Films Company (a manufacturer), is reviewing a new account with his credit analyst, Jane Dough. The customer, Compania Swift, Inc., has been in business for about 41 years. They had refused to provide financial information at first but finally agreed to release a ten-month interim balance sheet and income statement. Compania Swift is a market leader in Mexico in the design of plastic food wrappers and has had great success in areas that Locktight could not penetrate. Anticipated additional sales for Locktight as reflected in its sales manager's report on Compania Swift would be between $1 million to $1 million per year. Its paying habits are good. Compania Swift's initial order is for $150,000 to be shipped in the next 30 days. Locktight's margin on the order is 55%, which is high for the industry. Standard terms of sale for customized products to Mexico are cash in advance or confirmed letter of credit. The customer is asking for open account with net 60-day terms with a credit limit of $150,000. An international credit report and financial analysis are available for review.

INSTRUCTIONS

1. Analyze all data available on the case, summarizing your findings using the following:
   A. Common-size analysis and ratio analysis
   B. Summarize the information available in the credit report and information available above
2. What is your credit decision?
3. If approved, will open account terms be offered? Is security needed? If so, what type? Or should the order be declined?
4. What facts would you use to defend your decision to management and to the customer?
5. If overridden by management, what steps would you take to prevent a possible loss?

<u>CREDIT REPORT</u>

FILE #123456789   DATE PRINTED   SUMMARY
         NOV 23, 1996   RATING ---
COMPANIA SWIFT INC.   STARTED 1956
400 RUNDOWN LANE   PRINTS &   SALES $5,581,479
MEXICO CITY, MEXICO   ENGRAVES   WORTH $3,471,665
 TEL: 011 555-9000   SIC NO.
          5212

Legal: Private Corporation   Inc. Date: 1956
Major Shareholder: Lic. Jorge Simon   Financial Data in $
Employees: 180   Bank Rating: Good

Negative data: None   Authorized Capital: unknown

Federal Tax ID# (RFC) ISI-123456623

Managers: Lic. Jorge Simon   Owners: Lic. Jorge Simon

Activities: Prints, engraves and does lithographs. Imports 15% from the USA
    Exports indirectly to the USA and Central America

Mr. A.B. Aberto commented that the Subject belongs to a group of 8 companies in the same field.

Facility size: 6,783 Sq. meters in an owned space

The general offices and a plant are located at the above noted address

Bank: Bancomer
 Suc. 12
 Mexico, D.F.
 Tel: 525226-9399

Account Manager: Lic. Jose Gonzalez
Account # 598114-7
Account opened 1988
Average balance: $40,000
Line of Credit: $60,000
Bank rating: Good

There is nothing unfavorable with regard to the company's commercial reputation or financial situation.

Compania Swift Inc.

The following information supplied by the customer:

Cartones Ponderosa, S.A. DE C.V.   Tintas Sanchez
San Juan del Rio, QRO   Mexico, D.F.
Tel: 52 555 19-690   Tel: 52 5 555-6936

Contact Ms. Guadalupe Morales   Contact Mr. Poncho Cisco
Customer Since: 1984
Line of Credit: $100,000
Terms: 30 days   History: Excellent
The supplier confirmed the above   We have contacted Mr. Cisco,
Average monthly purchase: $100,000 who was unavailable to comment
           about the Company

J.F. Helmold & Bro. Inc.
901 Morse Ave. Elk Wood, TX 51248
Tel. 512 555-7085
Fax. 512 555-8695
Customer since: 1/29/83
Credit limit: $4,800
High Credit Utilized: $1,000
Terms: Check in Advance
Date of Last sale: 7/30/96
Rating Satisfactory

Foreplay South, Inc.
11896 Big Mouth Lane
Swallowdown, ME 12665
Tel. 235 555-5689
Fax. 235 555-5694

We have contacted the Company and have not received a response to date.

Komora Corporation
12-1, Azumabashi 3-Chome Sumida-ku
Tokyo Japan

Conclusion:
The Company is well established and has been doing business for 40 years; therefore, although it has suffered fiscal losses during the last two economic periods, we believe that it may be possible to have good trade relations with the Company.

Person Contacted: Mr. Alberto Gonzalez, Accountant, verified the information in this report.

Compania Swift Inc.
400 Rundown Lane
Mexico City, Mexico

SIC   5322
10/31/96

$5,581,479.09
$3,471,665.40

ACCOUNT #   123456

	$	% Change	% Assets	Ind % Assets	$	% Change	% Assets	Ind % Assets	$	% Change	% Assets	Ind % Assets
Cash	$245,699.12	100.00	5.64	0.00	$0.00	0.00	0.00	0.00	$0.00	0.00	0.00	0.00
Accounts Receivable	$763,349.94	100.00	17.53	0.00	$0.00	0.00	0.00	0.00	$0.00	0.00	0.00	0.00
Inventory	$1,235,620.66	100.00	28.37	0.00	$0.00	0.00	0.00	0.00	$0.00	0.00	0.00	0.00
Due from Shareholder	$0.00	0.00	0.00	---	$0.00	0.00	0.00	---	$0.00	0.00	0.00	---
Due From Affiliate	$16,196.71	100.00	0.37	---	$0.00	0.00	0.00	---	$0.00	0.00	0.00	---
Other Current	$349,380.37	100.00	8.02	0.00	$0.00	0.00	0.00	0.00	$0.00	0.00	0.00	0.00
Total Current	$2,610,246.80	100.00	59.93	0.00	$0.00	0.00	0.00	0.00	$0.00	0.00	0.00	0.00
Fixed Assets	$1,733,311.25	100.00	39.80	0.00	$0.00	0.00	0.00	0.00	$0.00	0.00	0.00	0.00
Notes Receivable	$10,839.80	100.00	0.25	---	$0.00	0.00	0.00	---	$0.00	0.00	0.00	---
Deposits	$405.58	100.00	0.01	---	$0.00	0.00	0.00	---	$0.00	0.00	0.00	---
Cash Value of Life Insur.	$0.00	0.00	0.00	0.00	$0.00	0.00	0.00	0.00	$0.00	0.00	0.00	0.00
Intangible Assets	$408.87	100.00	0.01	100.00	$0.00	0.00	0.00	100.00	$0.00	0.00	0.00	100.00
Total Assets	$4,355,212.30	100.00	100.00	100.00	$0.00	0.00	0.00	100.00	$0.00	0.00	0.00	100.00
Account Payable	$604,152.75	100.00	13.87	0.00	$0.00	0.00	0.00	0.00	$0.00	0.00	0.00	0.00
Bank Loans + N.P.	$109,584.00	100.00	2.52	0.00	$0.00	0.00	0.00	0.00	$0.00	0.00	0.00	0.00
Cur. Mat.-L.T.D.	$0.00	0.00	0.00	0.00	$0.00	0.00	0.00	0.00	$0.00	0.00	0.00	0.00
Income Tax Payables	$79,560.33	100.00	1.83	0.00	$0.00	0.00	0.00	0.00	$0.00	0.00	0.00	0.00
Accrued Expenses	$82,885.05	100.00	1.90	0.00	$0.00	0.00	0.00	0.00	$0.00	0.00	0.00	0.00
Total Current	$876,182.13	100.00	20.12	0.00	$0.00	0.00	0.00	0.00	$0.00	0.00	0.00	0.00
Long Term Debt	$7,364.77	100.00	0.17	0.00	$0.00	0.00	0.00	0.00	$0.00	0.00	0.00	0.00
Deferred Taxes	$0.00	0.00	0.00	0.00	$0.00	0.00	0.00	0.00	$0.00	0.00	0.00	0.00
All Other L.T. Debt	$0.00	0.00	0.00	0.00	$0.00	0.00	0.00	0.00	$0.00	0.00	0.00	0.00
Net Worth	$3,471,665.40	100.00	79.71	100.00	$0.00	0.00	0.00	100.00	$0.00	0.00	0.00	100.00
Total Liab & Equity	$4,355,212.30	100.00	100.00	100.00	$0.00	0.00	0.00	100.00	$0.00	0.00	0.00	100.00
Net Sales	$5,581,479.09	100.00	100.00	100.00	$0.00	0.00	0.00	100.00	$0.00	0.00	0.00	100.00
Cost of Goods Sold	$5,090,226.61	100.00	91.20	100.00	$0.00	0.00	0.00	100.00	$0.00	0.00	0.00	100.00
Gross Profit	$491,252.48	100.00	8.80	0.00	$0.00	0.00	0.00	0.00	$0.00	0.00	0.00	0.00
Depreciation	$0.00	0.00	0.00	---	$0.00	0.00	0.00	---	$0.00	0.00	0.00	---
Lease Payments	$0.00	0.00	0.00	---	$0.00	0.00	0.00	---	$0.00	0.00	0.00	---
Other Operating Exps.	$1,141,200.13	100.00	20.45	0.00	$0.00	0.00	0.00	0.00	$0.00	0.00	0.00	0.00
Tot. Operating Exps.	$1,141,200.13	100.00	20.45	0.00	$0.00	0.00	0.00	0.00	$0.00	0.00	0.00	0.00
Operating Profit	($649,947.65)	100.00	-11.64	0.00	$0.00	0.00	0.00	0.00	$0.00	0.00	0.00	0.00
Interest Inc.//(Exp.)	$19,529.54	100.00	0.35	0.00	$0.00	0.00	0.00	0.00	$0.00	0.00	0.00	0.00
G/(L) on sale of Fxd Assets	$0.00	0.00	0.00	---	$0.00	0.00	0.00	---	$0.00	0.00	0.00	---
Profit Before Taxes	($630,418.11)	100.00	-11.29	0.00	$0.00	0.00	0.00	0.00	$0.00	0.00	0.00	0.00
Taxes	$0.00	100.00	0.00	---	$0.00	0.00	0.00	---	$0.00	0.00	0.00	---
Net Profit	($630,418.11)	100.00	-11.29	---	$0.00	0.00	0.00	---	$0.00	0.00	0.00	---
Other Data:												
Working Capital	$1,734,064.67	100.00	39.82	0.00	$0.00	0.00	0.00	0.00	$0.00	0.00	0.00	0.00
Tangible Equity	$3,471,256.53	100.00	79.70	0.00	$0.00	0.00	0.00	0.00	$0.00	0.00	0.00	0.00
Recommended Credit Limit:	$402,665.76	100.00	---	---	$0.00	0.00	---	---	$0.00	0.00	---	---

Compania Swift Inc.
400 Rundown Lane
Mexico City, Mexico

RATIOS

10/31/96

		Value	% Change	UQ	Med	LQ	% Change	UQ	Med	LQ	% Change	UQ	Med	LQ
SOLVENCY														
Current Ratio	($)	2.98	100.00	0.00	0.00	0.00	0.00	0.00	0.00	0.00	0.00	0.00	0.00	0.00
Quick Ratio	($)	1.15	100.00	0.00	0.00	0.00	0.00	0.00	0.00	0.00	0.00	0.00	0.00	0.00
Net Profit B4 Tax + Depr./Cur LTD	(X)	0.00	0.00	0.00	0.00	0.00	0.00	0.00	0.00	0.00	0.00	0.00	0.00	0.00
Sales to Fixed Assets	(X)	3.22	100.00	0.00	0.00	0.00	0.00	0.00	0.00	0.00	0.00	0.00	0.00	0.00
Sales to Total Assets	(X)	1.28	100.00	0.00	0.00	0.00	0.00	0.00	0.00	0.00	0.00	0.00	0.00	0.00
Total Liab. to NW	(X)	0.25	100.00	0.00	0.00	0.00	0.00	0.00	0.00	0.00	0.00	0.00	0.00	0.00
Fixed Assets to NW	(X)	0.50	100.00	N/A	N/A	N/A	0.00	N/A	N/A	N/A	0.00	N/A	N/A	N/A
Tot. Liab. to Tot. Assets	(%)	20.29	100.00	N/A	N/A	N/A	0.00	N/A	N/A	N/A	0.00	N/A	N/A	N/A
Oper. Prof. to Int. Exp.	(X)	-33.28	100.00	N/A	N/A	N/A	0.00	N/A	N/A	N/A	0.00	N/A	N/A	N/A
Oper Prof+Lease Py to Int Exp+LP	(X)	-33.28	100.00	0.00	0.00	0.00	0.00	0.00	0.00	0.00	0.00	0.00	0.00	0.00
EFFICIENCY														
Sales to Receivables	(X)	7.31	100.00	0.00	0.00	0.00	0.00	0.00	0.00	0.00	0.00	0.00	0.00	0.00
Days Sales Outstanding	(D)	42	100.00	0	0	0	0.00	0	0	0	0.00	0	0	0
Cost of Sales to Inv.	(X)	4.12	100.00	0	0	0	0.00	0	0	0	0.00	0	0	0
Days' Sales in Inventory	(D)	74	100.00	0.00	0.00	0.00	0.00	0.00	0.00	0.00	0.00	0.00	0.00	0.00
Sales to Net Working Cap.	(X)	3.22	100.00	0.00	0.00	0.00	0.00	0.00	0.00	0.00	0.00	0.00	0.00	0.00
Cost of Sales/Payables	(X)	8.43	100.00	0	0	0	0.00	0	0	0	0.00	0	0	0
A/P Turnover	(D)	36	100.00	0	0	0	0.00	0	0	0	0.00	0	0	0
PROFITABILITY														
Depreciation to Sales	(%)	0.00	0.00	0.00	0.00	0.00	0.00	0.00	0.00	0.00	0.00	0.00	0.00	0.00
Prof bef Tax to Tot Assets	(%)	-14.48	100.00	0.00	0.00	0.00	0.00	0.00	0.00	0.00	0.00	0.00	0.00	0.00
Profit before Taxes to TNW	(%)	-18.16	100.00	0.00	0.00	0.00	0.00	0.00	0.00	0.00	0.00	0.00	0.00	0.00

OTHER RATIOS NOT AVAILABLE WITH INDUSTRY STANDARDS

		Value	% Change	UQ	Med	LQ	% Change	UQ	Med	LQ	% Change	UQ	Med	LQ
SOLVENCY														
Inv. to Net Work. Capital	(X)	0.71	100.00	N/A	N/A	N/A	0.00	N/A	N/A	N/A	0.00	N/A	N/A	N/A
Current Liab. to NW	(X)	0.25	100.00	N/A	N/A	N/A	0.00	N/A	N/A	N/A	0.00	N/A	N/A	N/A
LT Debt to Tot. Debt & Capital	(%)	0.17	100.00	N/A	N/A	N/A	0.00	N/A	N/A	N/A	0.00	N/A	N/A	N/A
Fixed Assets to LT Debt	(X)	235.35	100.00	N/A	N/A	N/A	0.00	N/A	N/A	N/A	0.00	N/A	N/A	N/A
EFFICIENCY														
Net Sales to NW	(X)	1.61	100.00	N/A	N/A	N/A	0.00	N/A	N/A	N/A	0.00	N/A	N/A	N/A
Net Sales to Inventory	(X)	4.52	100.00	N/A	N/A	N/A	0.00	N/A	N/A	N/A	0.00	N/A	N/A	N/A
Cost of Sales/Working Capital	(X)	2.94	100.00	N/A	N/A	N/A	0.00	N/A	N/A	N/A	0.00	N/A	N/A	N/A
Short Term Loan Turnover	(X)	7.00	100.00	N/A	N/A	N/A	0.00	N/A	N/A	N/A	0.00	N/A	N/A	N/A
LT Liabilities Payback *	($)	($630.42)	100.00	--	0.00	--	$0.00	--	0.00	--	0.00	--	--	--
PROFITABILITY														
Gross Profit on Net Sales	(%)	8.80	100.00	N/A	N/A	N/A	0.00	N/A	N/A	N/A	0.00	N/A	N/A	N/A
Net Oper Inc on Net Sales	(%)	-11.64	100.00	--	0.00	--	0.00	--	0.00	--	0.00	--	0.00	--
Net Profit on Net Sales	(%)	-11.29	100.00	N/A	N/A	N/A	0.00	N/A	N/A	N/A	0.00	N/A	N/A	N/A
Net Prof on Total Assets	(%)	-14.48	100.00	N/A	N/A	N/A	0.00	N/A	N/A	N/A	0.00	N/A	N/A	N/A
Tot Assets to Equity	(X)	1.25	100.00	N/A	N/A	N/A	0.00	N/A	N/A	N/A	0.00	N/A	N/A	N/A
Net Prft on Stkhlrs Eqty	(%)	-18.16	100.00	N/A	N/A	N/A	0.00	N/A	N/A	N/A	0.00	N/A	N/A	N/A

(X)=TIMES   (D) = DAYS   (%) = PRECENT   (%) = PRECENT   ($) = DOLLARS

* IN THOUSANDS

OVERVIEW

Let us look at the financial condition and the credit status of this customer. Here we have only a ten-month interim unaudited statement from a foreign country. Also, it is not valid to review their numbers against industry comparisons of U.S. companies. How much credence can we give these financials? Not much, but at least they can be a starting point to work from.

The liquidity ratio reflects a $1.15 to $1.00 level, which in general is not bad. Coupled with a DSO that is 42 days, it would be better than average if terms to customers were net 30 or longer. A debt-to-worth ratio of $0.25 to $1.00 is exceptional, assuming that the assets are not inflated, which would give a company a much higher net worth.

A/P turnover of 36 days likewise would be good if the terms extended to the company was net 30 days. The credit report at least has one firm that did sell to it on net 30 days terms. The firm had a negative operating income, which would be a problem in the United States, but it did have a high net worth compared to the volume of sales.

According to the credit report, Compania Swift has been in business for 41 years, and it owns its facilities. It has a $60,000 (U.S.) working capital line of credit from its bank with a $40,000 (U.S.) balance, which is being paid satisfactorily. The report reflects two trade references, one with a high credit of $100,000 that is being paid satisfactorily and one that is paid cash in advance. The credit report states that it is a "well-established firm" but has had negative earnings for the last two years.

WHAT OTHER CREDIT PROFESSIONALS THOUGHT

Now let us see how the students will deal with this case. They will tie questions 2, 3, and 4 together.

Student One

Linda L., corporate credit manager for a Fortune 500 multinational fiber optics manufacturer, was not comfortable with the limited amount of information that was available on this firm. The positives in this case are the product's profit margin, the new sales in a tough market that would help Locktight, and the customer's "appearance" of being a well-established firm. The downside to this deal is that the financial information is limited and unaudited, the credit information is sketchy, and open account 60 days in Mexico are not her firm's usual terms. She would be willing to do a letter of credit confirmed by her bank. Locktight will pay the letter-of-credit fees, and she will go the 60 days if that would help get her firm in the door with Compania Swift. As far as convincing top management, she feels that since their terms to Mexico normally are confirmed letter of credit, and she would be willing to go to 60-day terms, she will have their support.

The fact that Locktight is giving Compania Swift the 60 days that it wanted and that Locktight is willing to pay the letter-of-credit charges should help to show Locktight's desire to do this business.

Student Two

Michael P., a credit and collections manager for an international electronics firm, was really bothered by the fact that Compania Swift was reluctant to provide any financial information. Providing financial information is not as commonplace in Mexico as it is in the United States; Compania Swift reluctantly provided Locktight with interim financial statements, which reflected a third loss in a row. Coupled with the limited amount of available credit information and the risk of extending credit in Mexico, this deal seems less and less interesting as the day progresses. The fact that Compania Swift has a 55% margin and Locktight would like to break into the market that Compania Swift currently covers is the only reason he is willing to consider this deal at all. He would be willing to take a 25% down payment with the order (to cover costs), a 50% wire transfer at the time of shipment, the final 25% in 30 days, and would offer a 2% cash discount for the entire amount if the last 25% was paid in ten days.

Top management is aware of the difficulties of selling in Mexico and realizes that while some risk has to be taken to break into a new market, there is a limit to how much the company is willing to lose. Michael will advise Compania Swift that as it builds a relationship with Locktight over time, a higher open account limit can be established.

Student Three

Robert S., a supervisor of credit and collections from a global minerals company, was a little less taken aback by the lack of information or the customer is resistance to turning over financial information. He was impressed by the fact that the firm had been in business for 40+ years and that the financials looked as good as they did. He did realize that the information was not audited, and even if it was it would not be at the level of audit that a U.S. firm must endure. The fact that Compania Swift had a reference from a firm selling to it on open account up to $100,000 on net 30 days terms gave him some additional comfort.

The biggest concern he had revolved around doing business in Mexico with a firm that they had no past experience with in a market that they really wanted to break into. He decided that he would offer terms of 25% with order, 25% at the time of shipment, 25% in 30 days, and 25% at 60 days, all sent by wire transfer. This would give them at least 50% paid before the goods ever left the dock, which would cover its costs and a 5% profit even if no additional funds could be collected. This at least balances the risk between both firms. He also feels that since his firm is covering its costs yet giving the customer some open account, top management would not object to his decision. Robert felt that he would discuss the fact that he had not done business with Compania Swift before and that by sharing the risk he was providing an act of faith and asking for the same on that company's part.

BEING OVERRIDEN BY TOP MANAGEMENT

Student One

Linda L. felt that as a team player she would accept this entrance into new business with Compania Swift but would be very alert to when this invoice became due. She would make sure that it knew that money was due via wire transfer on the 60th day and not a minute later. She would make a PR call at 30 days to confirm that the goods arrived intact and that they had cleared customs. She also would confirm that all items were as ordered, that Compania Swift had the invoice, and that it knew the payment was due via wire transfer into her bank on the 60th day from invoice date. During this time frame, she would be looking for the best possible collection agency that could handle bad debt accounts in Mexico and learning how difficult it would be to sue there. She planned to be on the phone to Compania Swift on the 61st day after the invoice date and also would be in touch with Locktight's local sales rep to make sure he or she was involved in the follow-up of this customer if Compania Swift went past due. No additional orders would be released until the payment was wired and received; if the company went past due, then all future shipments would be under a confirmed letter of credit after this payment was received.

Student Two

Michael P. would not be happy that his firm would take this risk regardless of its chances of successfully entering a market it was desperate to break into. He would hold any new orders until this one was paid in full via wire transfer. As a show of good faith on his part, he would plan a trip to Compania Swift on the 65th day from the invoice date, just to make sure that people there had liked doing business with Locktight and to get a look at the firm. He also would see if the firm had a year-end statement available at that time. If payment had not been made by then, he would attempt to obtain a certified check in U.S. dollars drawn on a local branch of a U.S. bank in Mexico. He also would schedule a meeting with a local collection agency in Mexico to see its operation and to prepare it for this account if the need ever occurred.

Student Three

Robert S. had more faith in the customer and felt that it was unlikely that a loss would occur. He did, however, locate a local attorney in Mexico that specialized in commercial international claims. He also notified the international sales manager that if this account ended up in collections, the costs for this attorney would come out of her budget. He planned to contact Compania Swift early, as did Linda, to say that if it paid this invoice in 10 days, he would give a 2% cash discount and would pay for the wire transfer (a small concession on top management's part due to the profit margin and the reasons stated earlier).

WHAT REALLY HAPPENED

When this order first came to my attention, I was told that the owner of Compania Swift was in town and wanted to meet with me on the order that he wished to place with Locktight. Always pleased to meet our customers (especially before I extend credit to them), I asked if I could meet with him over lunch. However, I wanted to meet with the international sales manager first to get the background on this order and any information that I could get out of her on Compania Swift. I asked her to do the introductions. As long as the owner spoke fluent English our sales rep could excuse herself and let us talk alone about his firm's financial numbers.

She agreed though she was not 100% sure whether she should trust me with him alone or not. At lunch, the owner and I discussed many aspects of concern that I had with this deal. The Mexican peso was in free fall and while we certainly wanted to break into the market that he was in, we had never done business together before and we wanted to start out on the right foot. He agreed and understood our concern with the peso problem. I asked him about a letter of credit, and he stated that for the very same reason that I was concerned over the peso, he was concerned about the effort that he would have to expend to get a letter of credit.

As an alternative to a confirmed letter of credit, I suggested two courses of action. Step one would be to obtain a standby letter of credit through a Mexican branch of a U.S. bank for $100,000 confirmed and payable at the bank's U.S. headquarters; we would extend a $150,000 line of credit to Compania. Using it as collateral for one year would give us some security during the first year. After that, if all the numbers looked good, if payments were on time and no problems had occurred, the letter of credit would be waived. Step two of the plan was that he would pay us out of a U.S. bank account that he had established in Houston.

Paying from the bank account in the United States saved the trouble of having the funds transferred via wire transfer and gave us a real opportunity to see how the company would pay us. We discussed the request for 60 days terms and settled for payment receipt in 45 days as an acceptable compromise. It took him about two weeks to work out all the details, but after receiving the standby letter of credit, we began shipping and received our payment on the 45th day. Locktight has been doing business with Compania Swift on an unsecured basis for about five years.

I hope that you have enjoyed analyzing the data and coming up with your own solutions to each case as well as reading my students' solutions and the real outcomes. While I always encourage my students to be creative in their decisions, I also advocate that they make sound business credit decisions, which involves looking at more than just credit as a source of help in rendering that all-important judgment call. While we can second-guess ourselves until we are blue in the face, only careful consideration of all the facts can give us the necessary guidance that we need to make the best call. Are we going to get it right 100% of the times? Definitely not, but at the end of the day, if we feel that we made the best decisions possible with what information we had, then we have indeed done our job to the best of our ability. Good luck to you in all of your credit experiences.

INDEX